FLOWERPAEDIA

1000 flowers and their meanings

— ∾!∾ —

Cheralyn Darcey

ROCKPOOL

In joy or sadness, flowers are our constant friends.

KOZUKO OKAKURA

For Jared & Maddison,
the very finest treasures I ever helped to grow.
May you both always have a life
of true meaning, love and happiness.

Love, Mum

THANK YOU

This book of flowers really is the most special title I've ever created. It took me decades to research and years to write, and I deeply appreciate the support and encouragement of those who made it possible.

It is with much joy that I thank my family, friends and the supportive team at Rockpool Publishing who were there when it mattered most, and helped my dream to become a reality.

Immeasurable thanks and love to every one of you who I have met online and in person and with whom I share my passion for nature and flowers. I have adored our conversations and blossoming friendships over the years, and I greatly appreciate the wonderful support you have given my work.

Also thanks to those of you who are holding this book now – by doing so, you are helping me to continue my work with flowers now and into the future. I hope this book brings each one of you the bouquet of flower love, happiness and insight that you are looking for.

Thank you all for keeping me growing.
Bunches of love,
Cheralyn
www.cheralyndarcey.com

CONTENTS

PRIMROSE

EDELWEISS

FLANNEL FLOWER

TUBEROSE

INTRODUCTION

Are you trying to find the right flower to say I love you, I like you, cheer up, get well, I'm sorry, or congratulations? Perhaps you are planning an event and wish to infuse it with exactly the right emotion and atmosphere. Maybe you are gardening! Imagine creating an outdoor space that holds special meaning for you, or just knowing what the returning blossoms in your garden represent each season. Would you like to connect with the healing attributes of flowers and have a handy reference book to guide you? Did someone give you a bunch of flowers recently and you would like to know more about them? Do certain blooms seem to come to you in dreams, your daily life or thoughts? This book will tell you the meanings behind each flower.

After a lifetime spent researching the incredible language of flowers and plants, I have decided to create a title I haven't been able to find. I have long wanted a flower dictionary and a prescription of meanings to refer to – a flowerpaedia! A book I can carry with me and share with others, providing a quick and easy way to find the flowers that convey my intentions, a way to look up flowers and hear what they have to say.

You have in your hands this little book borne of these wishes. I hope that it is helpful for you when you are gardening, selecting bouquets, planning floral decorations for events, creating artworks, crafting, working with healing modalities and even perhaps making a little magic. I am sure that you will find many more ways to share and benefit from understanding the language of flowers, too.

May you always be a blessing to nature
Cheralyn

WHAT ARE FLOWER MEANINGS?

I AM A PASSIONATE GARDENER and lifetime student of ethnobotany, the exploration of the relationship between people and plants. What I have learned is that our botanical friends are very happy living their own lives, but they do connect with us and interact with us because we share the same ecosystem. A very positive additional layer to this relationship for us is that we may find personal assistance with healing, emotional support, physical nourishment and connections, which are tied to our spiritual beliefs.

How we can fully benefit from our relationship with nature and in turn assist her, is by understanding plant meanings. Flowers and plants describe the attributes that they hold through their form, function and behaviour. The way they grow and attract pollinators; the way they look, smell, taste, feel and even sound, are all indications of this. From closely observing these factors, we have an opening into the world of the language of plants.

We humans have been translating this plant language into flower and plant meanings in order to pass the information down to each generation. It benefits us because we learn which plants and flowers can heal, nourish, harm or delight us, and how we may care, in turn, for nature.

Some of the terms we have used for plant language are 'The Language of Flowers', 'The Language of Plants' and 'The Doctrine of Signatures', and there are thousands of verbal histories and folklore traditions the world over containing translation of these meanings.

Sometimes meanings are created to suit a fashion, fad or popular interest, but they are not in keeping with the true language of plants. A few collections are very lovely, but they are more concerned with pleasing a market and creating myth than exhibiting nature as the purest form of the flowers and plants themselves. I personally enjoy some of these publications – they are interesting from an ethnobotanical point of view as I explore the fascinating relationships between people and plants – but I have not included any meaning that does not relate directly to the true nature of the plant.

Within this book you will also notice that sometimes the various meanings seem to contradict each other. This is because everything has a light and shadow and, on occasion, the shadow side is stronger in certain flowers and can manifest as the complete opposite of the more positive meaning it contains. The shadow inclusion is therefore important, but the intention and the meaning you are focused on must be very carefully considered.

Finally, I'm often asked, 'Does a plant still have the meaning of the flower even if it isn't in bloom?' Yes, it does. The meaning is still there but it is tempered a little by the absence of the blossom. A bare rose bush still means 'love' but it could also mean that, right now, love is in a different stage than that first flush of petals and whirlwind romance. Perhaps it is a quieter love, steadily growing.

The meanings of flowers are there, you just need to quieten yourself and listen.

HOW TO USE THIS BOOK

IT WOULD BE IMPOSSIBLE TO LIST ALL THE FLOWERS of the world and all their meanings in one book, certainly not one you could carry. I have selected one thousand of what I hope are the most well-known flowers as well as a good cross-section of others in the floral world. The meanings I have gathered are the strongest associations available. They are not complete, however, and probably never will be – science and our own evolution opens us to more understanding of the natural world almost daily, and we are learning more and more through the generations.

I would love you to add to this book, scribble in the margins, keep your own journal, and join me and many others who are passionate about flowers and plants. Keep listening to and discussing the language of flowers, not only for yourself but

for nature. Flowers are the most visual way plants communicate with each other, across species and with the earth. If we listen closely, we may be the blessing nature really needs right now.

UNDERSTANDING THE LANGUAGE OF FLOWERS

I am looking for » If you know the sentiment and energy you would like to convey, or a healing outcome you are seeking to achieve with flowers, look through and find the meaning/s that you feel best match this in SECTION ONE Meanings.

You will find a list of flowers for each meaning. The botanical nomenclature (scientific name) is offered to ensure proper identification as common names do vary between areas, people and throughout history. Sometimes only the family or genus (the first parts of the scientific name) is given because the meaning is connected with all flowers of the type listed.

If the flower you are looking for is not available, look for similar meanings e.g. for 'happiness' try 'joy'. You can also look through the additional lists of floral correspondences at the end of this book for other inspirations.

I WANT TO KNOW WHAT A PARTICULAR FLOWER MEANS

If you are looking for the meanings of particular flowers, go to SECTION TWO Flowers. Here you can look up flowers and then explore the meanings. I have used the most common titles followed by the flowers' botanical names. To help you a little more, I have included an index of these botanical names at the back. For a quick search of the botanical name of a flower you are trying to identify and a dictionary of common plant names, I highly recommend Flora's Plant Names (Blooming Books, 2003).

If there are flowers you wish to know more about, visit www.florasphere.com and you will find links to connect to me as well as vibrant discussion groups. I enjoy nothing more than a good botanical exploration with like-minded friends.

GIVING FLOWERS

WHEN WE GIVE FLOWERS, most of us simply choose the blossoms and arrangements that we like rather than stopping and thinking of what the other person may like or, better still, choosing flowers that are fitting for the occasion or moment. Looking at an array of bouquets in a store can be overwhelming, however, so it is only natural that we tend to gravitate towards what we like as we struggle to make sense of this cornucopia of nature before us. We may, in fact, be drawn to certain flowers because of what they subconsciously mean to us at that time, rather than what they may mean to the recipient.

So, how do you select flowers for others? If you would like to give flowers you think the person may like, look up entries in SECTION ONE Meanings, which you think may reflect their personality. You may also look up meanings that align with the sentiments that you are hoping for the other person such as good luck, getting well, safe travels or love. If your floral gift is for an occasion or event, then search for entries in SECTION ONE that have something in common such as an anniversary, congratulations or longevity. At the end of the book, there are a few lists of correspondences for anniversaries and days, as well as zodiac and month lists.

Combinations of flowers can create wonderful, longer messages and were a favourites pastime of the English and Europeans in the Victorian era. Secret messages conveyed true feelings and elaborate plans between people during this ridgid time when sharing such sentiments openly was frowned upon. Today we may delight in the exchange of these bouquets of true meaning as a way of not only bringing our own wishes to another, but of connecting more closely with nature.

Any flowers are a welcome and much-adored gift, but by looking at the meaning of flowers you can create a bouquet, a plant gift, artwork or other floral gifts with greater depth, thoughtfulness, and positive energy to delight the receiver with a personally crafted message. Flowers and plants can even bring elements of healing. Look to the section, Healing with Flowers in this introduction for more information.

Perhaps you would like to give a plant as a gift. Be assured that even if the plant is not currently flowering, it still contains the same energy and message as if it were in bloom. Dried flowers, perfumes and botanical preparations all hold true to this as well.

Not everyone will have access to this book or have knowledge of the meanings of flowers, so you may perhaps like to include one of the following cards with your floral gift. Feel free to photocopy or create your own. More can be found at www.florasphere.com

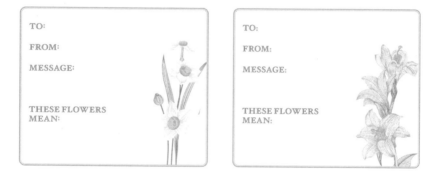

TO:		TO:	
FROM:		FROM:	
MESSAGE:		MESSAGE:	
THESE FLOWERS MEAN:		THESE FLOWERS MEAN:	

HEALING AND MEANINGFUL FLOWER GARDENS

CREATING A GARDEN TO EXPRESS YOUR HOPES, dreams and wishes, and perhaps even impart healing benefits upon those who visit, is so much easier once you understand the meanings of flowers. The botanical names of each and every flower are also listed in the back of this book in the 'Botanical Name Index' for easy and precise identification.

You may wish to have entire sections of your garden with the same theme and sentiments, or perhaps you could combine various flower meanings to craft a very personal healing and meaningful space suited for a particular purpose.

Other ideas include borders, which provide protection/welcome, trees that speak of the hopes you have for your future, garden beds planted by family and friends that express their personalities and dreams, and your own very special reflection, relaxation or meditation place, perhaps even a secret garden containing the wishes that only you truly know.

Why not create a container garden for a friend that expresses how you feel about them or what you wish for them – a small healing garden of love and hope? I find myself often making sweet fairy gardens for myself and for others, and I love exploring the world of smaller plants and their language for just the right blend of happiness and magic.

Don't forget vegetables! They, too, hold meaning. I have tried to include as many of the world's popular culinary favourites as possible in this book. Why don't you try plotting a veggie patch of your intentions for the season this year? I'm always fascinated to see which vegetables go together to say something quite unique, and I'm delighted by the clever and creative explorations of those who share my passion for the language of plants.

When visiting public gardens, this book can also be used very easily to explore the secret whispers of the blossoms you discover. Most gardeners can assist you in finding the name of your discovery, and larger institutions have very extensive resources to give you even more help. Oh, but be careful! You may be lost for days in botanical bliss!

CREATING WITH FLOWERS

How can you bring the power of flowers into your space or even to yourself permanently? Through art of course! The Impressionist painters developed a technique to quickly impart the impression, the emotional heart of the subject, and it is perhaps why so many of them selected flowers as their focus. They knew the change in mood and the familiar connections that flowers instantly bring to people. Many artists throughout history have focused on flowers as a subject. And they will forever more.

Those creating floral artworks for clients – like tattoo artists, florists and garden designers – can look up the sentiments and meanings their clients want to express in their designs. They may also wish to share the meanings of the flowers that their clients have selected as possibilities for their floral work.

Whether you are an artist or a crafter or both, this book will help you to create with flowers and invest far more meaning into your creative explorations. Imagine painting a picture, creating a sculpture or forming any artwork with flowers that perfectly capture the feelings and hopes that you may wish to bring into a home or space, or that you wish to provide for a person. If you craft, imagine the joy a creation filled with the deep meanings of particular flowers that you made could impart on those who enjoy your work. Card making, scrapbooking, quilting, sewing, textiles – the list goes on.

To inspire your creativity, simply look through SECTION ONE for the meanings you wish to convey in your work. To find your flower references to work with – either in person, through books or image libraries and the like – try using the botanical names I have included for exact identification. Do not rely completely on random internet searching. Consult resources such as gardening and plant identification books and websites, botanic gardens, flower and gardening groups and other reliable resources.

FLOWER BLESSINGS AND DREAMS

THIS BOOK ALSO WORKS AS A FLORAL DREAM DICTIONARY. Simply look up the flower that featured in your dream to find an indication of what the dream may mean. To expand on the meaning, you may then wish to look up a dream dictionary with the meanings you have found here.

To enrich your dream time and improve your sleep, look up the feelings and outcomes you are wanting to achieve. Perhaps you could obtain floral essences, botanical and herbal creations, or even gather these flowers in some other form – either fresh or in artworks in your bedroom to instill your sleep time with flower support.

FLOWER READING

CONSULTING FLOWERS FOR DIVINATION is known by various terms, including floramancy, floromancy and flower reading, and has been practised throughout history across most cultures.

The meanings of a flower can indicate something personal for us when we first ask a question and are willing to connect with nature. The flowers, however, are happy doing their own thing; they are not here to be of complete service to us. Their meanings are for their benefit, not ours, but as with any healing outcome, we are very lucky that we can benefit from their energy being around us.

I am sure that you may have asked a blossom the outcome of a romance in the childhood game of 'he/she loves me/loves me not', and if a flower blooms unexpectantly or comes into your life with repeated great passion, do you not wonder why that is?

The meanings in this book can all be used to better understand the true meanings of flowers when consulting nature as an oracle. You may like to reference the flowers that come to you by chance, for a deeper understanding. You could also use the knowledge of flower meanings that you develop through this book as the foundation of a flower reading practice for other people or even combine this knowledge with other modalities.

Simply opening the book to a random page while asking a question can connect you with flowers as oracles. Read what the selected flower's properties are for indications to your current situation.

If you are reading for others, ask your client which flowers are their favourites and which keep presenting to them in their lives or those they have found challenging. These flower appearances can provide a very good foundation for a divination reading once you consult with the meanings and correspondences in this book.

I have also provided zodiac flowers, days of the week flowers, the month and other correspondences, at the back of this book, to provide even more layers in your readings for yourself or others.

When reading flowers for others, I like to suggest that the person connect with a particular flower in order to manifest the outcome they desire. This is easily achieved by referring to SECTION ONE and looking through possible energies in the meanings I have listed. Once found, you might like to create essences, give the client an image of the flower, or even create a meditation or story for them to enhance their experience and deepen their connection with their flower reading.

HEALING WITH FLOWERS

WHILE DIRECTLY INGESTING or applying herbal remedies provides healing, simply being in the flowers' presence also offers support.

Healing happens because flowers and plants change an individual's energy or space and, through this, the healing response begins. Simply giving someone fresh flowers or bringing them into a space enables the emotional change that leads to healing. By looking at specific flowers and their individual healing qualities, we can also bring focused change.

The possible healing outcomes suggested via the flower meanings in this book are based on the applications described. Most will naturally align with herbal medicine possibilities, but medicinal applications are beyond the scope of the suggestions in this book. The entries here are a starting point for the exploration of herbal remedies and, as always, you must ensure correct botanical identification and the expert guidance of a registered professional when using flowers and plants for medicinal use.

To select flowers for healing outcomes for yourself or others, define the outcome you want to achieve. Look up these qualities in SECTION ONE Meanings. These flowers would be perfect as floral gifts and plants in healing gardens, as subjects for art or craft, and could be utilised in flower essence and aromatherapy work by a qualified and experienced practitioner.

Many flowers listed in this book (or any other such list) are poisonous and may even cause death if consumed or used topically (on your skin). So while most flowers and plants can indeed be consumed and used in lotions and potions for medicinal, culinary, healing and cosmetic creations, it is your responsibility to ensure that they are correctly identified, are organic and non-toxic, and do not present an allergy issue for your purpose. The information supplied in this book does not replace the care and advice of a qualified medical practitioner. If you wish to use the information in this book as a complimentary therapy, you should first seek a professional herbalist's advice.

TUBEROSE
Arum Harchil
isquodipsam
vendestia

SECTION ONE

MEANINGS

A

A token » Laurustinus (Viburnum tinus)

A tribute to your beauty and spirituality » Lilac, White (Syringa)

Absence » Wormwood (Artemisia absinthium), Zinnia (Zinnia elegans)

Ability » Money Plant (Lunaria annua)

Ability to be happy » Iris, Blue Flag (Iris versicolor)

Ability to cope » Skullcap (Scutellaria)

Ability to see » Clary Sage (Salvia sclarea)

Ability, healing » Rose, Cherokee (Rosa laevigata)

Abilities, hidden » Larch (Larix decidua)

Abilities, psychic » Mugwort (Artemisia vulgaris)

Abundance » Mesquite (Prosopis)

Abuse » Red Hot Poker (Kniphofia)

Abuse, do not » Safflower (Carthamus tinctorius)

Abuse, overcoming » Chinese Lantern (Physalis heterophylla)

Absolute authority » Black Orchid (Trichoglottis brachiata)

Abundance » Rabbit Orchid (Leptoceras menziesii), Carnation (Dianthus caryophyllus), Jasmine (Jasminum officinale), Peruvian Lily (Alstroemeria), Grape (Vitis), Roman Chamomile (Chamaemelum nobile), Stargazer Lily, Pink (Lilium orientalis), Marsh Marigold (Caltha palustris), Honesty (Lunaria annua), Golden Trumpet Tree (Tabebuia alba), Maple (Acer), Strawberry (Fragaria x ananassa), Pumpkin (Cucurbita pepo), Sesame (Sesamum indicum)

Acceptance » Sydney Rock Rose (Boronia serrulata), Magnolia (Magnolia campbellii), Scottish Primrose (Primula scotica), Crown Vetch (Securigera varia), Oregon Grape (Mahonia aquifolium), Jacobinia (Jacobinia), Mountain

Pride (Penstemon newberryi), Tall Yellow Top (Senecio magnificus)

Accepting change » Solomon's Seal (Polygonatum)

Accommodating disposition » Valerian (Polemonium caeruleum)

Accuracy » Rosemary (Rosmarinus officinalis)

Achieving greatness » Eggplant (Solanum melongena)

Achievement » Honey Grevillea (Grevillea eriostachya), Rose, Cecil Brunner (Rosa Mlle. Cecile Brunner)

Achievement, great » Oak (Quercus robur)

Acknowledgment » Canterbury Bells (Campanula medium)

Action, energy to » Cayenne (Capsicum frutescens)

Action, decisive » Artichoke, Jerusalem (Helianthus tuberosus)

Action, positive » Scotch Thistle (Onopordum acanthium)

Activation » Mandrake (Mandragora officinarum)

Activity » Thyme (Thymus vulgaris)

Activity, increase » Castor Oil Plant (Ricinus communis)

Acquaintance » Pelargonium (Pelargonium cucullatum)

Adaptability » Rose, Cherokee (Rosa laevigata), Arfaj (Rhanterium epapposum)

Adaptation » Native Passionflower (Passiflora herbertiana), Statice (Limonium)

Addiction, release love » Jack-in-the-Pulpit (Arisaema triphyllum)

Adjustment, attitude » Skunk Cabbage (Symplocarpus foetidus)

Admiration » Lavender (Lavandula stoechas), Heather, Lavender (Calluna vulgaris), Scabiosa (Scabiosa), Purple Orchid (Cattleya skinneri)

Admire you, I » Heather, Lavender (Calluna vulgaris)

Admire you but cannot love you, I » Laurel (Laurus nobilis)

Adorable, you are » Camellia, White (Camellia)

Adoration » Heliconia (Heliconia)

Adroitness » Spider Orchid (Caladenia)

Adversity, cheerfulness in » Xeranthemum (Xeranthemum bracteatum)

Adversity, constancy in » Pine (Pinus sylvestris)

Adversity, fidelity in » Wallflower (Erysimum)

Adversity, patience in » Chamomile, German (Matricaria chamomilla)

A

Adversity, solace in » Firethorn (Pyracantha)

Adversity, strength in » Walnut (Juglans regia)

Adversity, victory through » Spurge Laurel (Daphne laureola)

Advice » Rhubarb (Rheum rhabarbarum)

Affection » Thyme (Thymus vulgaris), Stock (Matthiola incana), Mistletoe (Viscum album), Celosia (Celosia), Crown Vetch (Securigera varia), Morning Glory (Ipomoea purpurea), Pear (Pyrus communis), Sorrel (Rumex acetosa)

Affection, enduring » Gorse (Ulex europaeus), Locust, Green (Gleditsia triacanthos)

Affection for you, I have » Stock (Matthiola incana)

Affection, lasting » Kalanchoe (Kalanchoe)

Affection, paternal » Sorrel (Rumex acetosa)

Affection, pure » Carnation, White (Dianthus caryophyllus)

Affection, true » Cereus (Cereus)

Affinity » Vanilla (Vanilla planifolia)

Afterthought » Aster (Aster), Michaelmas Daisy (Aster amellus)

Again, begin » Rose, Miniature (Rosa)

Against you, I declare » Liquorice (Glycyrrhiza glabra)

Age » Guelder-Rose (Viburnum opulus)

Age, old » Arborvitae (Thuja), Tree of Life (Guaiacum officinale)

Aggression, balance » Astilbe (Astilbe)

Aggressive energy » Peanut (Arachis hypogaea)

Agitation » Moving Plant (Mimosa pudica), Sainfoin (Onobrychis)

Agree with you, I » Rose, Dark Pink (Rosa)

Agreement » Rose, Dark Pink (Rosa), Phlox (Phlox)

Alchemy » Honesty (Lunaria annua)

Alchemy, plant » Hellebore (Helleborus)

Alert, be » Sundew (Drosera auriculata)

A

Alert mind » Peppermint (Mentha piperita)

Alignment » Five Corners (Styphelia laeta), Hoya (Hoya australis)

Alignment, chakras » Lilac (Syringa vulgaris)

Alignment, female » Easter Lily (Lilium longiflorum)

Altruism » Peach Blossom (Prunus persica)

Always lovely » Pink (Dianthus plumarius)

All else, place you above » Ash (Fraxinus)

All heal » Mistletoe (Viscum album)

All I have, I offer you » Wheat (Triticum)

All, I offer you my » Shepherd's Purse (Capsella bursa-pastoris)

Alleviate » Loveage (Levisticum officinale)

Alone, you are not » Sydney Rock Rose (Boronia serrulata)

Am I forgiven? » Holly (Ilex aquifolium)

Am I forgotten? » Holly (Ilex aquifolium)

Ambassador of love » Rose, Cabbage (Rosa x centifolia)

Ambition » Hollyhock (Alcea rosea), Stargazer Lily, Pink (Lilium orientalis), Ivy (Hedera), Pomegranate Blossom (Punica granatum)

Ambition, female » Hollyhock, White (Alcea rosea)

Ambition, modest » Trillium (Trillium)

Amiability » Fuchsia (Fuchsia magellanica)

Animosity » St John's Wort (Hypericum perforatum)

Anger » Gorse (Ulex europaeus), Petunia (Petunia), Fumitory (Fumaria officinalis)

Anger dissipated » Althea (Hibiscus syriacus)

Anger, release » Burdock (Arctium), Firethorn (Pyracantha)

Anniversary, happy » Tree Peony (Paeonia suffruticosa)

Answer, I need an » Pink Heath (Epacris impressa)

Answers » Cooktown Orchid (Vappodes phalaenopsis), Rafflesia (Rafflesia arnoldii)

A

Answers within » Violet, Blue (Viola sororia)

Answered, prayers » Frog Orchid (Coeloglossum)

Anticipation » Gooseberry (Ribes uva-crispa), Anemone (Anemone), Forsythia (Forsythia), Red Whortleberry (Vaccinium)

Anti-sorcery » Boneset (Eupatorium perfoliatum)

Anti-theft » Juniper (Juniperus), Caraway (Carum carvi)

Anxiety » Scottish Primrose (Primula scotica), Columbine (Aquilegia vulgaris), American Pasqueflower (Pulsatilla hirsutissima)

Anxiety, calm » Motherwort (Leonurus cardiaca)

Anxiety relief » Clary Sage (Salvia sclarea)

Anxiousness » Grey Spider Flower (Grevillea buxifolia)

Anything is possible » Delphinium (Delphinium)

Apathy » Hop (Humulus lupulus)

Aphrodisiac » Garlic (Allium sativum), Celery (Apium graveolens)

Apology » Flannel Flower (Actinotus helianthi)

Appreciate » Achimenes (Achimenes)

Appreciate you, I » Gerbera Daisy (Gerbera jamesonii), Lisianthus (Eustoma grandiflorum), Rose, Peach (Rosa)

Appreciation » Poinsettia (Euphorbia pulcherrima), Gerbera Daisy (Gerbera jamesonii), Lisianthus (Eustoma grandiflorum), Rose, Dark Pink (Rosa)

Appreciation for life » Forsythia (Forsythia)

Aquiring knowledge » Opoponax (Commiphora erythraea)

Ardent love » Himalayan Balsam (Impatiens glandulifera), Carnation, White (Dianthus caryophyllus)

Ardour » Broom (Genisteae), Cactus (Cactaceae), Fraxinella (Dictamnus), Lords and Ladies (Arum maculatum)

Argument » Fig (Ficus carica)

Arguments, end » Honeysuckle (Lonicera)

Articulation » Celandine (Ficaria verna)

A

Art » White Nun Orchid (Lycaste skinneri alba), Auricula (Primula auricular)

Artistic expression » Owl's Clover (Orthocarpus purpurascense)

Arts » Acanthus (Acanthus mollis)

Arts, dark » Blackthorn (Prunus spinosa)

Ascension » Princess Flower Tree (Tibouchina semidecandra)

Aspects, feminine » Sego Lily (Calochortus nuttallii)

Aspire » Harebell (Campanula rotundifolia)

Assertiveness » Geraldton Wax (Chamelaucium uncinatum), Sunflower (Helianthus annuus)

Assistance » Ageratum (Ageratum)

Assuredness » Karee (Rhus pendulina)

Astral projection » Mugwort (Artemisia vulgaris), Motherwort (Leonurus cardiaca)

Astral travel » Broom (Genisteae)

Attachment » Grape (Vitis)

Attachments, release » Trumpet Creeper (Campsis radicans)

Attachments, unfortunate » Mournful Widow (Scabiosa atropurpurea)

Attack, protection from physical » Bitter Root (Lewisia rediviva)

Attainment » Tea Tree (Leptospermum myrsinoides)

Attention seeking » Heliconia (Heliconia)

Attitude » Cooktown Orchid (Vappodes phalaenopsis), Red Hot Poker (Kniphofia)

Attitude adjustment » Skunk Cabbage (Symplocarpus foetidus)

Attitude, happy » Trout Lily (Erythronium americanum)

Attitude, open » Vervain (Verbena officinalis)

Attract good spirits » Marshmallow (Althea officinalis)

Attract love » Lady's Mantle (Alchemilla vulgaris), Loveage (Levisticum officinale), Chamomile, German (Matricaria chamomilla)

Attract money » Aspen (Populus tremula)

A

Attract wealth » Chamomile, Roman (Chamaemelum nobile)

Attraction » Moon Orchid (Phalaenopsis amabilis)

Attraction, beauty is your only » Rose, Beach (Rosa rugosa)

Attractiveness » Ranunculus (Ranunculus), Lemon Verbena (Aloysia triphylla)

Attunement » Dayflower (Commelina)

Austerity » Thistle, Common (Cirsium vulgare), Sea Holly (Eryngium maritimum)

Austerity, in love » Chamomile, Roman (Chamaemelum nobile)

Authentic spirituality » Jack-in-the-Pulpit (Arisaema triphyllum)

Authenticity » Antarctic Pearlwort (Colobanthus quitensis), Wormwood (Artemisia absinthium)

A

Authority, absolute » Black Orchid (Trichoglottis brachiata)

Autumn love » Guelder-Rose (Viburnum opulus)

Available, I am » Cranes-Bill (Geranium maculatum)

Availability » Cranes-Bill (Geranium maculatum)

Avarice » Auricula, Scarlet (Primula auricular)

Avert envy » Garlic (Allium sativum)

Await your return, I happily » Red Whortleberry (Vaccinium)

Awaken » Trillium (Trillium), American Pasqueflower (Pulsatilla hirsutissima)

Awaken magical powers » Okra (Abelmoschus esculentus)

Awakening » Bearberry (Arctostaphylos uva-ursi)

Aware of present » Horse-Chestnut (Aesculus hippocastanum)

Awareness » Gymea Lily (Doryanthes excelsa), Gardenia (Gardenia jasminoides), Lupin (Lupinus perennis), Queen Anne's Lace (Daucus carota), Bells of Ireland (Moluccella laevis), Rose, Prairie (Rosa arkansana), Butterfly Orchid (Psychopsis), Pentas (Pentas lanceolata)

Awareness of the divine » Aspen (Populus tremula)

Awareness of personal value » Cloudberry (Rubus chamaemorus)

Awareness, psychic » Rosemary (Rosmarinus officinalis), Wild Banana

Orchid (Schomburgkia thomsoniana), Cauliflower (Brassica oleracea), Lemongrass (Cymbopogon citratus)

Awareness, self » Clubmoss (Lycopodium), Gotu Kola (Hydrocotyle asiatica)

Awareness, sensory » Ginger (Zingiber officinale), Texas Bluebonnet (Lupinus texensis)

Awareness, spatial » Pink Knotweed (Persicaria capitata)

Away, go » Chilli (Capsicum)

Awkwardness » Mugwort (Artemisia vulgaris)

B

Baby blessing, mother and » Fir (Abies)

Bad, I will stay with you in good times and » Virginia Creeper (Parthenocissus quinquefolia)

Bad to good, from » Service Tree (Sorbus)

Balance » Bottlebrush (Callistemon linearis), Hawthorn (Crataegus monogyna), Meadowsweet (Filipendula ulmaria), Ginseng (Panax), Red Clover (Trifolium pratense), Maple (Acer), Hickory (Carya), Redwood (Sequoiadendron giganteum), Vanilla (Vanilla planifolia), Quinoa (Chenopodium quinoa)

Balance, emotional » Cat's Tail Grass (Phleum pratense), Showy Lady Slipper (Cypripedium reginae), Ipecac (Gillenia stipulata)

Balance emotions » Lemon Balm (Melissa officinalis), Prairie Crocus (Pulsatilla patens)

Balance, female » Evening Primrose (Oenothera)

Balance of mind » Holly (Ilex aquifolium)

Balance, relationship » Gloxinia (Gloxinia), Motherwort (Leonurus cardiaca)

Balance, spiritual » Passion Flower (Passiflora incarnate)

Balance, male and female energies » Quince (Cydonia oblonga)

Balanced aggression » Astilbe (Astilbe)

Balanced emotions » Native Passionflower (Passiflora herbertiana), Coconut (Cocus nucifera)

Balanced energy » Pasqueflower (Pulsatilla vulgaris)

Balanced relationships » Breadfruit (Artocarpus altilis)

Balancing male and female energies » Crepe Myrtle (Lagerstroemia indica)

Balancing sexuality » Wild Banana Orchid (Schomburgkia thomsoniana)

Banish evil spirits » Soy Bean (Glycine max)

Banish fear » Birch (Betula)

Banill ill will » Sheep Sorrel (Rumex acetosella)

Banish negative thoughts » Lemon (Citrus limon)

Banishing » Hellebore (Helleborus), Yarrow (Achillea millefolium)

Banishing unwanted spirits » Solomon's Seal (Polygonatum)

B

Bantering » Southernwood (Artemisia abrotanum)

Barriers, release » Lady's Mantle (Alchemilla vulgaris)

Bashful love » Rose, Deep Red (Rosa)

Bashfulness » Blushing Bride (Tillandsia ionantha), Primrose (Primula vulgaris)

Be alert » Sundew (Drosera auriculata)

Be brave » Waratah (Telopea speciosissima), Heather, White (Calluna vulgaris)

Be cautious » Goldenrod (Solidago virgaurea)

Be happy » Shasta Daisy (Leucanthemum maximum), Lily of the Valley (Convallaria majalis), Honeysuckle (Lonicera)

Be mine » Carnation, Red (Dianthus caryophyllus)

Be mine again » Willow (Salix alba)

Be my support » Bryony, Black (Dioscorea communis)

Be patient » Flax (Linum usitatissimum)

Be present in this moment » Baby's Breath (Gypsophila paniculata)

Be quiet » Belladonna (Atropa belladonna)

Be still » Belladonna (Atropa belladonna), Aconite (Aconite)

Be strong » Sunflower (Helianthus annuus)

Be true to yourself » Aster (Aster)

Be with you, I want to » Rose, Dark Pink (Rosa), Petunia (Petunia)

Beautiful » Hibiscus, Red (Hibiscus rosa-sinensis)

Beautiful complexion » Rose, Damask (Rosa x damascena)

Beautiful eyes » Tulip, Variegated (Tulipa)

Beautiful relationships » Gloxinia (Gloxinia)

Beautiful, you are » Frangipani (Plumeria alba), Sweet Pea (Lathyrus odoratus), Rose, Red (Rosa), Heather, Lavender (Calluna vulgaris), Apricot (Prunus armeniaca)

Beauty » Rose, Red (Rosa), Heather, Lavender (Calluna vulgaris), Cosmos (Cosmos), Ginseng (Panax), Opium Poppy (Papaver somniferum), Hazel (Corylus), Lime (Tilia europaea), Marguerite Daisy (Argyranthemum frutescens), Puti Tai Nobiu (Bougainvillea spectabilis), White Nun Orchid (Lycaste skinneri alba), Rosewood (Pterocarpus indicus), White Trillium (Trillium grandiflorum), Apricot (Prunus armeniaca), Ginkgo (Ginkgo biloba), Henna (Lawsonia inermis), Peanut (Arachis hypogaea), Rose, Beach (Rosa rugosa)

B

Beauty always new » Rose, China (Rosa chinensis)

Beauty and spirituality, a tribute to your » Lilac, White (Syringa)

Beauty, delicate » Hibiscus (Hibiscus)

Beauty, divine » Cowslip (Primula veris)

Beauty ever new » Rose, Damask (Rosa x damascena)

Beauty have charmed me completely, your grace and » Cowslip (Primula veris)

Beauty, I love your » Puerto Rican Hibiscus (Thespesia grandiflora)

Beauty, I see your » Tulip, Variegated (Tulipa)

Beauty, inner » Bird of Paradise (Strelitzia reginae)

Beauty is your only attraction » Rose, Beach (Rosa rugosa)

Beauty, lasting » Stock (Matthiola incana), Pink (Dianthus plumarius)

Beauty, mental » Kennedia (Kennedia)

Beauty, modest » Trillium (Trillium)

Beauty, natural » Sycamore (Acer pseudoplatanus)

Beauty, neglected » Throatwort (Trachelium caeruleum)

Beauty, pensive » Rose, Burgundy (Rosa)

Beauty, physical » Jojoba (Simmondsia chinensis)

Beauty, preservation of » Osmanthus (Osmanthus fragrans)

Beauty, rare » Hibiscus, Pink (Hibiscus rosa-sinensis)

Beauty, splendid » Amaryllis (Amaryllis)

Beauty, surround me in natural » Persimmon (Diospyros virginiana)

Beauty, transient » Cereus (Cereus)

Beauty, unconscious » Rose, Burgundy (Rosa)

Beauty, youthful » Tiare (Gardenia taitensis)

Begin again » Crowsfoot (Erodium crinitum), Rose, Miniature (Rosa)

Beginning » Spurge Laurel (Daphne laureola), Purple Saxifrage (Saxifraga oppositifolia)

Beginning, new » Mulla Mulla (Ptilotus exaltatus), Snowdrop (Galanthus nivalis), Rose, Yellow (Rosa), Jade (Crassula ovata), Bloodroot (Sanguinaria canadensis)

Belief » Grey Spider Flower (Grevillea buxifolia), Passion Flower (Passiflora incarnate)

Belief in own gifts » Iris, Fairy (Dietes grandiflora)

Belief in self » Mountain Avens (Dryas octopetala)

Belief in the future » Gentian (Gentiana)

Belief, self- » Star of Bethlehem (Ornithogalum), Lechenaultia (Lechenaultia formosa),

Believe in me » Tulip, Red (Tulipa)

Believe in you, I » Tree Spider Orchid (Dendrobium tetragonum), Antarctic Pearlwort (Colobanthus quitensis), Foxglove (Digitalis purpurea), Iris, Blue Flag (Iris versicolor)

Belong here, you » Hibiscus, White (Hibiscus arnottianus)

Belonging » Hibiscus, White (Hibiscus arnottianus), Primrose (Primula vulgaris)

B

Beneficence » Marshmallow (Althea officinalis)

Benefits, fringe » Radish (Raphanus sativus)

Benevolence » Potato (Solanum tuberosum)

Best days are over, my » Meadow Saffron (Colchicum autumnale)

Betrayal » Rose, Wild (Rosa acicularis)

Betrayed, confidences » Iris, Fairy (Dietes grandiflora)

Betrothal » Herb Paris (Paris quadrifolia)

Better, change for the » Yellow Elder (Tecoma stans)

Better times » Kumquat (Citrus japonica)

Beware » Foxglove (Digitalis purpurea), Heath Bell (Erica cinerea)

Beware of excess » Rhododendron (Rhododendron)

Beyond limits » Great Rhododendron (Rhododendron maximum)

Binding » Goosegrass (Galium aparine), Knotweed (Polygonum aviculare)

Birth » Tree Peony (Paeonia suffruticosa), Trillium (Trillium), Purple
     Saxifrage (Saxifraga oppositifolia), Dittany (Origanum dictamnus), Peanut
     (Arachis hypogaea)

Birth of a baby, congratulations on » Rabbit Orchid (Leptoceras menziesii)

Birth, support » Trillium (Trillium)

Bitter feelings, release » Harvest Brodiaea (Brodiaea elegans)

Blessing » Frankincense (Boswellia sacra)

Blessing, bride » Queen of the Meadow (Filipendula ulmaria)

Blessing, mother and baby » Fir (Abies)

Blessings, wedding » Sweet Bugle (Lycopus virginicus)

Blocks, release » Iris, Blue Flag (Iris versicolor)

Blocks, release emotional » Lime (Tilia x europaea)

Blockage release » Bearberry (Arctostaphylos uva-ursi)

Blockages cleared » Star of Bethlehem (Ornithogalum), Cayenne (Capsicum
     frutescens)

Blood » Beetroot (Beta vulgaris)

B

Bluntness » Borage (Borago officinalis)

Blush, you make me » Marjoram (Origanum majorana)

Boldness » Pink (Dianthus plumarius), Spruce (Picea)

Bond, love » Mistletoe (Viscum album)

Bond between worlds » tabacco (Nicotiana tabacum)

Bond with creator » tabacco (Nicotiana tabacum)

Bonds » Ivy (Hedera), Bindweed, Field (Convolvulus arvensis)

Boost, enthusiasium » Cabbage (Brassica oleracea var. capitata)

Boundaries » Rose, Cecil Brunner (Rosa Mlle. Cecile Brunner)

Boundaries, protective » Broccoli (Brassica oleracea var. italica)

Boundary protection » Chrysanthemum, Yellow (Chrysanthemum)

B   Boundary setting » Gladiola (Gladiolus)

Brave, be » Waratah (Telopea speciosissima), Heather, White (Calluna vulgaris)

Bravery » Waratah (Telopea speciosissima), Edelweiss (Leontopodium alpinum), Thyme (Thymus vulgaris), Brussels Sprout (Brassica oleracea), Pyrethrum (Anacyclus pyrethrum)

Break connections » Kinnick-Kinnick (Arctostaphylos ursi)

Break hexes » Capsicum (Capsicum annuum), Chilli (Capsicum), Galangal (Alpinia galangal)

Breaking, curse » Okra (Abelmoschus esculentus)

Breaking free » Tomato (Solanum lycopersicum)

Breaking, link » Walnut (Juglans regia)

Breaking negative patterns » Native Passionflower (Passiflora herbertiana)

Break through » Flame of the Forest (Butea monosperma)

Breakthroughs » Hoya (Hoya australis), Dagger's Log (Agave karatto miller), Yesterday, Today and Tomorrow (Brunfelsia)

Breakup, healing » Bleeding Heart (Lamprocapnos spectabilis)

Breath » Hyssop (Hyssopus officinalis)

Breathe » Baby's Breath (Gypsophila paniculata), Crocus (Crocus)

Bride, blessing » Queen of the Meadow (Filipendula ulmaria)

Bright, ever » Cineraria (Cineraria)

Brightness » Kowhai (Sophora)

Brilliance, transient » Rose, China (Rosa chinensis)

Broad perspective » Venus Flytrap (Dionaea muscipula)

Broken heart » Love Lies Bleeding (Amaranthus caudatus)

Broken promises » Hoya (Hoya australis)

Brotherly love » Lilac (Syringa vulgaris)

Brusqueness » Borage (Borago officinalis)

Build courage » Birch (Betula)

Bulkiness » Pumpkin (Cucurbita pepo)

Burn, I » Cactus (Cactaceae)

Business » Ginkgo (Ginkgo biloba), Spanish Moss (Tillandsia usneoides)

Busybody » Cardinal Vine (Ipomoea quamoclit)

B

C

Calculated risks » Oleander (Nerium oleander)

Calling spirits » Ginkgo (Ginkgo biloba)

Calm » Flannel Flower (Actinotus helianthi), Daisy (Bellis perennis), Camellia, Japanese (Camellia japonica), Geranium, Rose (Pelargonium graveolens), Evening Primrose (Oenothera), Feverfew (Tanacetum parthenium), Crown Vetch (Securigera varia), Tree Houseleek (Aeonium), Chamomile, Roman (Chamaemelum nobile), Statice (Limonium), Lemon Balm (Melissa officinalis), Sweet Marjoram (Origanum marjorana), Cat's Tail Grass (Phleum pratense), Star Anise (Illicium verum), Rockmelon (Cucumis melo)

Calm anxiety » Motherwort (Leonurus cardiaca)

Calm down » Geranium, Rose (Pelargonium graveolens), Pasqueflower (Pulsatilla vulgaris), Chamomile, German (Matricaria chamomilla), Ipecac (Gillenia stipulata)

Calm hysteria » Catnip (Nepeta cataria)

Calm, inner » Tiger Lily (Lilium tigrinum), Wood Betony (Stachys betonica)

Calm repose » Buckbean (Menyanthes)

Calm transition » Bee Balm (Monarda)

Calmative, mental » Rock Rose (Helianthemum)

Calming » Lily of the Valley (Convallaria majalis), Lisianthus (Eustoma grandiflorum), Pasqueflower (Pulsatilla vulgaris), Speedwell (Veronica officinalis)

Calmness » Red Clover (Trifolium pratense)

Calms fears » Elder (Sambucus nigra)

Calumny » Madder (Rubia tinctorum)

Can we be friends? » Shasta Daisy (Leucanthemum maximum)

Care » Safflower (Carthamus tinctorius), Xu Duan (Dipsacus japonica)

Care, emotional » Downy Hawthorn (Crataegus mollis)

Care, I do not » Plum (Prunus domestica)

Career » Rabbit Orchid (Leptoceras menziesii)

Catalyst » Mandrake (Mandragora officinarum)

Caution » Oleander (Nerium oleander), Bittersweet (Solanum dulcamara)

Cautious, be » Goldenrod (Solidago virgaurea)

Celebration » Lechenaultia (Lechenaultia formosa), Gerbera Daisy (Gerbera jamesonii), Trillium (Trillium)

Celibacy » Wood Betony (Stachys betonica), Rosebay Willowherb (Chamerion angustifolium)

Centred » Shepherd's Purse (Capsella bursa-pastoris), Statice (Limonium)

Chakra alignment » Lilac (Syringa vulgaris)

Challenge/s » Lantern Bush (Abutilon halophilum), Larch (Larix decidua), Violet Nightshade (Solanum brownii), Cayenne (Capsicum frutescens)

Challenge you, I » Cayenne (Capsicum frutescens)

Challenged, clarity when » Mountain Laurel (Kalmia latifolia)

Challenges, embrace » Ceibo (Erythrina crista-galli)

C

Challenges, fun » Nasturtium (Tropaeolum majus)

Challenges, new » Coltsfoot (Tussilago farfara)

Challenges, strength for » Mint (Mentha)

Changing needs » Statice (Limonium)

Chance/s, second » Sacred Blue Lily (Nymphaea caerulea)

Change/s » Bee Balm (Monarda), Scarlet Pimpernel (Anagallis arvensis), Mayflower (Epigaea repens), Fireweed (Chamerion angustifolium), Snowplant (Sarcodes sanquinea), Crowsfoot (Erodium crinitum), Magnolia (Magnolia campbellii)

Change, accepting » Solomon's Seal (Polygonatum)

Change but in death, I » Laurel (Laurus nobilis)

Change, courage to » Thorn Apple (Datura stamonium)

Change, failure to » Siberian Iris (Iris sibirica)

Change for the better » Yellow Elder (Tecoma stans)

Change habits » Yellow Dock (Rumex crispus)

Change in goals » Iris Croatica (Iris perunika)

Change, major » Mistletoe (Viscum album)

Change, positive » Dog Rose (Rosa canina), Edelweiss (Leontopodium alpinum), Radish (Raphanus sativus)

Change, support during » Walnut (Juglans regia)

Changed opinion » Cooktown Orchid (Vappodes phalaenopsis)

Changing, ever » Virginia Creeper (Parthenocissus quinquefolia)

Changing sex » Persimmon (Diospyros virginiana)

Channel opening » Hepatica (Hepatica)

Character, strength of » Pine (Pinus sylvestris)

Charity » Turnip (Brassica rapa subsp. rapa):

Charm » Ranunculus (Ranunculus), Cowslip (Primula veris)

Charms, your qualities surpass your » Mignonette (Reseda odorata)

Charmed me completely, your grace and beauty have » Cowslip (Primula veris)

C

Charming » Spindle (Euonymus)

Charisma » Moon Orchid (Phalaenopsis amabilis)

Chaste love » Rose, Pink (Rosa)

Chastity » Lily of the Valley (Convallaria majalis), Sweet Chestnut (Castanea sativa), Camphor (Cinnamomum camphora), Cucumber (Cucumis sativus), Lettuce (Lactuca sativa), Pineapple (Ananas comosus), Prickly Pear (Opuntia ficus-indica)

Cheer up » Buttercup (Ranunculus acris), Guava (Psidium guajava)

Cheerfulness » Buttercup (Ranunculus acris), Chrysanthemum, Florist's (Chrysanthemum morifolium), Shasta Daisy (Leucanthemum maximum), Gerbera Daisy (Gerbera jamesonii), Crocus (Crocus), Holly (Ilex aquifolium), Chocolate Flower (Berlandiera lyrata), Hibiscus, Native Yellow (Hibiscus brackenridgei), Desert Marigold (Baileya)

Cheerfulness in adversity » Xeranthemum (Xeranthemum bracteatum)

Cheerfulness in old age » Michaelmas Daisy (Aster amellus), Starwort (Stellaria)

Childhood » Scarlet Pimpernel (Anagallis arvensis)

Childhood healing » Cyclamen (Cyclamen)

Childhood memories » Rose, Miniature (Rosa)

Children » Coltsfoot (Tussilago farfara)

Christianity » Cedar of Lebanon (Cedrus libani)

Chivalry » Monkshood (Aconitum)

Choices, clear » Nettle (Urtica)

Choices, positive » African Daisy (Osteospermum)

Choose » Pyramidal Orchid (Anacamptis pyramidalis)

Choose you, I » Geranium, Ivy-Leafed (Pelargonium peltatum)

Choose, you need to » Pyramidal Orchid (Anacamptis pyramidalis)

Choose the right path » Lily of the Valley (Convallaria majalis)

Christianity » Dogwood (Cornus)

Clairvoyance » Monkshood (Aconitum), Mugwort (Artemisia vulgaris), Cinnamon (Cinnamomum verum), Lobelia (Lobelia inflata)

C

Clarity » Boronia (Boronia ledifolia), Grass Tree (Xanthorrhoea resinosa), Sweet Alyssum (Alyssum maritimum), Hemp (Cannabis sativa), Angel'sTrumpet (Brugmansia candida), Dandelion (Taraxacum officinale), Petunia (Petunia), Hippeastrum (Hippeastrum), Rosemary (Rosmarinus officinalis), Trout Lily (Erythronium americanum), Greater Celandine (Chelidonium majus), Peppermint (Mentha piperita), Catnip (Nepeta cataria), Clary Sage (Salvia sclarea), Red Clover (Trifolium pratense), Ginger (Zingiber officinale), Carrot (Daucus carota subsp. sativus), Grapefruit (Citrus parasisi), Coffee (Coffea arabica)

Clarity, emotional » Love-in-a-Mist (Nigella damascena), Gerbera Daisy, Yellow (Gerbera jamesonii)

Clarity, mental » Eyebright (Euphrasia officinalis)

Clarity of mind » Hawkweed (Hieracium)

Clarity of purpose » Deer Grass (Trichophorum cespitosum)

Clarity, visual » Ox-Eye Daisy (Leucanthemum vulgare)

Clarity when challenged » Mountain Laurel (Kalmia latifolia)

Cleanliness » Hyssop (Hyssopus officinalis)

Cleansing » Bottlebrush (Callistemon linearis), Lechenaultia (Lechenaultia formosa)Lavender(Lavandulastoechas),Bittersweet(Solanumdulcamara), Calendula (Calendula officinalis), Primrose (Primula vulgaris), Juniper (Juniperus), Sage (Salvia officinalis), Hepatica (Hepatica), Lemon Blossom (Citrus x limon), Oregon Grape (Mahonia aquifolium), Red Clover (Trifolium pratense), Broom (Genisteae), Crab Apple Tree (Malus sylvestris), Sagebrush (Artemisia tridentate), Lettuce (Lactuca sativa), Marjoram (Origanum majorana)

Cleansing, etheric » Dutchman's Breeches (Dicentra cucullaria)

Cleansing, physical » Cedar of Lebanon (Cedrus libani), Luffa (Luffa aegyptiaca)

Cleansing, ritual » Vervain (Verbena officinalis)

Cleansing, space » Alkanet (Alkanna tentoria), Lemon (Citrus limon)

Clear choices » Nettle (Urtica)

Clear expression » Chickweed (Stellaria media)

C

Clear negative emotions » Gerbera Daisy, Orange (Gerbera jamesonii)

Clear negativity » Red Clover (Trifolium pratense), Sandalwood (Santalum album)

Clear personal energies » Purple Saxifrage (Saxifraga oppositifolia)

Clear perspective » Eyebright (Euphrasia officinalis), Pine Drops (Pterospora andromedea)

Clear stagnant energy » Skunk Cabbage (Symplocarpus foetidus)

Clear thinking » Chickweed (Stellaria media), Peppermint (Mentha piperita)

Clear vision » Carrot (Daucus carota subsp. sativus)

Cleared blockages » Star of Bethlehem (Ornithogalum)

Cleared, misunderstandings » Yellow Jessamine (Gelsemium sempervirens)

Clearing » Spanish Moss (Tillandsia usneoides)

C

Clearing, mind » Horehound (Marrubium vulgare)

Clearing, negative environment » Dutchman's Breeches (Dicentra cucullaria)

Clearing, space » Lilac (Syringa vulgaris)

Clever, you are » Clematis (Clematis)

Clinging love » Wisteria (Wisteria sinensis)

Closer to you, I want to be » Flannel Flower (Actinotus helianthi)

Closure » Artichoke, Globe (Cynara scolymus)

Co-dependency » Bee Balm (Monarda)

Coherency » Cosmos (Cosmos)

Come back » Rose, Yellow (Rosa)

Come back to me » Japanese Cherry (Prunus serrulata), Rose, Yellow (Rosa)

Come home » Native Geranium (Geranium solanderi)

Comfort » Sweet Pea (Lathyrus odoratus), Lisianthus (Eustoma grandiflorum), Geranium, Rose (Pelargonium graveolens), Ithuriel's Spear (Triteleia laxa), Heartsease (Viola tricolor), Sweet Marjoram (Origanum marjorana), Mullein (Verbascum thapsus), Pear (Pyrus communis), Sweet Potato (Ipomoea batatas)

Comfort grief » Sweet Marjoram (Origanum marjorana)

Comfort in social situations » White Flag (Spathiphyllum)

Comfort the heart » Cranes-Bill (Geranium maculatum)

Comfort you, I will » Geranium, Rose (Pelargonium graveolens)

Comforting » Geranium, Scarlet (Pelargonium)

Coming together » Pot of Gold (Winteria aureispina)

Command » Scotch Thistle (Onopordum acanthium)

Commitment » Wedding Bush (Ricinocarpos pinifolius), Ranunculus (Ranunculus), Pussytoes (Antennaria), Goosegrass (Galium aparine), Flame Tree (Brachychiton acerifolius)

Commitments, fulfillment of » Oak (Quercus robur)

Common ground » Linnaea (Linnaea borealis)

Communication » Jade Vine (Strongylodon macrobotrys), Delphinium (Delphinium), Stephanotis (Stephanotis floribunda), Monkshood (Aconitum), Hippeastrum (Hippeastrum), Cosmos (Cosmos), Celandine (Ficaria verna), Bulrush (Scirpoides holoschoenus), Redwood (Sequoiadendron giganteum), Moth Orchid (Phalaenopsis), Bush Fuchsia (Epacris longiflora)

Communication, telepathic » Greater Celandine (Chelidonium majus)

Compassion » Carnation, Red (Dianthus caryophyllus), Peony (Paeonia officinalis), Rose, Musk (Rosa moschata), Bleeding Heart (Lamprocapnos spectabilis), Bee Balm (Monarda), Heartsease (Viola tricolor), Basil (Ocimum basilicum), Scottish Primrose (Primula scotica), Trillium (Trillium), Rosewood (Pterocarpus indicus), Saguaro Cactus Blossom (Carnegiea gigantean), Mesquite (Prosopis), Raspberry (Rubus idaeus), Air Plant (Tillandsia), Noble Star Cactus (Stapelia nobilis), Quinoa (Chenopodium quinoa), Scottish Primrose (Primula scotica)

Competence » Blanket Flower (Gaillardia grandiflora)

Competition » Lantern Bush (Abutilon halophilum)

Competition, healthy » Tiger Lily (Lilium tigrinum)

Completion » Godetia (Clarkia amoena)

Completion of projects » Stock (Matthiola incana)

C

Complexion, beautiful » Rose, Damask (Rosa x damascena)

Complication » Chocolate Flower (Berlandiera lyrata)

Concealed love » Motherwort (Leonurus cardiaca)

Concealed merit » Valerian (Polemonium caeruleum)

Consecration » Star Anise (Illicium verum)

Conceit » Poet's Narcissus (Narcissus poeticus)

Concentration » Clematis (Clematis), Camellia, Japanese (Camellia japonica), Celery (Apium graveolens), Peppermint (Mentha piperita)

Concern » Coltsfoot (Tussilago farfara)

Concerned for you, I am » Coltsfoot (Tussilago farfara)

Confidence » Frangipani (Plumeria alba), Poet's Narcissus (Narcissus poeticus), Sunflower (Helianthus annuus), Dahlia (Dahlia), Lilac (Syringa vulgaris), Heather, White (Calluna vulgaris), Foxglove (Digitalis purpurea), Pink Knotweed (Persicaria capitata), Blue Pimpernel (Lysimachia monelli), Chickweed (Stellaria media), Hepatica (Hepatica), Artichoke, Jerusalem (Helianthus tuberosus), Aspen (Populus tremula), Christmas Orchid (Cattleya trianae), Liverwort (Marchantiophyta), Monkey Flower (Mimulus guttatus), Bee Orchid (Ophrys apifera), Zedoary (Curcuma zedoaria), Hibbertia (Hibbertia pedunculata), Flame Tree (Brachychiton acerifolius)

Confidence, female » Christmas Orchid (Cattleya trianae)

Confidence in communication » Celandine (Ficaria verna)

Confidence in decisions » Mayflower (Epigaea repens)

Confidence in you, I have » Poet's Narcissus (Narcissus poeticus)

Confidence, inner » Alder (Alnus)

Confidence, male » Banana Flower (Musa)

Confidence, physical » Banana Flower (Musa)

Confidence, self » Larch (Larix decidua), Mountain Avens (Dryas octopetala), Puerto Rican Hibiscus (Thespesia grandiflora), Cerato (Ceratostigma willmottianum), Suncup (Lonicera ovata), Wake Robin (Trillium pendulum)

Confidences betrayed » Iris, Fairy (Dietes grandiflora)

C

Confiding love » Fuchsia (Fuchsia magellanica)

Conflict resolution » White Pine (Pinus strobus)

Conflicts, inner » Linnaea (Linnaea borealis)

Conflicts, resolve » Wood Betony (Stachys betonica)

Confusion, ease » Thorn Apple (Datura stamonium)

Congratulations » Sundew (Drosera auriculata), Tea Tree (Leptospermum myrsinoides), Jasmine (Jasminum officinale), Amaryllis (Amaryllis), Bouvardia (Bouvardia), Olive (Olea europaea)

Congratulations on birth of baby » Rabbit Orchid (Leptoceras menziesii)

Conjungal love » Lime (Tilia x europaea)

Connection » Old Maid (Catharanthus roseus)

Connection, cosmic » Sego Lily (Calochortus nuttallii)

Connection to earth » Marsh Marigold (Caltha palustris)

Consciousness » Rafflesia (Rafflesia arnoldii), Sacred Blue Lily (Nymphaea caerulea), Shooting Star (Dodecatheon meadia)

Consciousness, higher » Passion Flower (Passiflora incarnate), Meadow Saffron (Colchicum autumnale)

Consecration » Frankincense (Boswellia sacra)

Consequences » Gymea Lily (Doryanthes excelsa)

Consideration » Hibiscus, White (Hibiscus arnottianus)

Consistency » Morning Glory (Ipomoea purpurea)

Consolation » Rhododendron (Rhododendron), Sweet Marjoram (Origanum marjorana), Geranium, Scarlet (Pelargonium)

Constancy » Bluebell, Common (Hyacinthoides non-scripta), Gladiola (Gladiolus), Canterbury Bells (Campanula medium), Columbine (Aquilegia vulgaris), Cranes-Bill (Geranium maculatum), Sweet Violet (Viola odorata), Bellflower (Campanula), Southernwood (Artemisia abrotanum)

Constancy in adversity » Pine (Pinus sylvestris)

Contentment » Papaya (Carica papaya)

C

Consumed by love » Althea (Hibiscus syriacus)

Contented existence » Stock (Matthiola incana)

Contentment » Calendula (Calendula officinalis)

Continuance » Field Poppy (Papaver rhoeas)

Continuity » Chaconia (Warszewiczia coccinea)

Contracts » Rose, Wild (Rosa acicularis)

Control » Black Orchid (Trichoglottis brachiata), Willowherb (Epilobium)

Control, energy » King's Mantle (Thunbergia erecta)

Cooperation » Stephanotis (Stephanotis floribunda)

Cope, ability to » Skullcap (Scutellaria)

Coping » Thistle, Common (Cirsium vulgare)

Coquetry » Daylily (Hemerocallis), Mezereum (Daphne mezereum)

Coquettes, you are the Queen of » Queen's Rocket (Hesperis matronalis)

Core issues » Burdock (Arctium)

Cosmic connection » Sego Lily (Calochortus nuttallii)

Courage » Thyme (Thymus vulgaris), Grey Spider Flower (Grevillea buxifolia) Sturt's Desert Rose (Gossypium sturtianum), Waratah (Telopea speciosissima), King Protea (Protea cynaroides), Rose, Red (Rosa), Heather, White (Calluna vulgaris), Primrose (Primula vulgaris), Garlic (Allium sativum), Mullein (Verbascum thapsus), Borage (Borago officinalis), Tomato (Solanum lycopersicum), Thistle, Common (Cirsium vulgare), Rock Rose (Helianthemum), Lemon Balm (Melissa officinalis), Pine (Pinus sylvestris), Oak (Quercus robur), Elder (Sambucus nigra), Copihue (Lapageria rosea), Frankincense (Boswellia sacra), Masterwort (Peucedanum ostruthium), Tea (Camellia sinensis), Tonka (Dipteryx odorata), Kiwi (Actinidia chinensis)

Courage, build » Birch (Betula)

Courage, I admire your » Chamomile, Roman (Chamaemelum nobile)

Courage in difficulties » Basil (Ocimum basilicum)

Courage, man of » Borage (Borago officinalis)

Courage, take » Mullein (Verbascum thapsus)

C

Courage to change » Thorn Apple (Datura stamonium)

Courage to explore » Trilobed Violet (Viola palmata)

Courtesy » Mimosa (Acacia dealbata)

Counterfeit » Mock Orange (Philadelphus)

Creation » Honey Grevillea (Grevillea eriostachya), Water Lily (Nymphaea)

Creative arts » Lupin (Lupinus perennis)

Creative energy » Watermelon (Citrullus lanatus)

Creative expansion » Wisteria (Wisteria sinensis)

Creative freedom » Nasturtium (Tropaeolum majus), Carrot (Daucus carota subsp. sativus)

Creative growth » Gladiola (Gladiolus)

Creative ideas, success with » Iris, Fairy (Dietes grandiflora)

Creative opportunities, new » Iris, Fairy (Dietes grandiflora)

Creative power » Iris, Black (Iris nigricans)

Creative thought » Great Maple (Acer pseudoplatanus)

Creative visualisation » Mugwort (Artemisia vulgaris)

Creativity » Grevillea (Grevillea banksii), Turkey Bush (Calytrix exstipulata), Honey Grevillea (Grevillea eriostachya), King Protea (Protea cynaroides) Siberian Iris (Iris sibirica), Dahlia (Dahlia), Foxglove (Digitalis purpurea), Hazel (Corylus), Iris, Blue Flag (Iris versicolor), Great Maple (Acer pseudoplatanus), Auricula (Primula auricular), Cinnamon (Cinnamomum verum), Mace (Myristica fragrans), Spider Flower (Cleome), Sky Vine (Thunbergia alata), Breadfruit (Artocarpus altilis), Marigold (Tagetes evecta)

Creator, bond with the » tabacco (Nicotiana tabacum)

Crime » Tamarisk (Tamarix)

Criticism » King Protea (Protea cynaroides)

Critique » Yellow Elder (Tecoma stans)

Crone » Blackthorn (Prunus spinosa)

Cruel, you are » Nettle (Urtica)

C

Cruelty » Nettle (Urtica)

Cure » Althea (Hibiscus syriacus), Bouvardia (Bouvardia), Balm of Gilead (Commiphora gileadensis)

Cure, insanity » Hellebore (Helleborus)

Cure, possession » Periwinkle (Vinca minor)

Cure, to » Marshmallow (Althea officinalis)

Curiosity » Sycamore (Acer pseudoplatanus)

Curse breaking » Okra (Abelmoschus esculentus)

Curses, protection from » Mullein (Verbascum thapsus)

Curses, removal of » Yucca (Yucca filamentosa)

C   D

Daintiness » Michaelmas Daisy (Aster amellus)

Danger » Rhododendron (Rhododendron)

Danger, protection from » Red Clover (Trifolium pratense)

Dangerous, love is » Rose, Carolina (Rosa carolina)

Dangerous pleasures » Tuberose (Polianthes tuberosa)

Dangerous situation » Bindweed, Great (Convolvulus major)

Dark arts » Blackthorn (Prunus spinosa)

Dark emotions » Bladder-Fucus (Fucus vesiculosus)

Dark, light in the » Skunk Cabbage (Symplocarpus foetidus)

Dark thoughts » Nightshade (Solanaceae)

Darkness, light in the » Evening Primrose (Oenothera)

Darkness, transform » Mustard (Sinapis arvensis)

Dauntlessness » Thrift (Armeria maritima)

Daydreaming » Hawkweed (Hieracium)

Deal » Rose, Peach (Rosa)

Death » Yew (Taxus baccata), California Poppy (Eschscholzia californica), Jonquil (Narcissus jonquilla), Red Hot Poker (Kniphofia), Blackberry (Rubus fruticosus)

Death, I change but in » Laurel (Laurus nobilis)

Death, you will be my » Hemlock (Conium maculatum)

Deceit » Mock Orange (Philadelphus), Venus Flytrap (Dionaea muscipula), Lewis Mock Orange (Philadelphus lewisii), Dogbane (Apocynum cannabinum), Fly Orchid (Ophrys insectifera), Rocket (Eruca sativa)

Deception, protection from » Sweet Violet (Viola odorata)

Decide » Scleranthus (Scleranthus annus)

Decision/s » Sturt's Desert Rose (Gossypium sturtianum), Hawkweed (Hieracium), Coffee (Coffea arabica)

Decision-making » Karee (Rhus pendulina), Nettle (Urtica)

Decision, quick » Iris Croatica (Iris perunika)

Decisions, confidence in » Mayflower (Epigaea repens)

Decisions, difficult » Solomon's Seal (Polygonatum)

Decisive action » Artichoke, Jerusalem (Helianthus tuberosus)

Declaration of love » Red Tulip (Tulipa)

Declaration of war » Tansy (Tanacetum vulgare)

Dedication » Wedding Bush (Ricinocarpos pinifolius), Edelweiss (Leontopodium alpinum)

Deeds, good » Variegated Box (Buxus sempervirens)

Deepen relationships » Pussytoes (Antennaria)

Defeat » Mulberry, White (Morus alba)

Defense » Holly (Ilex aquifolium), Mayflower (Epigaea repens), Cinnamon (Cinnamomum verum), Patchouli (Pogostemon cablin), Privet (Ligustrum vulgare)

Dejection » Lupin (Lupinus perennis)

Delay/s » Ageratum (Ageratum), Boneset (Eupatorium perfoliatum), Lantern Bush (Abutilon halophilum)

D

Delicacy » Cornflower (Centaurea cyanus)

Delicate beauty » Hibiscus (Hibiscus)

Delight » Caladium (Caladium), Cineraria (Cineraria), Pink Poui (Tabebuia pentaphylla)

Delight, exuberant » Flame Lily (Gloriosa rothschildiana)

Delight me, you » Chocolate Flower (Berlandiera lyrata)

Denial » California Pitcher Plant (Darlingtonia californica)

Departure » Rose, China (Rosa chinensis)

Depression » Gentian (Gentiana)

Depression recovery » Mustard (Sinapis arvensis)

Depression, reduce » Air Plant (Tillandsia)

Depression support » Black Cohosh (Cimicifuga racemosa)

Desertion » Love Lies Bleeding (Amaranthus caudatus)

Deserve my love, only you » Campion Rose (Silene coronaria)

Desire » Red Tulip (Tulipa), Althea (Hibiscus syriacus), Tulip, Wild (Tulipa sprengeri), Jonquil (Narcissus jonquilla), Hibiscus, Red (Hibiscus rosa-sinensis)

Desire for riches » Marsh Marigold (Caltha palustris)

Desire, returned » Jonquil (Narcissus jonquilla)

Desire, romantic » Lisianthus (Eustoma grandiflorum)

Desire, strengthen » Purple Orchid (Cattleya skinneri)

Desire to travel » Stephanotis (Stephanotis floribunda)

Desire to please » Cranes-Bill (Geranium maculatum), Mezereum (Daphne mezereum)

Desire you above all else, I » Ivy (Hedera)

Desire you, I » Tuberose (Polianthes tuberosa), Moon Orchid (Phalaenopsis amabilis)

Desires, spiritual » Thistle, Common (Cirsium vulgare)

Despair, do not » Chamomile, Roman (Chamaemelum nobile)

Despair, end » Wood Betony (Stachys betonica)

D

Destiny » Texas Bluebonnet (Lupinus texensis)

Destiny is in your hands, my » Camellia, Japanese (Camellia japonica)

Detachment » Sacred Lotus (Nelumbo nucifera), Bleeding Heart (Lamprocapnos spectabilis), Thorn Apple (Datura stamonium), Wood Betony (Stachys betonica)

Determination » Cattle Bush (Trichodesma zelanicum), Amaryllis (Amaryllis), Ginger (Zingiber officinale), Alder (Alnus), Christmas Plant (Euphorbia)

Determination, self » Maltese Centaury (Paleocyanus crassifoleus)

Detox » Hippeastrum (Hippeastrum), Onion (Allium cepa), Spirulina (Arthrospira)

Development » Five Corners (Styphelia laeta), Rose, Prairie (Rosa arkansana)

Development, emotional » Gerbera Daisy, White (Gerbera jamesonii)

Development, intuition » Native Wood Violet (Viola odorata)

Development, personal » Kowhai (Sophora)

Development, psychic » Water Lily, Purple (Nymphaea), Cinnamon (Cinnamomum verum), Frankincense (Boswellia sacra), Galangal (Alpinia galangal), Kava-Kava (Piper methysticum), Purslane (Portulaca oleracea)

Devil, summon the » Heath Bell (Erica cinerea)

Devil, the » Firethorn (Pyracantha)

Deviousness » Snapdragon (Antirrhinum majus)

Devoted to you, I am » Peruvian Lily (Alstroemeria), Honeysuckle (Lonicera), Grape (Vitis), Heliotrope (Heliotropium)

Devotion » Peruvian Lily (Alstroemeria), Grape (Vitis), Crown Vetch (Securigera varia), Pussytoes (Antennaria), Heliotrope (Heliotropium), Broom (Genisteae), Cabbage (Brassica oleracea var. capitata), Carnation, White (Dianthus caryophyllus)

Devotion to duty » Oak (Quercus robur)

Die if neglected, I » Laurustinus (Viburnum tinus)

Die for you, I would » Opium Poppy (Papaver somniferum)

Die, never say » Xeranthemum (Xeranthemum bracteatum)

Difference, respect for » Stephanotis (Stephanotis floribunda)

D

Difficult decisions » Solomon's Seal (Polygonatum)

Difficult times, optimism during » Willowherb (Epilobium)

Difficulties, overcoming » Mistletoe (Viscum album)

Difficulty, courage in » Basil (Ocimum basilicum)

Dignity » Calla Lily (Zantedeschia aethiopica), Dahlia (Dahlia), Echinacea (Echinacea purpurea), Cloves (Eugenia caryophyllata), Elm (Ulmus), Pink, Clove-Scented (Dianthus caryophyllus)

Direction » Pink Heath (Epacris impressa)

Direction, new » Edelweiss (Leontopodium alpinum)

Discipline » Astilbe (Astilbe), Rabbit Bush (Chrysothamnus nauseosus)

Disconnection » Ginseng (Panax)

Discovery » Siberian Iris (Iris sibirica), Amaryllis (Amaryllis)

Discretion » Lemon (Citrus limon)

Discrimination » Alder (Alnus)

Discussion, healing » Lime, Key West (Citrus aurantifolia)

Disdain » Rue (Ruta graveolens), Solomon's Seal (Polygonatum)

Disease, protection from » Wood Anemone (Anemone nemerosa), Larch (Larix decidua), Laurel (Laurus nobilis), Ratchaphruek (Cassia fistula)

Disguise » Alkanet (Alkanna tinctoria), Stamonium (Datura stramonium)

Disgust » Frog Orchid (Coeloglossum)

Dislike » Lobelia, Blue (Lobelia)

Dispel evil spirits » Marshmallow (Althea officinalis)

Dispel negativity » Tangerine (Citrus tangerina)

Disposition, accommodating » Valerian (Polemonium caeruleum)

Dissension » Pride of China (Koelreuteria bipinnata)

Dissipated, anger » Althea (Hibiscus syriacus)

Dissolve negative ideas » Larch (Larix decidua)

Distance healing » Wild Yam (Dioscorea villosa)

Distinction » Cardinal Flower (Lobelia cardinalis)

D

Distraction » Avens (Geum)

Distractions, protection from » Thistle, Common (Cirsium vulgare)

Distrust » Apricot (Prunus armeniaca)

Diversity » Teuila (Alpinia purpurata)

Divination » Mugwort (Artemisia vulgaris), Meadowsweet (Filipendula ulmaria), Witchhazel (Hamamelis virginiana), Aspen (Populus tremula), Vervain (Verbena officinalis), Camphor (Cinnamomum camphora), Cinnamon (Cinnamomum verum), Fig (Ficus carica), Frankincense (Boswellia sacra), Lettuce (Lactuca sativa), Lilac (Syringa vulgaris), Mace (Myristica fragrans), Meadow Rue (Thalictrum)

Divine, awareness of the » Aspen (Populus tremula)

Divine beauty » Cowslip (Primula veris)

Divine communication » Monkshood (Aconitum)

Divine guidance » Gardenia (Gardenia jasminoides)

Divine hope » Melati (Jasminum sambac)

Divine intervention » Iris Croatica (Iris perunika)

Divine light » Scots Pine (Pinus syvestris)

Divine love » Rose, Briar (Rosa rubiginosa)

Divine messages » Gardenia (Gardenia jasminoides)

Divine union » Mistletoe (Viscum album)

Discouraged, do not be » Wormwood (Artemisia absinthium)

Disconnection » Sacred Blue Lily (Nymphaea caerulea)

Discretion » Lemon (Citrus limon)

Docility » Bulrush (Scirpoides holoschoenus), Rush (Juncaceae)

Domestic happiness » Holly (Ilex aquifolium)

Domestic life » Flax (Linum usitatissimum)

Domestic virtue » Sage (Salvia officinalis), Clover (Trifolium)

Do not abuse » Safflower (Carthamus tinctorius)

Do not be discouraged » Wormwood (Artemisia absinthium)

Do not despair » Chamomile, Roman (Chamaemelum nobile)

D

Do not forget me » Forget-Me-Not (Myosotis)

Do not forget me » Speedwell (Veronica officinalis)

Do not give up » Cattle Bush (Trichodesma zelanicum), Water Ribbons (Triglochin procerum)

Do not give up hope » Petunia (Petunia)

Do not touch me » Burdock (Arctium)

Do not worry » Crowea (Crowea exalata), Agrimony (Agrimonia eupatoria)

Do not worry » Loquat (Eriobotrya japonica)

Do this, you can » Vanilla (Vanilla planifolia)

Doubt » Apricot (Prunus armeniaca)

Down, calm » Ipecac (Gillenia stipulata)

Drama, releasing emotional » Prairie Crocus (Pulsatilla patens)

Dreams » Columbine (Aquilegia vulgaris), Ginkgo (Ginkgo biloba)

Dream of you, I » Queen of the Night (Selenicereus grandiflorus), California Poppy (Eschscholzia californica)

Dreaming, day » Hawkweed (Hieracium)

Dreams » Queen of the Night (Selenicereus grandiflorus) California Poppy (Eschscholzia californica), Monkshood (Aconitum), Cinnamon (Cinnamomum verum), Purslane (Portulaca oleracea), Ginkgo (Ginkgo biloba)

Dreams, sweet » Lemon Verbena (Aloysia triphylla)

Dreams come true, you make my » Himalayan Blue Poppy (Meconopsis grandis)

Dreams, prophetic » Mugwort (Artemisia vulgaris), Bracken (Pteridium)

Dreams, protection from bad » Cedar (Cedrus)

Dreams, understanding » Greater Celandine (Chelidonium majus)

Duality » Hawthorn (Crataegus monogyna), Larch (Larix decidua), Aspen (Populus tremula)

Dull virtues » Mignonette (Reseda odorata)

Duplicity » Geranium, Scarlet (Pelargonium)

Durability » Oak (Quercus robur), Tamarind (Tamarindus indica)

Duty, devotion to » Oak (Quercus robur)

E

Earth, connection to » Marsh Marigold (Caltha palustris)

Earth healing » Fireweed (Chamerion angustifolium)

Earth to heaven connection » Mulberry, White (Morus alba), Pine (Pinus sylvestris)

Eagerness » Pelargonium (Pelargonium cucullatum)

Ease » Meadow Rue (Thalictrum)

Ease confusion » Thorn Apple (Datura stamonium)

Ease nightmares » Chamomile, German (Matricaria chamomilla)

Ease of worry » Jonquil (Narcissus jonquilla)

Ecstasy » Moss Rose (Portulaca grandiflora)

Education » Edelweiss (Leontopodium alpinum), Orange Banksia (Banksia ashbyi)

Ego » Gladiola (Gladiolus)

Ego, healthy » Witchhazel (Hamamelis virginiana)

Ego, unchecked » Madder (Rubia tinctorum)

Elation » Clary Sage (Salvia sclarea)

Elegance » Yarrow (Achillea millefolium), Geranium (Geranium), Aster (Aster), Ivy (Hedera), Locust (Gleditsia triacanthos)

Elegance, mature » Pomegranate Blossom (Punica granatum)

Elemental energies » Cow Parsley (Anthriscus sylvestris)

Eliminate negative feelings » Iris, Blue Flag (Iris versicolor)

Elevation » Fir (Abies)

Elope with me » Spider Flower (Cleome)

Eloquence » Ice Plant (Carpobrotus edulis), Crepe Myrtle (Lagerstroemia indica)

E

Elves » Ambrosia (Ambrosia), Shamrock (Trifolium dubium)

Embrace challenges » Ceibo (Erythrina crista-galli)

Emotion of love, first » Lilac (Syringa vulgaris)

Emotional balance » Cat's Tail Grass (Phleum pratense), Showy Lady Slipper (Cypripedium reginae), Ipecac (Gillenia stipulata)

Emotional blocks, release » Lime (Tilia x europaea)

Emotional breakthrough/s » Belladonna (Atropa belladonna)

Emotional care » Downy Hawthorn (Crataegus mollis)

Emotional clarity » Love-in-a-Mist (Nigella damascena), Gerbera Daisy, Yellow (Gerbera jamesonii)

Emotional development » Gerbera Daisy, White (Gerbera jamesonii)

Emotional drama, releasing » Prairie Crocus (Pulsatilla patens)

Emotional healing » Gentian (Gentiana), Mahogany (Swietenia macrophylla)

Emotional hurt, release » Cuckoo Flower (Cardamine pratensis)

Emotional maturity » Avocado (Persea americana)

Emotional release » Dutchman's Breeches (Dicentra cucullaria), Yerba Santa (Eriodictyon glutinosum), Blue-Eyed Grass (Sisyrinchium montanum)

Emotional strength » Artichoke, Globe (Cynara scolymus), Gerbera Daisy, Red (Gerbera jamesonii)

Emotional warmth » Evening Primrose (Oenothera)

Emotional wellbeing » Wood Betony (Stachys betonica)

Emotions, clear negative » Gerbera Daisy, Orange (Gerbera jamesonii)

Emotions, transform » Rose, Prairie (Rosa arkansana)

Emotions, balance » Lemon Balm (Melissa officinalis), Prairie Crocus (Pulsatilla patens)

Emotions, balanced » Native Passionflower (Passiflora herbertiana), Coconut (Cocus nucifera)

Emotions, dark » Bladder-Fucus (Fucus vesiculosus)

Emotions, expressing » Bleeding Heart (Lamprocapnos spectabilis)

Emotions, expression of » Snapdragon (Antirrhinum majus)

E

Emotions, freeing deep » Fuchsia (Fuchsia magellanica)

Emotions, purity of » Apple Blossom (Malus domestica)

Emotions, released » Mulberry, Black (Morus nigra)

Emotions, stabilises » Blackthorn (Prunus spinosa)

Emotions, suppressed » Firethorn (Pyracantha)

Emotions, lift » Turmeric (Cucurma longa)

Empathy » Poinciana (Delonix regia)

Employment » Lucky Hand (Orchis)

Empowerment » Hibiscus, Native Yellow (Hibiscus brackenridgei)

Empowerment, self- » Saguaro Cactus Blossom (Carnegiea gigantean)

Enchant me, you » Rose, Mauve (Rosa)

Enchantment » Vervain (Verbena officinalis), Orchid (Orchidaceae), Rose, Mauve (Rosa), Bittersweet (Solanum dulcamara), Nightshade (Solanaceae), Bracken (Pteridium)

Enchantment, protection from » Rowan (Sorbus aucuparia)

Encourage healing » Calamus Root (Acorus calamus)

Encourage love » Cedar (Cedrus)

Encourage trust » Fennel (Foeniculum vulgare)

Encouragement » Madonna Lily (Lilium candidum), Carnation, Pink (Dianthus caryophyllus), Dahlia (Dahlia), Goldenrod (Solidago virgaurea), Black-Eyed Susan (Rudbeckia hirta), Campion, Red (Silene), Bayberry (Myrica), Watermelon (Citrullus lanatus), Butterfly Lily (Hedychium coronarium)

Encouragement, joyful » Pride of Barbados (Poinciana pulcherrima)

End arguments » Honeysuckle (Lonicera)

End despair » Wood Betony (Stachys betonica)

End misfortune » Shallot (Allium cepa var. aggregatum)

End sadness » Poke Weed (Phytolacca americana)

End self-sabotage » Red Hot Poker (Kniphofia)

End, this must » Hemlock (Conium maculatum), Angel's Trumpet (Brugmansia candida), Begonia (Begonia)

E

Ending relationships » Turnip (Brassica rapa subsp. rapa)

Ending unwanted friendships » Chilli (Capsicum)

Endurance » Everlasting Daisy (Rhodanthe chlorocephala), Kalanchoe (Kalanchoe), Tomato (Solanum lycopersicum), Wisteria (Wisteria sinensis), Chinese Plum (Prunus mume), Oak (Quercus robur), Wood of Life (Guaiacum sanctum), Saguaro Cactus Blossom (Carnegiea gigantean), Prairie Crocus (Pulsatilla patens), Cactus (Cactaceae), Prickly Pear (Opuntia ficus-indica), Sarsaparilla, Wild (Aralia nudicaulis)

Enduring affection » Gorse (Ulex europaeus), Locust, Green (Gleditsia triacanthos)

Enduring love » Wisteria (Wisteria sinensis)

Energies, balance of male and female » Quince (Cydonia oblonga)

Enemies, immunity from » Vervain (Verbena officinalis)

Energies, clear personal » Purple Saxifrage (Saxifraga oppositifolia)

Energies, elemental » Cow Parsley (Anthriscus sylvestris)

Energies, female » Cauliflower (Brassica oleracea)

Energies, male » Banana Flower (Musa)

Energies, release » Rose, Meadow (Rosa blanda)

Energy » Swamp Lily (Crinum pedunculatum), Forsythia (Forsythia), Chocolate Flower (Berlandiera lyrata), Chamomile, German (Matricaria chamomilla), Peppermint (Mentha piperita), Castor Oil Plant (Ricinus communis), Borage (Borago officinalis), Frankincense (Boswellia sacra), Guarana (Paullinia cupana), Stevia (Stevia rebaudiana)

Energy, aggressive » Peanut (Arachis hypogaea)

Energy, balanced » Pasqueflower (Pulsatilla vulgaris)

Energy boost » Rosella Flower (Hibiscus heterophyllus)

Energy, clear stagnant » Skunk Cabbage (Symplocarpus foetidus)

Energy control » King's Mantle (Thunbergia erecta)

Energy, creative » Watermelon (Citrullus lanatus)

Energy expansion » Jade (Crassula ovata)

Energy, good use of » Forsythia (Forsythia)

Energy, great » Great Maple (Acer pseudoplatanus)

Energy, hibernating » Onion (Allium cepa)

Energy, life » Osmanthus (Osmanthus fragrans)

Energy, male » Peanut (Arachis hypogaea)

Energy, positive » Mastic (Pistacia lentiscus)

Energy protection » Rue (Ruta graveolens)

Energy, protection from negative » Okra (Abelmoschus esculentus)

Energy, renewal of » Elder (Sambucus nigra)

Energy, stabilising inner » Elder (Sambucus nigra)

Energy, strengthen » Pepper (Piper nigrum)

Energy to action » Cayenne (Capsicum frutescens)

Energy, ungrounded » Sweet Pea (Lathyrus odoratus)

E

Enhanced self-awareness » Red Clover (Trifolium pratense)

Enhancement » Psyllium (Plantago ovata)

Enjoyment » Chocolate Flower (Berlandiera lyrata)

Enlightenment » Grass Tree (Xanthorrhoea resinosa), Water Lily, White (Nymphaea), Water Lily (Nymphaea), Mango (Mangifera indica), Persimmon (Diospyros virginiana), Tea (Camellia sinensis), Hibiscus, White (Hibiscus rosa-sinensis), Golden Chalice (Solandra nitida zucs)

Ensure survival » Goosegrass (Galium aparine)

Entertainment » Parsley (Petroselinum crispum)

Enthral me, you » Bracken (Pteridium)

Enthusiasm » Orange Banksia (Banksia ashbyi), Rose, Orange (Rosa), Orange Blossom (Citrus x sinensis), Petunia (Petunia), Morning Glory (Ipomoea purpurea), Dog Rose (Rosa canina), Gayfeather (Liatris), Old Man Banksia (Banksia serrata)

Enthusiasm boost » Cabbage (Brassica oleracea var. capitata)

Enthusiasm, religious » Maltese Cross (Lychnis chalcedonica)

Enticement » Quince (Cydonia oblonga)

Environment clearing, negative » Dutchman's Breeches (Dicentra cucullaria)

Envy » Blackberry (Rubus fruticosus), Raspberry (Rubus idaeus)

Envy, avert » Garlic (Allium sativum)

Equal challenges, opportunities with » Variegated Box (Buxus sempervirens)

Equilibrium » Chamomile, German (Matricaria chamomilla)

Error » Bee Orchid (Ophrys apifera), Fly Orchid (Ophrys insectifera)

Error, paternal » Cuckoo Flower (Cardamine pratensis)

Esteem » Sage (Salvia officinalis)

Esteem but not love » Spiderwort (Tradescantia), Tradescantia (Tradescantia zebrina)

Estranged love » Water Lily, Red (Nymphaea)

Eternal happiness » Straw Flower (Xerochrysum bracteatum)

Eternal love » Orange Blossom (Citrus x sinensis), Heliotrope (Heliotropium), Mexican Orange Blossom (Choisya ternata)

Etheric cleansing » Dutchman's Breeches (Dicentra cucullaria)

Euphoria » Clary Sage (Salvia sclarea)

Evening » Campion, White (Silene)

Ever bright » Cineraria (Cineraria)

Ever changing » Virginia Creeper (Parthenocissus quinquefolia)

Everlasting love » Baby's Breath (Gypsophila paniculata), Ranunculus (Ranunculus)

Everlasting loveliness » Rose, China (Rosa chinensis)

Evil, protection from » Meadowsweet (Filipendula ulmaria), Dill (Anethum graveolens), Yucca (Yucca filamentosa), Centaury (Erythraea centaurium), Cranes-Bill (Geranium maculatum), Elder (Sambucus nigra), Vervain (Verbena officinalis), Rowan (Sorbus aucuparia), Teasel (Dipsacus)

Evil, repel » Fennel (Foeniculum vulgare)

Evil spirits, banish » Soy Bean (Glycine max)

Evil spirits, expel » Wood Betony (Stachys betonica)

Evil spirits, protection against » Nettle (Urtica)

E

Evil spirits, protection from » Mustard (Sinapis arvensis), Chives (Allium schoenoprasum), Bean (Phaseolus vulgaris), Tormentil (Potentilla erecta)

Evil spirits, removal of » St John's Wort (Hypericum perforatum)

Evil, ward off » Xu Duan (Dipsacus japonica)

Evolution, personal » Sagebrush (Artemisia tridentate)

Exam support » Larch (Larix decidua)

Exams, good luck with your » Clematis (Clematis)

Excellence » Camellia, Japanese (Camellia japonica), Bird of Paradise (Strelitzia reginae), Calendula (Calendula officinalis)

Excellence, unpretending » Camellia, Red (Camellia), Camellia, White (Camellia)

Excess, beware of » Rhododendron (Rhododendron)

Excite me, you » Orange Banksia (Banksia ashbyi)

Exorcism » Juniper (Juniperus), Hellebore (Helleborus), Cloves (Eugenia caryophyllata), Bean (Phaseolus vulgaris), Boneset (Eupatorium perfoliatum), Frankincense (Boswellia sacra), Fumitory (Fumaria officinalis)

Expanded horizons » Stargazer Lily, Pink (Lilium orientalis), Purslane (Portulaca oleracea)

Expanding awareness » Butterfly Orchid (Psychopsis)

Expansion » Ash (Fraxinus), Lime (Tilia x europaea)

Expansion, creative » Wisteria (Wisteria sinensis)

Expansion, energy » Jade (Crassula ovata)

Expansion, mental » Jerusalem Thorn (Parkinsonia aculeata)

Expansive thinking » Banana Flower (Musa)

Expectation » Anemone (Anemone), Zephyr Lily (Zephyranthes)

Expel evil spirits » Wood Betony (Stachys betonica)

Experience, wisdom from » Clary Sage (Salvia sclarea)

Explore, courage to » Trilobed Violet (Viola palmata)

Expression » Coast Rhododendron (Rhododendron macrophyllum)

Expression, artistic » Owl's Clover (Orthocarpus purpurascense)

E

Expression, clear » Chickweed (Stellaria media)

Expression, free » Chickweed (Stellaria media)

Expression, freedom of » Tropicbird Orchid (Angraecum eburneum)

Expression of emotions » Snapdragon (Antirrhinum majus)

Expressing emotions » Bleeding Heart (Lamprocapnos spectabilis)

Extended potential » Rock Rose (Helianthemum)

Extension, over » Tree Peony (Paeonia suffruticosa)

Extinguish hopes » Bindweed, Great (Convolvulus major)

Exuberance » Pride of Barbados (Poinciana pulcherrima), Golden Trumpet Tree (Tabebuia alba)

Exuberant delight » Flame Lily (Gloriosa rothschildiana)

Eye, gladdens the » Eyebright (Euphrasia officinalis)

Eyes, beautiful » Tulip, Variegated (Tulipa)

E

F

Facing the unknown » Angelica (Angelica archangelica)

Facts » Bittersweet (Solanum dulcamara)

Fae, working with the » Iris, Fairy (Dietes grandiflora)

Fairy realm access » Hazel (Corylus)

Fairy-realm entrance » Heath Bell (Erica cinerea)

Fairies » Cow Parsley (Anthriscus sylvestris), Elm (Ulmus), Lobelia (Lobelia inflata), Pear (Pyrus communis), Ambrosia (Ambrosia), Shamrock (Trifolium dubium)

Failure to change » Siberian Iris (Iris sibirica)

Fairness » Emu Bush (Eremophila duttonii)

Faith » Grey Spider Flower (Grevillea buxifolia), Turkey Bush (Calytrix exstipulata), Dahlia (Dahlia), Gladiola (Gladiolus), Heather, White (Calluna vulgaris), Canterbury Bells (Campanula medium), Tomato (Solanum lycopersicum), Columbine (Aquilegia vulgaris), Gentian

(Gentiana), Iris, Blue Flag (Iris versicolor), Marguerite Daisy (Argyranthemum frutescens), Iris, German (Iris germanica)

Faith in you, I have » Canterbury Bells (Campanula medium)

Faith, strengthen » Basil (Ocimum basilicum)

Faithful heart » Frankincense (Boswellia sacra)

Faithful, I remain » Speedwell (Veronica officinalis)

Faithful to you, I am » Dandelion (Taraxacum officinale)

Faithlessness » Evening Primrose (Oenothera), Scarlet Pimpernel (Anagallis arvensis), Heliotrope (Heliotropium), Pine (Pinus sylvestris), Bulrush (Scirpoides holoschoenus), Tamarind (Tamarindus indica)

Faithfulness » Blue Violet (Viola sororia)

Falling in love with you, I am » Rose, Yellow (Rosa)

Falsehood » Alkanet (Alkanna tentoria), Nightshade (Solanaceae), Dogbane (Apocynum cannabinum)

Fame » Tulip Tree (Liriodendron)

Family » Maguey (Agave americana)

Fantasy » Guava (Psidium guajava)

Farewell » Michaelmas Daisy (Aster amellus), Spruce (Picea)

Fascinate me, you » Rose, orange (Rosa), Honesty (Lunaria annua)

Fascination » Rose, orange (Rosa), Honesty (Lunaria annua)

Fashionable » Queen's Rocket (Hesperis matronalis)

Fate » Hemp (Cannabis sativa), Flax (Linum usitatissimum)

Fatigue » Jade (Crassula ovata)

Favour » Geranium, Ivy-Leafed (Pelargonium peltatum)

Favours » Chicory (Cichorium intybus)

Fear, banish » Birch (Betula)

Fear, have no » Grey Spider Flower (Grevillea buxifolia)

Fear, inner » Agrimony (Agrimonia eupatoria)

Fear, let go of » Sweet Marjoram (Origanum marjorana)

F

Fear, release » Okra (Abelmoschus esculentus)

Fear, release of » Mountain Avens (Dryas octopetala)

Fears, calm » Elder (Sambucus nigra)

Fears, hidden » Betony (Stachys officinalis)

Fears, still » Aspen (Populus tremula)

Fearlessness » Monkshood (Aconitum)

Feast » Parsley (Petroselinum crispum)

Feel, I want to tell you how I » Bleeding Heart (Lamprocapnos spectabilis)

Feeling, warmth of » Mint (Mentha)

Feelings for you, I have new » Delphinium (Delphinium)

Feelings, inner » Manzanita (Arctostaphylos manzanita)

Feelings, natural » Yerba Santa (Eriodictyon glutinosum)

Feelings, release bitter » Harvest Brodiaea (Brodiaea elegans)

Feelings, true » Fuchsia (Fuchsia magellanica), Poinsettia (Euphorbia pulcherrima),

Feelings, unfaded » Amaranthus (Amaranth)

Feelings, warm » Ginger (Zingiber officinale)

Feelings, warming of » Mulberry, Red (Morus rubra)

Felicity » Sweet Sultan (Amberboa moschata)

Female alignment » Easter Lily (Lilium longiflorum)

Female ambition » Hollyhock, White (Alcea rosea)

Female balance » Evening Primrose (Oenothera)

Female confidence » Christmas Orchid (Cattleya trianae)

Female energies » Magnolia (Magnolia campbellii), Queen Anne's Lace (Daucus carota), Cauliflower (Brassica oleracea)

Female energies, balancing male and » Crepe Myrtle (Lagerstroemia indica)

Female fertility » Peony (Paeonia officinalis)

Female healing » Hibiscus, White (Hibiscus arnottianus), Lady's Mantle (Alchemilla vulgaris), Motherwort (Leonurus cardiaca), Black Cohosh

F

(Cimicifuga racemosa), Tiger Lily (Lilium tigrinum), Catnip (Nepeta cataria), Pride of Barbados (Poinciana pulcherrima), Christmas Orchid (Cattleya trianae), Rose, Cherokee (Rosa laevigata), Purple Pitcher Plant (Sarracenia purpurea), Cotton (Gossypium)

Female loveliness, perfection of » Shrimp Plant (Justicia)

Female protection » Purple Pitcher Plant (Sarracenia purpurea)

Feminine aspects » Sego Lily (Calochortus nuttallii)

Feminine grace » Rosewood (Pterocarpus indicus)

Feminine strength » Lady's Mantle (Alchemilla vulgaris), Rose, Cherokee (Rosa laevigata)

Feminine qualities » Mock Orange (Philadelphus)

Femininity » Love-in-a-Mist (Nigella damascena)

Fertility » Rabbit Orchid (Leptoceras menziesii), Lily (Lilium), St John's Wort (Hypericum perforatum), Orange Blossom (Citrus x sinensis), Wisteria (Wisteria sinensis), Opium Poppy (Papaver somniferum), Hazel (Corylus), Walnut (Juglans regia), Sweet Marjoram (Origanum marjorana), Red Clover (Trifolium pratense), Clover (Trifolium), Crab Apple Tree (Malus sylvestris), Scots Pine (Pinus syvestris), Asparagus (Asparagus officinalis), Carrot (Daucus carota subsp. sativus), Cucumber (Cucumis sativus), Eggplant (Solanum melongena), Fig (Ficus carica), Geranium (Geranium), Ginkgo (Ginkgo biloba), Maguey (Agave americana), Mango (Mangifera indica), Oats (Avena sativa), Strawberry (Fragaria x ananassa), Patchouli (Pogostemon cablin), Red Dock (Rumex sanguineus), Spirulina (Arthrospira), Celtic Bean (Vicia faba celtica)

Fertility, female » Peony (Paeonia officinalis), Asparagus (Asparagus officinalis)

Fickleness » Evening Primrose (Oenothera)

Fidelity » Wallflower (Erysimum), Ivy (Hedera), Plum (Prunus domestica), Basil (Ocimum basilicum), Capsicum (Capsicum annuum), Liquorice (Glycyrrhiza glabra), Moneywort (Bacopa monnieri), Speedwell (Veronica officinalis), Brooklime (Veronica beccabunga), Rhubarb (Rheum rhabarbarum), Spruce (Picea)

Fidelity in adversity » Wallflower (Erysimum)

F

Fidelity in love » Lemon (Citrus limon)

Fiery passion » Teuila (Alpinia purpurata)

Fight or flight » Pennyroyal (Mentha pulegium)

Fighting, let's stop » Rose, Musk (Rosa moschata)

Finances » Dill (Anethum graveolens), Gorse (Ulex europaeus)

Financial gain » Buttercup (Ranunculus acris)

Find new paths » Purple Orchid (Cattleya skinneri)

Find it out, if you love me you will » Rose, Maiden's Blush (Rosa)

Fire » Fraxinella (Dictamnus)

First » Spurge Laurel (Daphne laureola)

First aid » Arnica (Arnica montana), Rock Rose (Helianthemum)

First emotion of love » Lilac (Syringa vulgaris)

First love » Dog Violet (Viola riviniana), Primrose (Primula vulgaris), Periwinkle (Vinca minor)

Fitness » Calamus Root (Acorus calamus)

Flamboyance » Pride of Barbados (Poinciana pulcherrima)

Flame of love » Marvel of Peru (Mirabilis jalapa)

Flame, old » Ice Plant (Carpobrotus edulis)

Flattery » Venus' Looking Glass (Triodanis perfoliata)

Flexibility » Feverfew (Tanacetum parthenium), Sallow (Salix cinerea), Hickory (Carya), Sarsaparilla, Wild (Aralia nudicaulis)

Flirtation » Daylily (Hemerocallis), London Pride (Saxifraga x urbium)

Flow » Primrose (Primula vulgaris)

Focus » Pink Heath (Epacris impressa), Sundew (Drosera auriculata), Stock (Matthiola incana), Catnip (Nepeta cataria), Gazania (Gazania), Bedstraw (Galium verum)

Focus, mental » Sandalwood (Santalum album)

Focus on life goals » Dagger's Log (Agave karatto miller)

Focused intention » Jade (Crassula ovata)

F

Folly » Columbine (Aquilegia vulgaris), Rocky Mountain Columbine (Aquilegia caerulea), Geranium, Scarlet (Pelargonium)

Food, protection of » Parsley (Petroselinum crispum)

Foolishness » Celosia (Celosia)

Forbearance » Tamarind (Tamarindus indica)

Force » Fennel (Foeniculum vulgare)

Foresight » Coreopsis (Coreopsis grandiflora)

Forget you, I will never » Pussytoes (Antennaria), Carnation, Pink (Dianthus caryophyllus)

Forget you, I will not » Forget-Me-Not (Myosotis)

Forget me, do not » Speedwell (Veronica officinalis)

Forget me, don't » Forget-Me-Not (Myosotis)

Forgetfulness » Daylily (Hemerocallis)

Forgive me » White Tulip (Tulipa), Kangaroo Paw (Anigozanthos manglesii) Sturt's Desert Rose (Gossypium sturtianum)

Forgive me for my hastiness » Blackberry (Rubus fruticosus)

Forgive me, please » Kantuta (Cantua buxifolia)

Forgive you, I » Hyssop (Hyssopus officinalis), Star of Bethlehem (Ornithogalum)

Forgiven?, am I » Holly (Ilex aquifolium)

Forgiveness » White Tulip (Tulipa), Kangaroo Paw (Anigozanthos manglesii), Calla Lily (Zantedeschia aethiopica), Scottish Primrose (Primula scotica), Hyssop (Hyssopus officinalis), Star of Bethlehem (Ornithogalum), Kantuta (Cantua buxifolia), Texas Bluebonnet (Lupinus texensis), Loosestrife, Purple (Lythrum salicaria), Clarkia (Clarkia purpurea), Lemon Mint (Monarda citriodora), Mountain Devil (Lambertia formosa), Dagger Hakea (Hakea teretifolia)

Forgiveness of hurt » Cinnamon (Cinnamomum verum)

Forgiveness, self- » Heartsease (Viola tricolor), Heliotrope (Heliotropium), Naked Lady (Lycoris squamigera)

F

Forgotten, am I? » Holly (Ilex aquifolium)

Forgotten you, I have not » Amaranthus (Amaranth)

Forlornness » Wood Anemone (Anemone nemerosa)

Forsaken love » Willow (Salix alba)

Forsaken memory » Lilac (Syringa vulgaris)

Fortitude » Everlasting Daisy (Rhodanthe chlorocephala), Chamomile (Chamaemelum nobile), Elder (Sambucus nigra), Dagger's Log (Agave karatto miller), Spinach (Spinacia oleracea)

Fortune » Clover (Trifolium)

Fortune, good » Goldenrod (Solidago virgaurea), Garlic (Allium sativum), Sweet Marjoram (Origanum marjorana), Red Clover (Trifolium pratense), Apricot (Prunus armeniaca), Bok Choy (Brassica rapa subsp. chinensis)

F

Foundation » Alder (Alnus)

Fragrance » Camphor (Cinnamomum camphora)

Frankness » Osier (Salix viminalis)

Fraternal love » Woodbine (Lonicera periclymenum)

Free, breaking » Tomato (Solanum lycopersicum)

Free expression » Chickweed (Stellaria media)

Free thought » Ragwort (Jacobaea vulgaris)

Freedom » Water Ribbons (Triglochin procerum), Frangipani (Plumeria alba), Grape (Vitis), Japanese Toad Lily (Tricyrtis tojen)

Freedom, creative » Nasturtium (Tropaeolum majus), Carrot (Daucus carota subsp. sativus)

Freedom of expression » Tropicbird Orchid (Angraecum eburneum)

Freeing deep emotions » Fuchsia (Fuchsia magellanica)

Freeze me, you » Ice Plant (Carpobrotus edulis)

Friend, I am your » Peruvian Lily (Alstroemeria), Rose, Yellow (Rosa)

Friends, I think we could be » Phlox (Phlox)

Friends?, can we be » Shasta Daisy (Leucanthemum maximum), Rose, Yellow (Rosa)

Friendship » Yarrow (Achillea millefolium), Peruvian Lily (Alstroemeria), Shasta Daisy (Leucanthemum maximum), Freesia (Freesia), Rose, Yellow (Rosa), Kalanchoe (Kalanchoe), Jade (Crassula ovata), Ivy (Hedera), Peppermint (Mentha piperita), Acacia (Acacia), Copihue (Lapageria rosea), Yellow Jessamine (Gelsemium sempervirens), Chrysanthemum, Bronze(Chrysanthemum),Lemongrass(Cymbopogoncitratus),Loosestrife, Purple (Lythrum salicaria), Love Seed (Adenanthera pavonina), Melissa (Melissa officinalis), Mullein, White (Verbascum thapsus), Passionfruit (Passiflora edulis), Phlox, Pink (Phlox), Rose, Pink (Rosa)

Friendship, I offer you » Jade (Crassula ovata)

Friendship, new » Cornflower (Centaurea cyanus), Periwinkle (Vinca minor)

Friendship, strengthen » Macadamia (Macadamia integrifolia)

Friendship, true » Geranium, Oak Leaf (Pelargonium quercifolium)

Friendship, unchanging » Arborvitae (Thuja)

Friendships, ending unwanted » Chilli (Capsicum)

Friendships, new » Loveage (Levisticum officinale)

Frigidity » Chicory (Cichorium intybus), Ice Plant (Carpobrotus edulis)

Fringe benefits » Radish (Raphanus sativus)

Frivolity » London Pride (Saxifraga x urbium)

Frivolous amusements » Bladder Senna (Colutea arborescens)

From bad to good » Service Tree (Sorbus)

Fruitfulness » Hollyhock (Alcea rosea), Orange Blossom (Citrus x sinensis), Mexican Orange Blossom (Choisya ternata), Wheat (Triticum)

Frugality » Endive (Cichorium endivia)

Fulfilment of commitments » Oak (Quercus robur)

Fullness » Watermelon (Citrullus lanatus)

Fun » Bladder Senna (Colutea arborescens)

Fun challenges » Nasturtium (Tropaeolum majus)

Fun, let's have » Nasturtium (Tropaeolum majus)

Fusion » Comfrey (Symphytum officinale)

F

Future » Meadow Rue (Thalictrum)

Future, belief in » Gentian (Gentiana)

Future joy » Celandine (Ficaria verna)

G

Gaiety » Butterfly Orchid (Psychopsis)

Gain » Cabbage (Brassica oleracea var. capitata)

Gallantry » Sweet William (Dianthus barbatus)

Game » Hyacinth (Hyacinthus)

Generosity » Royal Bluebell (Wahlenbergia gloriosa),Tree Peony (Paeonia suffruticosa), Dahlia (Dahlia), Maple (Acer), Raspberry (Rubus idaeus)

Genius » Plane Tree (Platanus)

Gentle healing » Scabiosa (Scabiosa), Iris, Fairy (Dietes grandiflora)

Gentle on self » Crown Vetch (Securigera varia)

Gentle question » Heath Bell (Erica cinerea)

Gentle strength » Wooly Sunflower (Eriophyllum lanatum)

Genteel » Rose, Pompon (Rosa)

Gentleness » Mock Orange (Philadelphus), Primrose (Primula vulgaris), Marguerite Daisy (Argyranthemum frutescens), Lewis Mock Orange (Philadelphus lewisii)

Get well » Blue Gum Flower (Eucalyptus globulus), Native Geranium (Geranium solanderi), Swamp Lily (Crinum pedunculatum), Sunflower (Helianthus annuus), Rose, pale pink (Rosa), Self-Heal (Prunella vulgaris), Arnica (Arnica montana)

Gifts, personal » Treasure Flower (Gazania rigens)

Give me your love » Marsh Marigold (Caltha palustris)

Give up, don't » Water Ribbons (Triglochin procerum)

Gladdens the eye » Eyebright (Euphrasia officinalis)

Gladness » Crocus (Crocus)

Glee » Crocus (Crocus)

Glory » Laurel (Laurus nobilis), Flame Lily (Gloriosa rothschildiana)

Go away » Chilli (Capsicum), Pennyroyal (Mentha pulegium)

Go, let me » Butterfly Weed (Asclepias tuberosa)

Go with the flow » Water Ribbons (Triglochin procerum)

Goal setting » Carrot (Daucus carota subsp. sativus)

Goals » Rose, Cecil Brunner (Rosa Mlle. Cecile Brunner)

Goals achieved, long-held » Amaryllis (Amaryllis)

Goals, change in » Iris Croatica (Iris perunika)

Goals, realistic » Rose, Cecil Brunner (Rosa Mlle. Cecile Brunner)

Goal setting » Pink Heath (Epacris impressa)

Good deeds » Variegated Box (Buxus sempervirens)

Good fortune » Peruvian Lily (Alstroemeria), Goldenrod (Solidago virgaurea),Garlic (Allium sativum), Sweet Marjoram (Origanum marjorana), Red Clover (Trifolium pratense), Apricot (Prunus armeniaca), Bok Choy (Brassica rapa subsp. chinensis)

Good, from bad to » Service Tree (Sorbus)

Good health » Tree Peony (Paeonia suffruticosa), Peony (Paeonia officinalis), Feverfew (Tanacetum parthenium), Sage (Salvia officinalis)

Good luck » Lechenaultia (Lechenaultia formosa), Tea Tree (Leptospermum myrsinoides), Sweet Pea (Lathyrus odoratus), Tree Peony (Paeonia suffruticosa), Carnation Pink (Dianthus caryophyllus), Stephanotis (Stephanotis floribunda), Heather, Lavender (Calluna vulgaris), Bells of Ireland (Moluccella laevis), Holly (Ilex aquifolium), Jade (Crassula ovata), Calamus Root (Acorus calamus), Centaury (Erythraea centaurium), Elder (Sambucus nigra), Red Clover (Trifolium pratense), Clover (Trifolium), Bok Choy (Brassica rapa subsp. chinensis), Eggplant (Solanum melongena), Heal-All (Pedicularis canadensis), Peyote (Lophophora williamsii), Soy Bean (Glycine max)

Good luck, risky venture » Goldenrod (Solidago virgaurea)

Good luck with your exams » Clematis (Clematis)

G

Good nature » Mullein, White (Verbascum thapsus)

Good news » Guelder-Rose (Viburnum opulus)

Good spirits, attract » Marshmallow (Althea officinalis)

Good taste » Fuchsia (Fuchsia magellanica)

Good times and bad, I will stay with you in » Virginia Creeper (Parthenocissus quinquefolia)

Good to be true, too » Variegated Box (Buxus sempervirens)

Good use of energy » Forsythia (Forsythia)

Goodbye » Cyclamen (Cyclamen)

Goodness » Boxwood (Buxus), Dog's Mercury (Mercurialis perennis)

Goodwill » Oregon Grape (Mahonia aquifolium), Olive (Olea europaea)

G

Gossip, stop » Slippery Elm (Ulmus rubra)

Grateful, I am » Rose, Dark Pink (Rosa), Calendula (Calendula officinalis)

Gratitude » Sweet Pea (Lathyrus odoratus), Bluebell, Common (Hyacinthoides non-scripta), Carnation, Pink (Dianthus caryophyllus), Lisianthus (Eustoma grandiflorum), Rose, Dark Pink (Rosa), Calendula (Calendula officinalis), Canterbury Bells (Campanula medium), Venus' Looking Glass (Triodanis perfoliata), Copihue (Lapageria rosea), Kiwi (Actinidia chinensis), Ylang-Ylang (Cananga odorata), Canna (Canna generalis striatus)

Grace » Lavender (Lavandula stoechas), Orchid (Orchidaceae), Rose, pale pink (Rosa), Snapdragon (Antirrhinum majus), Water Lily, Pink (Nymphaea), Lime (Tilia x europaea), Puti Tai Nobiu (Bougainvillea spectabilis), Pomegranate Blossom (Punica granatum), Mallow (Malva sylvestris)

Grace and beauty have charmed me, your » Cowslip (Primula veris)

Grace, feminine » Rosewood (Pterocarpus indicus)

Grace under pressure » Snapdragon (Antirrhinum majus)

Gracefulness » Water Lily (Nymphaea)

Grandeur » Ash (Fraxinus), Beech (Fagus)

Great achievement » Oak (Quercus robur)

Great energy » Great Maple (Acer pseudoplatanus)

Great joy » Caladium (Caladium)

Greatness, achieving » Eggplant (Solanum melongena)

Greed » Sweet Pea (Lathyrus odoratus)

Grief » Sturt's Desert Pea (Swainsona formosa), Calendula (Calendula officinalis), Aloe (Aloe vera), Blackberry (Rubus fruticosus), Harebell (Campanula rotundifolia)

Grief, comfort » Sweet Marjoram (Origanum marjorana)

Grief, release of » Artichoke, Globe (Cynara scolymus)

Grief, unresolved » Yerba Santa (Eriodictyon glutinosum)

Grounding » Native Geranium (Geranium solanderi), Flax (Linum usitatissimum), Hawkweed (Hieracium), Crown Vetch (Securigera varia), Tree Houseleek (Aeonium), Shepherd's Purse (Capsella bursa-pastoris), Ginseng (Panax), Marsh Marigold (Caltha palustris), Clubmoss (Lycopodium), Bilberry (Vaccinium myrtillus), Elm (Ulmus), Peanut (Arachis hypogaea), Turnip (Brassica rapa subsp. rapa)

G

Growth » Kowhai (Sophora), Bloodroot (Sanguinaria canadensis), Rose, Prairie (Rosa arkansana), Maguey (Agave americana)

Growth, inner » Grape (Vitis), Water Hyacinth (Eichbornia crassipes)

Growth, new » Rose, Prairie (Rosa arkansana)

Growth, spiritual » Sacred Lotus (Nelumbo nucifera), Angel's Trumpet (Brugmansia candida), Frankincense (Boswellia sacra)

Guardian of love » Copihue (Lapageria rosea)

Guidance » Fairy Aprons (Utricularia dichotoma), Bee Balm (Monarda), Mountain Laurel (Kalmia latifolia), Live Forever (Dudleya farinosa)

Guidance, divine » Gardenia (Gardenia jasminoides)

Guidance, inner » Freesia (Freesia)

Guilt » Hyssop (Hyssopus officinalis)

H

Habit-breaking » Morning Glory (Ipomoea purpurea), Thistle, Common (Cirsium vulgare), Horse-Chestnut (Aesculus hippocastanum)

Habits, change » Yellow Dock (Rumex crispus)

Habits, new » Red Hot Poker (Kniphofia)

Happened, I wish this had not » Aster (Aster)

Happy, ability to be » Iris, Blue Flag (Iris versicolor)

Happy attitude » Trout Lily (Erythronium americanum)

Happy anniversary » Tree Peony (Paeonia suffruticosa)

Happy, be » Shasta Daisy (Leucanthemum maximum), Lily of the Valley (Convallaria majalis), Honeysuckle (Lonicera)

Happy for you, I am » Bouvardia (Bouvardia)

Happy life » Stock (Matthiola incana)

Happy love » Rose, Bridal (Rosa)

Happy marriage » Tree Peony (Paeonia suffruticosa)

Happy marriage, I wish you a » Peony (Paeonia officinalis), Stephanotis (Stephanotis floribunda)

Happy marriage, long and » Clover (Trifolium)

Happy memories » Straw Flower (Xerochrysum bracteatum)

Happy newborn » Daphne (Daphne odora)

Happy old age » Pine (Pinus sylvestris)

Happy with self » Chickweed (Stellaria media)

Happy wedding anniversary » Peony (Paeonia officinalis)

Happy work » Wand Flower (Sparaxis grandiflora)

Happy, your love makes me » Hepatica (Hepatica)

Happiness » Daisy (Bellis perennis), Sunflower (Helianthus annuus), Shasta Daisy (Leucanthemum maximum), Gerbera Daisy (Gerbera jamesonii), Lily of the Valley (Convallaria majalis), Rose, orange (Rosa), Honeysuckle (Lonicera), Hibiscus (Hibiscus), Meadowsweet (Filipendula ulmaria),

Cowslip (Primula veris), Lime (Tilia x europaea), Golden Trumpet Tree (Tabebuia alba), Copihue (Lapageria rosea), Trilobed Violet (Viola palmata), Prairie Lily (Lilium philadelphicum), Bamboo (Bambusoideae), Eggplant (Solanum melongena), Fir (Abies), Oregano (Origanum vulgare), Osmanthus (Osmanthus fragrans), Purslane (Portulaca oleracea), Queen of the Meadow (Filipendula ulmaria), Sweet Sultan (Amberboa moschata), Mountain Devil (Lambertia formosa)

Happiness, domestic » Holly (Ilex aquifolium)

Happiness, eternal » Straw Flower (Xerochrysum bracteatum)

Happiness, I wish you » Gerbera Daisy (Gerbera jamesonii)

Happiness, long-lasting » Dandelion (Taraxacum officinale)

Happiness, momentary » Tradescantia (Tradescantia zebrina)

Happiness, new » Cowslip (Primula veris)

Happiness, rural » Tulip Tree (Liriodendron), Violet, Yellow (Viola pubescens)

Happiness, transient » Spiderwort (Tradescantia)

Happiness, wealth does not always indicate » Auricula (Primula auricular)

Hardworking » Flamingo Flower (Anthurium)

Hardiness » Purple Saxifrage (Saxifraga oppositifolia)

Harmonious life » Vervain (Verbena officinalis)

Harmonious relationships » Tree Peony (Paeonia suffruticosa)

Harmony » Japanese Cherry (Prunus serrulata), Sweet Pea (Lathyrus odoratus), Meadowsweet (Filipendula ulmaria), Olive (Olea europaea), Basil (Ocimum basilicum), Fir (Abies), Loosestrife, Purple (Lythrum salicaria), Gilia-Scarlet (Ipomopsis aggregata)

Harmony, relationship » Tiger Lily (Lilium tigrinum)

Hastiness, forgive me for my » Blackberry (Rubus fruticosus)

Have faith » Turkey Bush (Calytrix exstipulata)

Heal » Swallow-Wort (Cynanchum louiseae)

Heal, all » Mistletoe (Viscum album)

Heal relationships » Ceibo (Erythrina crista-galli)

H

Heal wounds » Solomon's Seal (Polygonatum)

Healer, heart » Rhododendron (Rhododendron)

Healing » Blue Gum Flower (Eucalyptus globulus), Flannel Flower (Actinotus helianthi) Kangaroo Paw (Anigozanthos manglesii), Madonna Lily (Lilium candidum), Tree Peony (Paeonia suffruticosa), Rose, Pale Pink (Rosa), Self-Heal (Prunella vulgaris), Dandelion (Taraxacum officinale), Feverfew (Tanacetum parthenium), Juniper (Juniperus), Mugwort (Artemisia vulgaris), Meadowsweet (Filipendula ulmaria), Echinacea (Echinacea purpurea), Burdock (Arctium), Bloodroot (Sanguinaria canadensis), Ginseng (Panax), Hop (Humulus lupulus), Pepper (Piper nigrum), Broom (Genisteae), Rowan (Sorbus aucuparia), White Trillium (Trillium grandiflorum), Balm of Gilead (Commiphora gileadensis), Bracken (Pteridium), Cedar (Cedrus), Cinnamon (Cinnamomum verum), Cucumber (Cucumis sativus), Goat's Rue (Galega officinalis), Goldenseal (Hydrastis canadensis), Heal-All (Pedicularis canadensis), Henna (Lawsonia inermis), Job's Tears (Coix lacryma-jobi) Persimmon (Diospyros virginiana), Comfrey (Symphytum officinale), Fringed Violet (Thysanotus tuberosus)

Healing ability » Rose, Cherokee (Rosa laevigata)

Healing, breakup » Bleeding Heart (Lamprocapnos spectabilis)

Healing, childhood » Cyclamen (Cyclamen)

Healing, discussion » Lime, Key West (Citrus aurantifolia)

Healing, earth » Fireweed (Chamerion angustifolium)

Healing, emotional » Gentian (Gentiana), Mahogany (Swietenia macrophylla)

Healing, encourage » Calamus Root (Acorus calamus)

Healing, female » Hibiscus, White (Hibiscus arnottianus), Lady's Mantle (Alchemilla vulgaris), Motherwort (Leonurus cardiaca), Black Cohosh (Cimicifuga racemosa), Tiger Lily (Lilium tigrinum), Catnip (Nepeta cataria), Pride of Barbados (Poinciana pulcherrima), Christmas Orchid (Cattleya trianae), Rose, Cherokee (Rosa laevigata), Purple Pitcher Plant (Sarracenia purpurea), Cotton (Gossypium)

Healing, distant » Wild Yam (Dioscorea villosa)

Healing from past hurts » Zephyr Lily (Zephyranthes)

Healing, gentle » Scabiosa (Scabiosa), Iris, Fairy (Dietes grandiflora)

Healing, heart » Downy Hawthorn (Crataegus mollis)

Healing, heartbreak » Wild Pansy (Viola tricolor), Opium Poppy (Papaver somniferum)

Healing, intuitive » Rosewood (Pterocarpus indicus)

Healing, male » Sunflower (Helianthus annuus), Blue-Eyed Grass (Sisyrinchium montanum)

Healing, mental » Hellebore (Helleborus)

Healing, psychic » Skullcap (Scutellaria)

Healing, spiritual » Motherwort (Leonurus cardiaca)

Healing transformation » Yesterday, Today and Tomorrow (Brunfelsia)

Healing trauma » Arnica (Arnica montana)

Health » Juniper (Juniperus), Camphor (Cinnamomum camphora), Caraway (Carum carvi), Goat's Rue (Galega officinalis), Grapefruit (Citrus paradisi), Knotweed (Polygonum aviculare), Peyote (Lophophora williamsii), Spinach (Spinacia oleracea)

Health, good » Peony (Paeonia officinalis), Feverfew (Tanacetum parthenium), Sage (Salvia officinalis)

Health, inner » Apple Blossom (Malus domestica)

Health recovery » Nettle (Urtica)

Health, restore » Lemon Balm (Melissa officinalis)

Health, ward off ill- » Cranes-Bill (Geranium maculatum)

Healthy competition » Tiger Lily (Lilium tigrinum)

Healthy ego » Witchhazel (Hamamelis virginiana)

Heart-centred widom » Marguerite Daisy (Argyranthemum frutescens)

Heart, broken » Love Lies Bleeding (Amaranthus caudatus)

Heart, comfort the » Cranes-Bill (Geranium maculatum)

Heart, faithful » Frankincense (Boswellia sacra)

Heart healer » Rhododendron (Rhododendron)

H

Heart healing » Downy Hawthorn (Crataegus mollis)

Heart health, physical » Lily of the Valley (Convallaria majalis)

Heart, I hold you close to my » Ranunculus (Ranunculus)

Heart is full of passion, my » Lords and Ladies (Arum maculatum)

Heart, light » Dancing Lady Orchid (Oncidium)

Heart, open your » Wild Pansy (Viola tricolor), Basil (Ocimum basilicum)

Heart opening » Downy Hawthorn (Crataegus mollis)

Heart, protected » Gerbera Daisy, Pink (Gerbera jamesonii)

Heart protection » Hawthorn (Crataegus monogyna)

Heart, purity of » Lily of the Valley (Convallaria majalis), Rose, Lavender (Rosa)

Heart, strong » Wild Pansy (Viola tricolor)

Heart was mine until we met, my » Periwinkle (Vinca minor)

Heart, you are the flame in my » Camellia, Red (Camellia)

Heartache » Bee Balm (Monarda)

Heartache cure » Milkweed (Asclepias)

Heartbreak healing » Wild Pansy (Viola tricolor), Opium Poppy (Papaver somniferum)

Heartless, hopeless not » Love Lies Bleeding (Amaranthus caudatus)

Heartlessness » Hydrangea (Hydrangea)

Heaven connection, earth to » Mulberry, White (Morus alba), Pine (Pinus sylvestris)

Help you, I will » Swamp Lily (Crinum pedunculatum)

Helpful relationships » Trout Lily (Erythronium americanum)

Here, I am » King Protea (Protea cynaroides)

Here for you, I am » Straw Flower (Xerochrysum bracteatum)

Heritage » Oak (Quercus robur), Wood of Life (Guaiacum sanctum)

Hermitage » Milkwort (Polygala vulgaris)

Hexes, break » Capsicum (Capsicum annuum), Chilli (Capsicum), Galangal (Alpinia galangal)

Hibernating energy » Onion (Allium cepa)

Hidden abilities » Larch (Larix decidua)

Hidden fears » Betony (Stachys officinalis)

Hidden protection » Puti Tai Nobiu (Bougainvillea spectabilis)

High ideals » Oak (Quercus robur)

High ranking » Red Blossomed Heilala (Garcinia sessilis)

Higher consciousness » Passion Flower (Passiflora incarnate), Meadow Saffron (Colchicum autumnale)

Higher learning » African Violet (Saintpaulia)

Higher perspective » Ash (Fraxinus)

Higher purpose » Sage (Salvia officinalis)

Higher self » Rose, Musk (Rosa moschata), Echinacea (Echinacea purpurea), Rue (Ruta graveolens), Chervil (Anthriscus cerefolium)

Higher wisdom » Iris Croatica (Iris perunika)

Homemaking » Holly (Ilex aquifolium)

Home, protection of » Cornflower (Centaurea cyanus), Chives (Allium schoenoprasum)

Home, safe » Heather, White (Calluna vulgaris)

Homesickness » Honeysuckle (Lonicera)

Holy » Yerba Santa (Eriodictyon glutinosum)

Honesty » Chrysanthemum, White (Chrysanthemum), Rose, White (Rosa), Daphne (Daphne odora), Honesty (Lunaria annua), Bittersweet (Solanum dulcamara), Star of Bethlehem (Ornithogalum), Woodbine (Lonicera periclymenum)

Honour » Lily (Lilium), Peony (Paeonia officinalis), Wisteria (Wisteria sinensis), Speedwell (Veronica officinalis), Red Blossomed Heilala (Garcinia sessilis), Oregano (Origanum vulgare)

Hope » Jasmine (Jasminum officinale), Poet's Narcissus (Narcissus poeticus), Snowdrop (Galanthus nivalis), Freesia (Freesia), Daffodil (Narcissus pseudonarcissus), Hawthorn (Crataegus monogyna), Star of Bethlehem

H

(Ornithogalum), Bee Balm (Monarda), Easter Lily (Lilium longiflorum), Columbine (Aquilegia vulgaris), Bloodroot (Sanguinaria canadensis), Chinese Plum (Prunus mume), Olive (Olea europaea), Sweet Marjoram (Origanum marjorana), Kantuta (Cantua buxifolia), Blackthorn (Prunus spinosa), Rose, Cherokee (Rosa laevigata), Iris, German (Iris germanica), Fireweed (Chamerion angustifolium)

Hope, divine » Melati (Jasminum sambac)

Hope, do not give up » Petunia (Petunia)

Hopes, extinguish » Bindweed, Great (Convolvulus major)

Hopeless love » Yellow Tulip (Tulipa)

Hopeless not heartless » Love Lies Bleeding (Amaranthus caudatus)

Hoping for you, I am » Daffodil (Narcissus pseudonarcissus)

Horizons, expanded » Stargazer Lily, Pink (Lilium orientalis), Purslane (Portulaca oleracea)

Horror » Ebony (Diospyros crassiflora), Mandrake (Mandragora officinarum), Snakesfoot (Rauvolfia serpentina)

Hospitality » Tiare (Gardenia taitensis), Flamingo Flower (Anthurium)

Hot temper » Barberry (Berberis vulgaris)

House warming » Cornflower (Centaurea cyanus)

How sweet you are » Pink, Clove-Scented (Dianthus caryophyllus)

Human understanding » Artichoke, Globe (Cynara scolymus)

Humanity » Marshmallow (Althea officinalis)

Humility » Buttercup (Ranunculus acris), Lilac (Syringa vulgaris), Lily of the Valley (Convallaria majalis), Sweet Violet (Viola odorata), Melati (Jasminum sambac), Broom (Genisteae), Bulrush (Scirpoides holoschoenus), Bindweed, Small (Convolvulus minor), Broom (Genisteae), Strawberry (Fragaria x ananassa)

Humility, joyful » African Daisy (Osteospermum)

Hurt, forgiveness of » Cinnamon (Cinnamomum verum)

Hurt me, you have » Sturt's Desert Pea (Swainsona formosa)

Hurt, release emotional » Cuckoo Flower (Cardamine pratensis)

Hurt, release of » Puti tai nobiu (Bougainvillea spectabilis)

Hysteria, calm » Catnip (Nepeta cataria)

I

I admire you » Lavender (Lavandula stoechas), Heather, Lavender (Calluna vulgaris)

I admire you but cannot love you » Laurel (Laurus nobilis)

I admire your courage » Chamomile, Roman (Chamaemelum nobile)

I agree with you » Rose, Dark Pink (Rosa)

I am available » Cranes-Bill (Geranium maculatum)

I am concerned for you » Coltsfoot (Tussilago farfara)

I am devoted to you » Peruvian Lily (Alstroemeria), Honeysuckle (Lonicera), Grape (Vitis), Heliotrope (Heliotropium)

I am falling in love with you » Rose, Yellow (Rosa)

I am faithful to you » Dandelion (Taraxacum officinale)

I am grateful » Rose, Dark Pink (Rosa), Calendula (Calendula officinalis)

I am happy for you » Bouvardia (Bouvardia)

I am here » King Protea (Protea cynaroides)

I am here for you » Snowdrop (Galanthus nivalis), Straw Flower (Xerochrysum bracteatum)

I am hoping for you » Daffodil (Narcissus pseudonarcissus)

I am interested » Old Man Banksia (Banksia serrata)

I am intoxicated with pleasure » Heliotrope (Heliotropium)

I am leaving » Henbane (Hyoscyamus niger)

I am only dedicated to you » Edelweiss (Leontopodium alpinum)

I am pledged to another » Passion Flower (Passiflora incarnate)

I am proud of you » Lily (Lilium), Heliconia (Heliconia), Tiger Lily (Lilium tigrinum)

I am ready » Rosella Flower (Hibiscus heterophyllus), Pelargonium (Pelargonium cucullatum)

I am ready for you » Venus Flytrap (Dionaea muscipula)

I am ready to progress » Five Corners (Styphelia laeta)

I am receptive » Sego Lily (Calochortus nuttallii)

I am shy » Marvel of Peru (Mirabilis jalapa), Moving Plant (Mimosa pudica)

I am sincere » Rose, Dark Pink (Rosa)

I am sorry » Flannel Flower (Actinotus helianthi), Sturt's Desert Pea (Swainsona formosa), Sturt's Desert Rose (Gossypium sturtianum), Scottish Primrose (Primula scotica), Rose, pale pink (Rosa), Rose, Musk (Rosa moschata), Calendula (Calendula officinalis), Snapdragon (Antirrhinum majus), Kantuta (Cantua buxifolia), Loosestrife, Yellow (Lythrum salicaria), Clarkia (Clarkia purpurea), Dagger Hakea (Hakea teretifolia)

I am sorry you are hurt » Iris, Fairy (Dietes grandiflora)

I am staying with you » Pohutukawa (Metrosideros excelsa)

I am telling the truth » Rose, White (Rosa)

I am thinking of our love » Pansy (Viola tricolor var. hortensis)

I am thinking of you » Heartsease (Viola tricolor)

I am with you » Hoya (Hoya australis)

I am your friend » Peruvian Lily (Alstroemeria), Rose, Yellow (Rosa)

I appreciate you » Gerbera Daisy (Gerbera jamesonii), Lisianthus (Eustoma grandiflorum), Rose, Peach (Rosa)

I believe in you » Grey Spider Flower (Grevillea buxifolia), Tree Spider Orchid (Dendrobium tetragonum), Antarctic Pearlwort (Colobanthus quitensis), Foxglove (Digitalis purpurea), Iris, Blue Flag (Iris versicolor)

I believe you can succeed » Nasturtium (Tropaeolum majus)

I burn » Cactus (Cactaceae)

I cannot resist you » Quince (Cydonia oblonga)

I cannot be with you » Chrysanthemum, Yellow (Chrysanthemum)

I

I cannot wait to see you » Anemone (Anemone), Himalayan Balsam (Impatiens glandulifera)

I can see you » Eyebright (Euphrasia officinalis)

I challenge you » Cayenne (Capsicum frutescens)

I change but in death » Laurel (Laurus nobilis)

I choose you » Geranium, Ivy-Leafed (Pelargonium peltatum)

I declare against you » Liquorice (Glycyrrhiza glabra)

I desire you » Tuberose (Polianthes tuberosa), Moon Orchid (Phalaenopsis amabilis)

I desire you above all else » Ivy (Hedera)

I die if neglected » Laurustinus (Viburnum tinus)

I do not care » Plum (Prunus domestica)

I do not trust you » Geranium, Scarlet (Pelargonium)

I dream of you » Queen of the Night (Selenicereus grandiflorus), California Poppy (Eschscholzia californica)

I forgive you » Hyssop (Hyssopus officinalis), Star of Bethlehem (Ornithogalum)

I happily await your return » Red Whortleberry (Vaccinium)

I have affection for you » Stock (Matthiola incana)

I have confidence in you » Poet's Narcissus (Narcissus poeticus)

I have faith » Gentian (Gentiana)

I have faith in you » Canterbury Bells (Campanula medium), Gentian (Gentiana)

I have lost all » Mournful Widow (Scabiosa atropurpurea)

I have not forgotten you » Amaranthus (Amaranth)

I have not stopped loving you » Amaranthus (Amaranth)

I have noticed you » Gymea Lily (Doryanthes excelsa)

I hold you close to my heart » Ranunculus (Ranunculus)

I hope your wish is granted » Heather, White (Calluna vulgaris)

I hope your wishes are heard » Iris, Fairy (Dietes grandiflora)

I jest » Celosia (Celosia)

I know » Angel's Trumpet (Brugmansia candida), Opoponax (Commiphora erythraea)

I live for thee » Cedar (Cedrus)

I long for a tryst » Pea (Pisum sativum)

I love more than just your beauty » Sweet Alyssum (Alyssum maritimum)

I love you » Carnation (Dianthus caryophyllus), Native Passionflower (Passiflora herbertiana), Apple Blossom (Malus domestica), Chrysanthemum, Red (Chrysanthemum), Rose, Red (Rosa), Bloodroot (Sanguinaria canadensis), Tiare (Gardenia taitensis)

I love you completely » Waratah (Telopea speciosissima), Scottish Primrose (Primula scotica)

I love you unconditionally » Chicory (Cichorium intybus)

I love your beauty » Puerto Rican Hibiscus (Thespesia grandiflora)

I loved you at first sight » Rose, Mauve (Rosa), Gloxinia (Gloxinia)

I miss you » Statice (Limonium), Geranium (Geranium)

I need an answer » Pink Heath (Epacris impressa)

I need space » Cow Parsley (Anthriscus sylvestris)

I offer you all I have » Wheat (Triticum)

I offer you friendship » Jade (Crassula ovata)

I offer you my all » Shepherd's Purse (Capsella bursa-pastoris)

I only want you » Quince (Cydonia oblonga)

I promise » Madonna Lily (Lilium candidum), Chrysanthemum, White (Chrysanthemum)

I promise to be true » Lemon (Citrus limon)

I place you above all else » Ash (Fraxinus)

I prefer you » Geranium (Geranium)

I regret what I have done » Dogwood (Cornus)

I release you » Lechenaultia (Lechenaultia formas), Calendula (Calendula officinalis)

I remain faithful » Speedwell (Veronica officinalis)

I remember » Melilot (Melilotus officinalis), Mock Orange (Philadelphus)

I remember you » Rosemary (Rosmarinus officinalis)

I respect you » Hibiscus, White (Hibiscus arnottianus), Rose, Red (Rosa)

I respect your uniqueness » Purple Orchid (Cattleya skinneri)

I see your beauty » Tulip, Variegated (Tulipa)

I still love you » Kalanchoe (Kalanchoe)

I support you » Fairy Fan Flower (Scaevola aemula), Hoya (Hoya australis), Nasturtium (Tropaeolum majus)

I surrender » Crown Vetch (Securigera varia)

I think we could be friends » Phlox (Phlox)

I trust you » Rose, Wild (Rosa acicularis), Freesia (Freesia)

I understand » Boronia (Boronia ledifolia), Grass Tree (Xanthorrhoea resinosa), Kangaroo Paw (Anigozanthos manglesii), Sacred Blue Lily (Nymphaea caerulea), Sweet Alyssum (Alyssum maritimum), Poinciana (Delonix regia)

I understand you » Trout Lily (Erythronium americanum)

I want to be with you » Rose, Dark Pink (Rosa), Petunia (Petunia), Comfrey (Symphytum officinale)

I want to marry you » Valerian (Polemonium caeruleum)

I want to meet you » Geranium (Geranium)

I want to please you » Daphne (Daphne odora)

I want to share my intention with you » Hemp (Cannabis sativa)

I want to share my life with you » Tarragon (Artemisia dracunculus)

I want to tell you how I feel » Bleeding Heart (Lamprocapnos spectabilis)

I want you » Tulip, Wild (Tulipa sprengeri)

I want you to love me » Dutchman's Breeches (Dicentra cucullaria)

I will always love you » Magnolia (Magnolia campbellii)

I will always treasure you » Straw Flower (Xerochrysum bracteatum)

I will be ready » Astilbe (Astilbe)

I

I will comfort you » Geranium, Rose (Pelargonium graveolens)

I will help you » Swamp Lily (Crinum pedunculatum)

I will love you forever » Orange Blossom (Citrus x sinensis)

I will marry you » Blushing Bride (Tillandsia ionantha)

I will never forget you » Carnation, Pink (Dianthus caryophyllus), Pussytoes (Antennaria)

I will not forget you » Forget-Me-Not (Myosotis)

I will not survive you » Mulberry, Black (Morus nigra)

I will protect you » Rose, White (Rosa)

I will return » Rose, Yellow (Rosa)

I will stay with you in good times and bad » Virginia Creeper (Parthenocissus quinquefolia)

I will succeed » Hollyhock (Alcea rosea)

I will wait » Astilbe (Astilbe), Ageratum (Ageratum), Patience Dock (Rumex patientia)

I will win » Columbine (Aquilegia vulgaris)

I wish this had not happened » Aster (Aster)

I wish this moment would last forever » Everlasting Daisy (Rhodanthe chlorocephala)

I wish you a happy marriage » Peony (Paeonia officinalis), Stephanotis (Stephanotis floribunda)

I wish you good health » Tree Peony (Paeonia suffruticosa)

I wish you happiness » Gerbera Daisy (Gerbera jamesonii)

I wish you longevity » Bouvardia (Bouvardia)

I wish you peace » Holly (Ilex aquifolium)

I wish you success » Peruvian Lily (Alstroemeria), Mullein (Verbascum thapsus)

I wish you success in your studies » Clematis (Clematis)

I would die for you » Opium Poppy (Papaver somniferum)

Idea, realisation of an » Heliconia (Heliconia)

Ideals, high » Oak (Quercus robur)

Ideas, new » Indian Paintbrush (Castilleja miniata), Mock Orange (Philadelphus), Water Lily, White (Nymphaea), Alfalfa (Medicago sativa), Paw Paw (Asimina triloba)

Ideas » Swan Plant (Asclepias physocarpa)

Identity » Thorn Apple (Datura stamonium)

Idleness » Ice Plant (Carpobrotus edulis), Icicle Plant (Mesembryanthemum crystallinum)

If you love me you will find it out » Rose, Maiden's Blush (Rosa)

Ill at ease » Fumitory (Fumaria officinalis)

Ill health, ward off » Cranes-Bill (Geranium maculatum), Oak (Quercus robur)

Ill-timed » Sorrel, Wild (Rumex acetosella)

Ill will, banish » Sheep Sorrel (Rumex acetosella)

Illness, protection from » Mint (Mentha)

Illumination » King Protea (Protea cynaroides), Snowdrop (Galanthus nivalis)

Imagination » Turkey Bush (Calytrix exstipulata), Lupin (Lupinus perennis), Great Maple (Acer pseudoplatanus)

Improved relationships » Linnaea (Linnaea borealis)

Immortality » Ambrosia (Ambrosia), Ivy (Hedera), Periwinkle (Vinca minor), Motherwort (Leonurus cardiaca), Larch (Larix decidua), Pine (Pinus sylvestris), Oak (Quercus robur), Myrtle (Myrtus), Yew (Taxus baccata), Scots Pine (Pinus syvestris), Peach Blossom (Prunus persica), Chervil (Anthriscus cerefolium), Hornbeam (Carpinus)

Immune system, strengthen » Self-Heal (Prunella vulgaris)

Immunity » Pansy (Viola tricolor var. hortensis), Garlic (Allium sativum), Echinacea (Echinacea purpurea), Coltsfoot (Tussilago farfara)

Immunity from enemies » Vervain (Verbena officinalis)

Impartiality » Black-Eyed Susan (Rudbeckia hirta)

Impatience » Himalayan Balsam (Impatiens glandulifera)

Imperishability » Chaconia (Warszewiczia coccinea)

Importunity » Burdock (Arctium), Teasel (Dipsacus)

Improved relationships » Rose, Musk (Rosa moschata)

Improvement » Rabbit Orchid (Leptoceras menziesii)

Incorruptibility » Larch (Larix decidua)

Increase activity » Castor Oil Plant (Ricinus communis)

Increase positivity » Black Cohosh (Cimicifuga racemosa)

Increase, to » Pumpkin (Cucurbita pepo)

Increased intelligence » Hellebore (Helleborus)

Increased perception » Snapdragon (Antirrhinum majus)

Increased trust » Ithuriel's Spear (Triteleia laxa)

Increased wisdom » Solomon's Seal (Polygonatum)

Incorruptible » Cedar of Lebanon (Cedrus libani)

Independent success » Cranberry Heath (Astroloma humifusum)

Independence » Common Thistle (Cirsium vulgare), Geraldton Wax (Chamelaucium uncinatum), Self-Heal (Prunella vulgaris), Everlasting Daisy (Rhodanthe chlorocephala), Nasturtium (Tropaeolum majus), Grape (Vitis), Plum (Prunus domestica), Butterfly Jasmine (Mariposa), Native Wood Violet (Viola odorata), Native Violet (Viola papilionacea), Redwood (Sequoiadendron giganteum), Sea Holly (Eryngium maritimum)

Indifference » Plum (Prunus domestica), Candytuft (Iberis), Mustard (Sinapis arvensis)

Inebriation, protection from » Sweet Violet (Viola odorata)

Infection, protection from » Witchhazel (Hamamelis virginiana)

Influence » Southern Cross (Xanthosia rotundifolia)

Influences, protection from outside » Walnut (Juglans regia)

Information » Greater Celandine (Chelidonium majus)

Ingenuity » Clematis (Clematis)

Ingratitude » Gentian (Gentiana)

Initiation » Thorn Apple (Datura stamonium)

Injustice » Hop (Humulus lupulus), Blackberry (Rubus fruticosus)

Inner beauty » Bird of Paradise (Strelitzia reginae)

Inner beauty, I see your » Indian Paintbrush (Castilleja miniata)

Inner calm » Tiger Lily (Lilium tigrinum), Wood Betony (Stachys betonica)

Inner child » Buttercup (Ranunculus acris)

Inner confidence » Alder (Alnus)

Inner conflicts » Linnaea (Linnaea borealis)

Inner energy, stabilising » Elder (Sambucus nigra)

Inner fears » Agrimony (Agrimonia eupatoria)

Inner feelings » Manzanita (Arctostaphylos manzanita)

Inner growth » Grape (Vitis), Water Hyacinth (Eichbornia crassipes)

Inner guidance » Freesia (Freesia)

Inner health » Apple Blossom (Malus domestica)

Inner openness » Bells of Ireland (Moluccella laevis)

Inner peace » Snowdrop (Galanthus nivalis), Sage (Salvia officinalis), Corn (Zea mays)

Inner perception » Clary Sage (Salvia sclarea)

Inner quiet » Aconite (Aconite)

Inner stability » Mustard (Sinapis arvensis)

Inner strength » Pohutukawa (Metrosideros excelsa), Dahlia (Dahlia), Wild Pansy (Viola tricolor), Snapdragon (Antirrhinum majus), Scotch Thistle (Onopordum acanthium), Thistle, Common (Cirsium vulgare), Walnut (Juglans regia), Olive (Olea europaea), Lemon Balm (Melissa officinalis), Aspen (Populus tremula), Elder (Sambucus nigra), Arfaj (Rhanterium epapposum), Suncup (Lonicera ovata), Flame Tree (Brachychiton acerifolius)

Inner transformation » Sweet Chestnut (Castanea sativa)

Inner trust » Motherwort (Leonurus cardiaca)

Inner truth » Betony (Stachys officinalis)

Inner vision » Eyebright (Euphrasia officinalis)

Inner voice » Native Violet (Viola papilionacea), Wake Robin (Trillium pendulum)

Inner wisdom » Rhododendron (Rhododendron), Saguaro Cactus Blossom (Carnegiea gigantean)

Inner worries » Agrimony (Agrimonia eupatoria)

Innocence » Baby's Breath (Gypsophila paniculata), Chrysanthemum, White (Chrysanthemum), Shasta Daisy (Leucanthemum maximum), Freesia (Freesia), Lily of the Valley (Convallaria majalis), Daphne (Daphne odora), Orange Blossom (Citrus x sinensis), Star of Bethlehem (Ornithogalum), Easter Lily (Lilium longiflorum), Stargazer Lily, White (Lilium orientalis), Lilac, White (Syringa), Marjoram (Origanum majorana), Mexican Orange Blossom (Choisya ternata)

Innocence, youthful » Lilac, White (Syringa)

Insanity cure » Hellebore (Helleborus)

Insight » Speedwell (Veronica officinalis), Eyebright (Euphrasia officinalis), Evening Primrose (Oenothera), Cloudberry (Rubus chamaemorus), California Pitcher Plant (Darlingtonia californica), Coffee (Coffea arabica)

Insight, self- » Rhododendron (Rhododendron)

Insincerity » Foxglove (Digitalis purpurea)

Insignificance » Moschatel (Adoxa moschatellina)

Insinuation » Bindweed, Great (Convolvulus major)

Inspire me, you » Turkey Bush (Calytrix exstipulata), Siberian Iris (Iris sibirica)

Inspiration » Turkey Bush (Calytrix exstipulata) Indian Paintbrush (Castilleja miniata), Siberian Iris (Iris sibirica), Daffodil (Narcissus pseudonarcissus),Angelica (Angelica archangelica), Hazel (Corylus), Iris, Blue Flag (Iris versicolor), Peppermint (Mentha piperita), Fir (Abies), Bee Orchid (Ophrys apifera), Osmanthus (Osmanthus fragrans), Prickly Pear (Opuntia ficus-indica), Redwood (Sequoiadendron giganteum), Tamarisk (Tamarix)

Inspiration, quiet » Iris, Black (Iris nigricans)

Inspirational thoughts » Iris, Black (Iris nigricans)

Instability » Dahlia (Dahlia)

Integration » Shasta Daisy (Leucanthemum maximum)

Integrity » Royal Bluebell (Wahlenbergia gloriosa), Echinacea (Echinacea purpurea), Thistle, Scotch (Onopordum acanthium), Chinese Plum (Prunus mume), Liquid Amber (Liquidambar styraciflua)

Intellect, stimulation of » Artichoke, Jerusalem (Helianthus tuberosus)

Intelligence » Dandelion (Taraxacum officinale), Ginger (Zingiber officinale), Mace (Myristica fragrans)

Intelligence, increased » Hellebore (Helleborus)

Intention » Hemp (Cannabis sativa)

Intention, focused » Jade (Crassula ovata)

Intention with you, I want to share my » Hemp (Cannabis sativa)

Intentions are true, my » Blushing Bride (Tillandsia ionantha)

Interconnectedness » Hydrangea (Hydrangea)

Interest » Phlox, White (Phlox), Thrift (Armeria maritima)

Interest has changed, my » Cranes-Bill (Geranium maculatum)

Interested, I am » Old Man Banksia (Banksia serrata)

Interference, shield from » Native Wood Violet (Viola odorata)

Intervention, divine » Iris Croatica (Iris perunika)

Intimacy » Flannel Flower (Actinotus helianthi), Honeysuckle (Lonicera), Tuberose (Polianthes tuberosa), Purslane (Portulaca oleracea)

Intuition » Queen of the Night (Selenicereus grandiflorus), Angel's Trumpet(Brugmansia candida), Speedwell (Veronica officinalis), Sallow (Salix cinerea), Bearberry (Arctostaphylos uva-ursi), Opoponax (Commiphora erythraea), Prayer Plant (Maranta leuconeura)

Intuition development » Native Wood Violet (Viola odorata)

Intuitive healing » Rosewood (Pterocarpus indicus)

Intuition » Tree Spider Orchid (Dendrobium tetragonum)

Intuition, restoration of » Althea (Hibiscus syriacus)

Intuition, psychic » Rowan (Sorbus aucuparia)

Inutility » Diosma (Coleonema)

I

Invisibility » Chicory (Cichorium intybus), Monkshood (Aconitum), Hellebore (Helleborus), Fern (Tracheophyta)

Invitation » Chrysanthemum, Red (Chrysanthemum)

Irrational expectations » Marigold (Tagetes evecta)

Issue, unresolved » Almond (Prunus amygdalus)

Issues, core » Burdock (Arctium)

It hurts not to have a sweetheart » Puti Tai Nobiu (Bougainvillea spectabilis)

J

Jest » Nasturtium (Tropaeolum majus), Southernwood (Artemisia abrotanum)

Jest, I » Celosia (Celosia)

Job, new » Rabbit Orchid (Leptoceras menziesii)

Join me » Emu Bush (Eremophila duttonii), Wedding Bush (Ricinocarpos pinifolius)

Journey » Juniper (Juniperus)

Journey, new » Rose, Prairie (Rosa arkansana)

Joy » Golden Wattle (Acacia pycnantha), Chrysanthemum, Florist's (Chrysanthemum morifolium), Hollyhock (Alcea rosea), Daphne (Daphne odora), Hibiscus (Hibiscus), Orange Blossom (Citrus x sinensis), Chickweed (Stellaria media), Olive (Olea europaea), Sweet Marjoram (Origanum marjorana), Elder (Sambucus nigra), Mustard (Sinapis arvensis), Acacia (Acacia), Althea (Hibiscus syriacus), Blackthorn (Prunus spinosa), Yellow Jessamine (Gelsemium sempervirens), Coast Rhododendron (Rhododendron macrophyllum), Henna (Lawsonia inermis), Oregano (Origanum vulgare), Anemone (Anemone)

Joy, future » Celandine (Ficaria verna)

Joy, great » Caladium (Caladium)

Joy in new experiences » Wild Banana Orchid (Schomburgkia thomsoniana)

Joy, return of » Prairie Lily (Lilium philadelphicum)

Joy, ulitimate » Great Rhododendron (Rhododendron maximum)

Joy, you bring me » Orange Blossom (Citrus x sinensis)

Joyful encouragement » Pride of Barbados (Poinciana pulcherrima)

Joyful humility » African Daisy (Osteospermum)

Joyful living » Rockmelon (Cucumis melo)

Judgement » Monkshood (Aconitum)

Judgement, trust personal » Ceibo (Erythrina crista-galli)

Justice » Black-Eyed Susan (Rudbeckia hirta)

K

Keep going » Geraldton Wax (Chamelaucium uncinatum)

Keep your promise » Plum (Prunus domestica)

Kindness » Primrose (Primula vulgaris)

Kiss me » Mistletoe (Viscum album), Love-in-a-Mist (Nigella damascena)

Knight-errantry » Monkshood (Aconitum)

Know, I » Angel's Trumpet (Brugmansia candida), Opoponax (Commiphora erythraea)

Knowledge » Cornflower (Centaurea cyanus), Anemone (Anemone), Water Lily, Pink (Nymphaea), Hazel (Corylus), Yew (Taxus baccata), Beech (Fagus)

Knowledge, acquiring » Opoponax (Commiphora erythraea)

Knowledge, useful » Parsley (Petroselinum crispum)

Knowledge, sharing » Water Lily, Blue (Nymphaea)

Knowledge, spiritual » Silversword (Argyroxiphium sandwicense)

L

Lasting affection » Kalanchoe (Kalanchoe)

Lasting beauty » Stock (Matthiola incana), Pink (Dianthus plumarius)

Last forever, I wish this moment would » Everlasting Daisy (Rhodanthe chlorocephala)

Leadership » Delphinium (Delphinium), Jack-in-the-Pulpit (Arisaema triphyllum), Black Orchid (Trichoglottis brachiata)

Learn from mistakes » Horse-Chestnut (Aesculus hippocastanum)

Learning » Orange Banksia (Banksia ashbyi), Lime (Tilia x europaea), Rocky Mountain Columbine (Aquilegia caerulea), Beech (Fagus)

Learning, higher » African Violet (Saintpaulia)

Leave me quickly » Pennyroyal (Mentha pulegium)

Leaving, I am » Henbane (Hyoscyamus niger)

Laugh, to » Scarlet Pimpernel (Anagallis arvensis)

Laughter » Scarlet Pimpernel (Anagallis arvensis)

L

Learning » Paw Paw (Asimina triloba)

Legacy » Pyramidal Orchid (Anacamptis pyramidalis), Blue Pimpernel (Lysimachia monelli), White Pine (Pinus strobus)

Legal matters » Galangal (Alpinia galangal), Hickory (Carya)

Lessons » Spikenard (Aralia racemosa)

Lessons, old » Bear's Breech (Acanthus mollis)

Let down » Alkanet (Alkanna tinctoria)

Let go » Sacred Lotus (Nelumbo nucifera)

Let go of fear » Sweet Marjoram (Origanum marjorana)

Let go of pain » Crocus (Crocus)

Let go of the past » Lilac (Syringa vulgaris)

Let go, you must » Pasqueflower (Pulsatilla vulgaris)

Let me go » Henbane (Hyoscyamus niger), Skunk Cabbage (Symplocarpus foetidus), Butterfly Weed (Asclepias tuberosa)

Let's do something » Thyme (Thymus vulgaris)

Let's have fun » Nasturtium (Tropaeolum majus)

Let's move on » Lilac (Syringa vulgaris)

Let's play » Daisy (Bellis perennis), Hyacinth (Hyacinthus)

Let's start again » Crowsfoot (Erodium crinitum), Kantuta (Cantua buxifolia)

Let's stop fighting » Rose, Musk (Rosa moschata)

Let's travel » Stephanotis (Stephanotis floribunda)

Let's work it out » Grevillea (Grevillea banksii), Almond (Prunus amygdalus)

Letters, love » Agapanthus (Agapanthus praecox)

Letting go » Hemlock (Conium maculatum), Angel's Trumpet (Brugmansia candida), Bleeding Heart (Lamprocapnos spectabilis), Wood Anemone (Anemone nemerosa)

Liberty » Copihue (Lapageria rosea)

Lie, you » Nightshade (Solanaceae)

Life » Easter Lily (Lilium longiflorum), Olive (Olea europaea), Alfalfa (Medicago sativa), Peyote (Lophophora williamsii), Old Man Banksia (Banksia serrata)

Life, appreciation for » Forsythia (Forsythia)

Lift emotions » Turmeric (Cucurma longa)

Life energy » Osmanthus (Osmanthus fragrans)

Life force » Carnation (Dianthus caryophyllus), Marigold (Tagetes evecta), Forsythia (Forsythia), Althea (Hibiscus syriacus)

Life goals, focus on » Dagger's Log (Agave karatto miller)

Life, happy » Stock (Matthiola incana)

Lighten mood » Ice Plant (Carpobrotus edulis)

Life, harmonious » Vervain (Verbena officinalis)

Life is worthwhile » Freesia (Freesia)

Life, long » Sage (Salvia officinalis), Sweet Marjoram (Origanum marjorana), Chives (Allium schoenoprasum)

Life, love of » Karee (Rhus pendulina)

Life, new » Bloodroot (Sanguinaria canadensis)

Life nourishment » Bilberry (Vaccinium myrtillus)

Life, past » Bear's Breech (Acanthus mollis)

L

Life path » African Daisy (Osteospermum), Bee Orchid (Ophrys apifera), Wand Flower (Sparaxis grandiflora)

Life, prolong » Elder (Sambucus nigra)

Life purpose » Five Corners (Styphelia laeta), Wedding Bush (Ricinocarpos pinifolius), Edelweiss (Leontopodium alpinum), Lily of the Valley (Convallaria majalis), Hemp (Cannabis sativa), Jack-in-the-Pulpit (Arisaema triphyllum), Clary Sage (Salvia sclarea), Cloudberry (Rubus chamaemorus), Khat (Catha edulis)

Life restoration » Yerba Santa (Eriodictyon glutinosum)

Life, stages of » Primrose (Primula vulgaris)

Life, sweet » Honeysuckle (Lonicera)

Life with you, I want to share my » Tarragon (Artemisia dracunculus)

Lift negativity » Black Cohosh (Cimicifuga racemosa)

Lift mood » Bitter Root (Lewisia rediviva)

Lift spirits » Cranes-Bill (Geranium maculatum), Lemon Balm (Melissa officinalis), Red Bud (Cercis siliquastrum)

Light and shadow » Variegated Box (Buxus sempervirens)

Light, divine » Scots Pine (Pinus syvestris)

Light heart » Dancing Lady Orchid (Oncidium)

Light-heartedness » Bee Balm (Monarda), Chocolate Flower (Berlandiera lyrata), Anemone (Anemone)

Light in the dark » Skunk Cabbage (Symplocarpus foetidus)

Light in the darkness » Evening Primrose (Oenothera)

Lighten » Primrose (Primula vulgaris)

Lightning, protection from » Sweet Marjoram (Origanum marjorana), Oak (Quercus robur)

Lightness of being » Christmas Orchid (Cattleya trianae)

Limits » Rhododendron (Rhododendron), Coast Rhododendron (Rhododendron macrophyllum)

Limits, beyond » Great Rhododendron (Rhododendron maximum)

L

Link breaking » Walnut (Juglans regia)

Listen to me » Belladonna (Atropa belladonna)

Live for thee, I » Cedar (Cedrus)

Live, will to » Self-Heal (Prunella vulgaris), Saguaro Cactus Blossom (Carnegiea gigantean), Prairie Crocus (Pulsatilla patens)

Live for me » Arborvitae (Thuja)

Living, joyful » Rockmelon (Cucumis melo)

Longevity » Chrysanthemum, Florist's (Chrysanthemum morifolium), Wisteria (Wisteria sinensis), Sage (Salvia officinalis), Motherwort (Leonurus cardiaca), Walnut (Juglans regia), Pine (Pinus sylvestris), Ginseng (Panax), Maple (Acer), Yew (Taxus baccata), Peach Blossom (Prunus persica), Bamboo (Bambusoideae), Fig (Ficus carica), Ginkgo (Ginkgo biloba), Tagua (Phytelephas macrocarpa)

Longevity, I wish you » Bouvardia (Bouvardia), Maple (Acer)

Long and happy marriage » Clover (Trifolium)

Long-held goals achieved » Amaryllis (Amaryllis)

Long-lasting happiness » Dandelion (Taraxacum officinale)

Long-lasting relationships » Lily (Lilium)

Long life » Sage (Salvia officinalis), Sweet Marjoram (Origanum marjorana), Chives (Allium schoenoprasum)

Longing for you » Camellia, Pink (Camellia)

Loss, memory » Daylily (Hemerocallis)

Lost all, I have » Mournful Widow (Scabiosa atropurpurea)

Lost love » Love Lies Bleeding (Amaranthus caudatus)

Love » Carnation (Dianthus caryophyllus), Native Passionflower (Passiflora herbertiana), Apple Blossom (Malus domestica), Chrysanthemum, Red (Chrysanthemum), Rose, Red (Rosa), Daphne (Daphne odor), Juniper (Juniperus), Meadowsweet (Filipendula ulmaria), Love-in-a-Mist (Nigella damascena), Grape (Vitis), Cosmos (Cosmos), Wisteria (Wisteria sinensis), Lemon Verbena (Aloysia triphylla), Columbine (Aquilegia vulgaris), Morning Glory (Ipomoea purpurea), Bloodroot (Sanguinaria canadensis),

L

Ginseng (Panax), Water Lily, Red (Nymphaea), Loveage (Levisticum officinale), Chamomile, German (Matricaria chamomilla), Peppermint (Mentha piperita), Basil (Ocimum basilicum), Sweet Marjoram (Origanum marjorana), Sweet Violet (Viola odorata), Cloves (Eugenia caryophyllata), Maple (Acer), Tiare (Gardenia taitensis), Myrtle (Myrtus), Crab Apple Tree (Malus sylvestris), Iris, German (Iris germanica), Asparagus (Asparagus officinalis), Bean (Phaseolus vulgaris), Beetroot (Beta vulgaris), Cardamon (Elettario caramomum), Capsicum (Capsicum annuum), Cinnamon (Cinnamomum verum), Devil's Bit (Succisa pratensis), Elm (Ulmus), Endive (Cichorium endivia), Fennel (Foeniculum vulgare), Fig (Ficus carica), Frankincense (Boswellia sacra), Geranium (Geranium), Ginkgo (Ginkgo biloba), Hens and Chickens (Sempervivum tectorum), Lettuce (Lactuca sativa), Liquorice (Glycyrrhiza glabra), Lobelia (Lobelia inflata), Love Seed (Adenanthera pavonina), Michaelmas Daisy (Aster amellus), Strawberry (Fragaria x ananassa), Papaya (Carica papaya), Passionfruit (Passiflora edulis), Pear (Pyrus communis), Patchouli (Pogostemon cablin), Radish (Raphanus sativus), Tomato (Solanum lycopersicum), Vanilla (Vanilla planifolia), Ylang-Ylang (Cananga odorata), Jacaranda (Jacaranda acutifolia), Hibiscus, Red (Hibiscus rosa-sinensis), Avocado (Persea americana)

L

Love addiction, release » Jack-in-the-Pulpit (Arisaema triphyllum)

Love again, time to » Crocus (Crocus)

Love, ambassador of » Rose, Cabbage (Rosa x centifolia)

Love are at hand, the halcyon days of our » Beech (Fagus)

Love, ardent » Himalayan Balsam (Impatiens glandulifera), Carnation, White (Dianthus caryophyllus)

Love at first sight » Rose, Mauve (Rosa)

Love, attract » Lady's Mantle (Alchemilla vulgaris), Loveage (Levisticum officinale), Chamomile, German (Matricaria chamomilla)

Love, autumn » Guelder-Rose (Viburnum opulus)

Love, bashful » Rose, Deep Red (Rosa)

Love bond » Mistletoe (Viscum album)

Love, brotherly » Lilac (Syringa vulgaris)

Love burns for you, my » Marvel of Peru (Mirabilis jalapa)

Love, chaste » Rose, Pink (Rosa)

Love, clinging » Wisteria (Wisteria sinensis)

Love, complete » Waratah (Telopea speciosissima)

Love, concealed » Motherwort (Leonurus cardiaca)

Love, confiding » Fuchsia (Fuchsia magellanica)

Love, conjugal » Lime (Tilia x europaea)

Love, declaration of » Tulip, Red (Tulipa)

Love, divine » Rose, Briar (Rosa rubiginosa)

Love, encourage » Cedar (Cedrus)

Love, enduring » Wisteria (Wisteria sinensis)

Love, esteem but not » Spiderwort (Tradescantia), Tradescantia (Tradescantia zebrina)

Love, estranged » Water Lily, Red (Nymphaea)

Love, eternal » Orange Blossom (Citrus x sinensis), Heliotrope (Heliotropium), Mexican Orange Blossom (Choisya ternata)

Love, everlasting » Baby's Breath (Gypsophila paniculata), Ranunculus (Ranunculus)

Love, fraternal » Woodbine (Lonicera periclymenum)

Love, falling in » Rose, Yellow (Rosa)

Love, fidelity in » Lemon (Citrus limon)

Love, first » Dog Violet (Viola riviniana), Primrose (Primula vulgaris), Periwinkle (Vinca minor)

Love, first emotion of » Lilac (Syringa vulgaris)

Love, flame of » Marvel of Peru (Mirabilis jalapa)

Love, forsaken » Willow (Salix alba)

Love, give me your » Marsh Marigold (Caltha palustris)

Love, guardian of » Copihue (Lapageria rosea)

Love, happy » Rose, Bridal (Rosa)

L

Love has not faded, my » Agapanthus (Agapanthus praecox)

Love, hopeless » Yellow Tulip (Tulipa)

Love, I am thinking of our » Pansy (Viola tricolor var. hortensis)

Love me you will find it out, if you » Rose, Maiden's Blush (Rosa)

Love in austerity » Chamomile, Roman (Chamaemelum nobile)

Love in idleness » Pansy (Viola tricolor var. hortensis)

Love in vain » Morning Glory (Ipomoea purpurea)

Love is dangerous » Rose, Carolina (Rosa carolina)

Love is pure, our » Rose, Lavender (Rosa)

Love is reciprocated, your » Ambrosia (Ambrosia)

Love letters » Agapanthus (Agapanthus praecox)

Love lost » Love Lies Bleeding (Amaranthus caudatus)

Love, loyal » Marguerite Daisy (Argyranthemum frutescens)

Love, lucky in » Lily of the Valley (Convallaria majalis)

Love, magical » Agapanthus (Agapanthus praecox)

Love makes me happy, your » Hepatica (Hepatica)

Love, maternal » Coltsfoot (Tussilago farfara)

Love, mature-aged » Traveller's Joy (Clematis vitalba)

Love me, I want you to » Dutchman's Breeches (Dicentra cucullaria)

Love, message of » Iris, German (Iris germanica)

Love more than just your beauty, I » Sweet Alyssum (Alyssum maritimum)

Love, motherly » Carnation, Pink (Dianthus caryophyllus), Impatiens
     (Impatiens walleriana)

Love, mutual » Ambrosia (Ambrosia)

Love, never-fading » Agapanthus (Agapanthus praecox)

Love, new » Cornflower (Centaurea cyanus), Water Lily, Red (Nymphaea)

Love of life » Karee (Rhus pendulina)

Love of nature » Calendula (Calendula officinalis)

Love of others » Ithuriel's Spear (Triteleia laxa)

L

Love, only you deserve my » Campion Rose (Silene coronaria)

Love, openness to » Love-in-a-Mist (Nigella damascena)

Love, passion in » Puerto Rican Hibiscus (Thespesia grandiflora)

Love, passionate » Bleeding Heart (Lamprocapnos spectabilis), Lime, Key West (Citrus aurantifolia)

Love, platonic » Bittersweet (Solanum dulcamara), Acacia (Acacia)

Love, protection of » Tormentil (Potentilla erecta)

Love, rejected » Bleeding Heart (Lamprocapnos spectabilis)

Love, reluctance in » Toadflax (Linaria vulgaris)

Love returned » Ambrosia (Ambrosia)

Love, secret » Gardenia (Gardenia jasminoides), Acacia (Acacia), Toothwort (Lathraea squamaria)

Love, self- » Poet's Narcissus (Narcissus poeticus), Orchid (Orchidaceae), Oregon Grape (Mahonia aquifolium)

Love, sensitive » Mimosa (Acacia dealbata)

Love shall endure, our » Cactus (Cactaceae)

Love, shy » Moss Rose (Portulaca grandiflora)

Love spells » Dutchman's Breeches (Dicentra cucullaria)

Love, strength in » Quince (Cydonia oblonga)

Love, true » Forget-Me-Not (Myosotis), Teuila (Alpinia purpurata)

Love, trust in » Aspen (Populus tremula), Ceibo (Erythrina crista-galli)

Love, unconditional » Scottish Primrose (Primula scotica), Straw Flower(Xerochrysum bracteatum), Chicory (Cichorium intybus)

Love, undying » Purple Tulip (Tulipa)

Love, unrequited » Daffodil (Narcissus pseudonarcissus), Dogwood (Cornus)

Love, voluptuous » Moss Rose (Portulaca grandiflora)

Love will endure after death, our » Asphodel (Asphodelus)

Love, woman's » Carnation, White (Dianthus caryophyllus), Pink (Dianthus plumarius)

Love you forever, I will » Orange Blossom (Citrus x sinensis)

L

Love you, I » Carnation (Dianthus caryophyllus), Native Passionflower (Passiflora herbertiana), Apple Blossom (Malus domestica), Chrysanthemum, Red (Chrysanthemum), Rose, Red (Rosa), Bloodroot (Sanguinaria canadensis), Tiare (Gardenia taitensis)

Love you, I admire you but cannot » Laurel (Laurus nobilis)

Love you, I still » Kalanchoe (Kalanchoe)

Love you, I will always » Magnolia (Magnolia campbellii)

Love you more, no one could » Cosmos (Cosmos)

Love you unconditionally, I » Chicory (Cichorium intybus)

Love yourself » Orchid (Orchidaceae)

Loved, you are » Sydney Rock Rose (Boronia serrulata), Ginger (Zingiber officinale)

Loved you at first sight, I » Gloxinia (Gloxinia)

Loveliness, everlasting » Rose, China (Rosa chinensis)

Loveliness, perfect » Camellia, White (Camellia)

Loveliness, perfection of female » Shrimp Plant (Justicia)

Lovely » Carnation, White (Dianthus caryophyllus)

Lovely, always » Pink (Dianthus plumarius)

Lovely, mysteriously » Faeries' Fire (Pieris japonica)

Lovely, very » Rose, Austrian (Rosa)

Love's memory » Redbay (Persea borbonia)

Loving » Baby's Breath (Gypsophila paniculata)

Loving thoughts » Pansy (Viola tricolor var. hortensis)

Loving you, I have not stopped » Amaranthus (Amaranth)

Loyal love » Marguerite Daisy (Argyranthemum frutescens)

Loyal protection » Spring Onion (Allium fistulosum)

Loyalty » Opium Poppy (Papaver somniferum), Sweet Violet (Viola odorata)

Luck » Lechenaultia (Lechenaultia formas), Tea Tree (Leptospermum myrsinoides), Dill (Anethum graveolens), Clover (Trifolium), Peach Blossom (Prunus persica), Galangal (Alpinia galangal), Henna (Lawsonia inermis), Hens and Chickens (Sempervivum tectorum), Job's Tears (Coix lacryma-jobi), Kumquat (Citrus japonica), Cotton (Gossypium), Strawberry (Fragaria x ananassa), Pineapple (Ananas comosus), Shamrock (Trifolium dubium), Spanish Moss (Tillandsia usneoides), Jacaranda (Jacaranda acutifolia)

Luck always be with you, may » Bells of Ireland (Moluccella laevis)

Luck, good » Carnation, White (Dianthus caryophyllus), Heather, Lavender (Calluna vulgaris), Bells of Ireland (Moluccella laevis), Centaury (Erythraea centaurium), Elder (Sambucus nigra), Red Clover (Trifolium pratense), Clover (Trifolium), Bok Choy (Brassica rapa subsp. chinensis), Eggplant (Solanum melongena), Heal-All (Pedicularis canadensis), Peyote (Lophophora williamsii), Soy Bean (Glycine max)

Lucky in love » Lily of the Valley (Convallaria majalis)

Lucklessness » Mournful Widow (Scabiosa atropurpurea)

Lust » Oleander (Nerium oleander), Rose, Red (Rosa), Dill (Anethum graveolens), Celery (Apium graveolens), Ginseng (Panax), Water Lily, Red (Nymphaea), Asparagus (Asparagus officinalis), Caraway (Carum carvi), Cardamon (Elettaria caramomum), Endive (Cichorium endivia), Galangal (Alpinia galangal), Lemongrass (Cymbopogon citratus), Liquorice (Glycyrrhiza glabra), Pear (Pyrus communis), Vanilla (Vanilla planifolia), Sesame (Sesamum indicum)

M

Magic » Mistletoe (Viscum album), Wood of Life (Guaiacum sanctum), Yew (Taxus baccata) Marigold (Tagetes evecta), Betony (Stachys officinalis), Rose, Mauve (Rosa), Foxglove (Digitalis purpurea), Opium Poppy (Papaver somniferum), Wood Betony (Stachys betonica)

Magic, practical » Maple (Acer)

Magic, water » Cauliflower (Brassica oleracea)

Magical love » Agapanthus (Agapanthus praecox)

Magical powers » Aster (Aster)

Magical powers, awaken » Okra (Abelmoschus esculentus)

Magical protection » Rowan (Sorbus aucuparia)

Magical strength » Wood of Life (Guaiacum sanctum)

Magnificence » Bird of Paradise (Strelitzia reginae), Plane Tree (Platanus)

Magnificent beauty » Calla Lily (Zantedeschia aethiopica)

Magnificent, you are » Bird of Paradise (Strelitzia reginae)

Majesty » Lily (Lilium), Lilac, White (Syringa)

Major change » Mistletoe (Viscum album)

Male and female energies, balancing » Crepe Myrtle (Lagerstroemia indica)

Male energy » Peanut (Arachis hypogaea)

Male energies » Banana Flower (Musa)

Male healing » Sunflower (Helianthus annuus), Blue-Eyed Grass (Sisyrinchium montanum)

Male sexuality » Coconut (Cocus nucifera)

Male stamina » Asparagus (Asparagus officinalis)

Male strength » Spirulina (Arthrospira)

Malevolence » Lobelia (Lobelia inflata)

Manifestation » Boxwood (Buxus), Mastic (Pistacia lentiscus)

Manners » Mimosa (Acacia dealbata)

Man of courage » Borage (Borago officinalis)

Marital bliss » Stephanotis (Stephanotis floribunda)

Marriage » Mistletoe (Viscum album), Orange Blossom (Citrus x sinensis), Lemon Verbena (Aloysia triphylla), Ivy (Hedera), Myrtle (Myrtus), Crab Apple Tree (Malus sylvestris), Mexican Orange Blossom (Choisya ternata)

Marriage, happy » Tree Peony (Paeonia suffruticosa)

Marriage, long and happy » Clover (Trifolium)

Marry me?, will you » Wedding Bush (Ricinocarpos pinifolius), Honey Grevillea (Grevillea eriostachya), Rose, Wild (Rosa acicularis), Lisianthus (Eustoma grandiflorum), Blushing Bride (Tillandsia ionantha), Mistletoe (Viscum album), Orange Blossom (Citrus x sinensis), Myrtle (Myrtus),

M

Queen of the Meadow (Filipendula ulmaria)

Marry you, I want to » Valerian (Polemonium caeruleum)

Marry you, I will » Blushing Bride (Tillandsia ionantha)

Masculine strength » Oak (Quercus robur)

Mastery » Black Orchid (Trichoglottis brachiata)

Material objects » Woodbine (Lonicera periclymenum)

Maternal energies » Marshmallow (Althea officinalis)

Maternal love » Coltsfoot (Tussilago farfara)

Mature-aged love » Traveller's Joy (Clematis vitalba)

Mature elegance » Pomegranate Blossom (Punica granatum)

Maturity » Dagger's Log (Agave karatto miller), Pomegranate Blossom (Punica granatum)

Maturtiy, emotional » Avocado (Persea americana)

May luck always be with you » Bells of Ireland (Moluccella laevis)

May sweet sleep attend you » Buckbean (Menyanthes)

Meaningful secret » Ranunculus (Ranunculus)

Meditation » Heath (Erica), Champa (Calophyllum), Cinnamon (Cinnamomum verum), Yerba Buena (Satureja douglasii)

Meekness » Rush (Juncaceae)

Meet me?, will you » Scarlet Pimpernel (Anagallis arvensis)

Meet you, I want to » Geranium (Geranium)

Medicine » Swallow-Wort (Cynanchum louiseae)

Meditation » Clary Sage (Salvia sclarea), Frankincense (Boswellia sacra)

Melancholy » Weeping Willow (Salix babylonica)

Memories » Forget-Me-Not (Myosotis)

Memories, childhood » Rose, Miniature (Rosa)

Memories, happy » Straw Flower (Xerochrysum bracteatum)

Memories, sad » African Daisy (Osteospermum)

Memories, sweet » Evening Primrose (Oenothera), Periwinkle (Vinca minor)

M

Memory » Field Poppy (Papaver rhoeas), Rosemary (Rosmarinus officinalis), Eyebright (Euphrasia officinalis), Bear's Breech (Acanthus mollis), Caraway (Carum carvi)

Memory, forsaken » Lilac (Syringa vulgaris)

Memory loss » Daylily (Hemerocallis)

Memory, you are always in my » Field Poppy (Papaver rhoeas)

Mendacity » Alkanet (Alkanna tentoria)

Mental anguish, relief of » Sweet Alyssum (Alyssum maritimum)

Mental beauty » Kennedia (Kennedia)

Mental calmative » Rock Rose (Helianthemum)

Mental clarity » Eyebright (Euphrasia officinalis)

Mental expansion » Jerusalem Thorn (Parkinsonia aculeata)

Mental focus » Sandalwood (Santalum album)

Mental healing » Hellebore (Helleborus)

Mental powers » Celery (Apium graveolens), Ginseng (Panax), Horehound (Marrubium vulgare), Savory (Satureja hortensis), Tangerine (Citrus tangerina)

Mental peace » Rocky Mountain Columbine (Aquilegia caerulea)

Mental purity » Water Lily, White (Nymphaea)

Mental stability » Ranunculus (Ranunculus)

Mental strength » Rosemary (Rosmarinus officinalis), Caraway (Carum carvi)

Mental tension, relieve » Sweet Marjoram (Origanum marjorana)

Mental work » Mace (Myristica fragrans)

Mentorship » Violet Nightshade (Solanum brownii)

Merit » Laurel (Laurus nobilis)

Merit concealed » Valerian (Polemonium caeruleum)

Merriment » Heartsease (Viola tricolor)

Message » Butterfly Jasmine (Mariposa)

Message of love » Iris, German (Iris germanica)

M

Messages, divine » Gardenia (Gardenia jasminoides)

Messages, spirit » Iris, Blue Flag (Iris versicolor)

Mildness » Privet (Ligustrum vulgare)

Mind, alert » Peppermint (Mentha piperita)

Mind, clarity of » Hawkweed (Hieracium)

Mind, clearing » Horehound (Marrubium vulgare)

Mind, balance of » Holly (Ilex aquifolium)

Mind, peace of » Geranium (Geranium), Heartsease (Viola tricolor), Woodbine (Lonicera periclymenum), Daisy (Bellis perennis)

Mind, strengthen » Lemon Balm (Melissa officinalis)

Mindfulness » Willowherb (Epilobium)

Miracles » Hippeastrum (Hippeastrum)

Mirth » Crocus (Crocus), Scarlet Pimpernel (Anagallis arvensis), Hop (Humulus lupulus)

Misanthropy » Monkshood (Aconitum), Teasel (Dipsacus)

Misfortune » Wallflower (Erysimum)

Misfortune, end » Shallot (Allium cepa var. aggregatum)

Miss you, I » Statice (Limonium), Geranium (Geranium)

Missing you » Zinnia (Zinnia elegans)

Mistakes, learn from » Horse-Chestnut (Aesculus hippocastanum)

Misunderstandings cleared » Yellow Jessamine (Gelsemium sempervirens)

Modest ambition » Trillium (Trillium)

Modest beauty » Trillium (Trillium)

Modest worth » Woodruff (Galium odoratum)

Modesty » Shasta Daisy (Leucanthemum maximum), Violet, Blue (Viola sororia), Lilac, White (Syringa), Marjoram (Origanum majorana), Strawberry (Fragaria x ananassa)

Momentary happiness » Tradescantia (Tradescantia zebrina)

Momentum » Chicory (Cichorium intybus)

M

Money » Cloves (Eugenia caryophyllata), Bladder-Fucus (Fucus vesiculosus), Cashew (Anacardium occidentale), Cedar (Cedrus), Eggplant (Solanum melongena), Fumitory (Fumaria officinalis), Goldenseal (Hydrastis canadensis), Macadamia (Macadamia integrifolia), Pea (Pisum sativum), Red Dock (Rumex sanguineus)

Money, attract » Aspen (Populus tremula)

Mood, lighten » Ice Plant (Carpobrotus edulis)

Mood stabilisation » Artichoke, Jerusalem (Helianthus tuberosus)

Mood, lift » Bitter Root (Lewisia rediviva)

Moon » Cauliflower (Brassica oleracea), Pumpkin (Cucurbita pepo)

Mortality » Morning Glory (Ipomoea purpurea)

Mother » Lily (Lilium)

Mother and baby blessing » Fir (Abies)

Mother, new » Lily (Lilium)

Motherhood » Daylily (Hemerocallis)

Mothering » Lewis Mock Orange (Philadelphus lewisii)

Mothering issues » Motherwort (Leonurus cardiaca)

Motherly love » Carnation, Pink (Dianthus caryophyllus), Impatiens (Impatiens walleriana)

Motive, sincerity of » Deer Grass (Trichophorum cespitosum)

Motives » Deer Grass (Trichophorum cespitosum)

Motivation » Self-Heal (Prunella vulgaris), Black-Eyed Susan (Rudbeckia hirta), Neoporteria Cactus (Neoporteria paucicostata)

Mourning » Weeping Willow (Salix babylonica), Scabiosa (Scabiosa), Basil (Ocimum basilicum), Pine (Pinus sylvestris), Asphodel (Asphodelus), Bellflower (Campanula)

Move on » Mulla Mulla (Ptilotus exaltatus)

Move on, let's » Lilac (Syringa vulgaris)

Movement » Cayenne (Capsicum frutescens), Scarlet Fritillary (Fritillaria recurva)

M

Mutual love » Ambrosia (Ambrosia)

My best days are over » Meadow Saffron (Colchicum autumnale)

My destiny is in your hands » Camellia, Japanese (Camellia japonica)

My heart is full of passion » Lords and Ladies (Arum maculatum)

My heart was mine until we met » Periwinkle (Vinca minor)

My intentions are true » Blushing Bride (Tillandsia ionantha)

My interest has changed » Cranes-Bill (Geranium maculatum)

My love has not faded » Agapanthus (Agapanthus praecox)

My love burns for you » Marvel of Peru (Mirabilis jalapa)

My regrets will follow you to the grave » Asphodel (Asphodelus)

Mysteriously lovely » Faeries' Fire (Pieris japonica)

Mystical power » Redwood (Sequoiadendron giganteum)

N

N

Natural beauty » Sycamore (Acer pseudoplatanus)

Natural beauty, surround me in » Persimmon (Diospyros virginiana)

Natural feelings » Yerba Santa (Eriodictyon glutinosum)

Nature, good » Mullein, White (Verbascum thapsus)

Nature, love of » Calendula (Calendula officinalis)

Necromancy » Opoponax (Commiphora erythraea)

Needs, changing » Statice (Limonium)

Negative energies, removal of » Heather, Lavender (Calluna vulgaris), St John's Wort (Hypericum perforatum)

Negative energy, protection from » Okra (Abelmoschus esculentus)

Negative emotions, clear » Gerbera Daisy, Orange (Gerbera jamesonii)

Negative environment clearing » Dutchman's Breeches (Dicentra cucullaria)

Negative feelings, eliminate » Iris, Blue Flag (Iris versicolor)

Negative ideas, dissolve » Larch (Larix decidua)

Negative imbalances shifting » Belladonna (Atropa belladonna)

Negative patterns, breaking » Native Passionflower (Passiflora herbertiana)

Negative patterns, release » Macadamia (Macadamia integrifolia)

Negative thoughts, banish » Lemon (Citrus limon)

Negativity, clear » Red Clover (Trifolium pratense), Sandalwood (Santalum album)

Negativity, dispel » Tangerine (Citrus tangerina)

Negativity, lift » Black Cohosh (Cimicifuga racemosa)

Negativity, protection against » Madonna Lily (Lilium candidum)

Negativity, releasing » Fly Orchid (Ophrys insectifera)

Negativity, repels » Rose of Jerico (Anastatica hierochuntica)

Neglect, self » Snowdrop (Galanthus nivalis)

Neglected beauty » Throatwort (Trachelium caeruleum)

Neglected, I die if » Laurustinus (Viburnum tinus)

Nerve calmative » Black Cohosh (Cimicifuga racemosa)

Nervous system support » Chamomile, German (Matricaria chamomilla)

Never-fading love » Agapanthus (Agapanthus praecox)

Never give up » Gladiola (Gladiolus)

Never say die » Xeranthemum (Xeranthemum bracteatum)

New beginning » Mulla Mulla (Ptilotus exaltatus), Snowdrop (Galanthus nivalis), Rose, Yellow (Rosa), Jade (Crassula ovata), Bloodroot (Sanguinaria canadensis)

New challenges » Coltsfoot (Tussilago farfara)

New creative opportunities » Iris, Fairy (Dietes grandiflora)

New, beauty always » Rose, China (Rosa chinensis)

New, beauty ever » Rose, Damask (Rosa x damascena)

New direction » Edelweiss (Leontopodium alpinum), Lupin (Lupinus perennis)

New experiences, joy in » Wild Banana Orchid (Schomburgkia thomsoniana)

New feelings » Delphinium (Delphinium)

New friendship » Periwinkle (Vinca minor)

New friendships » Loveage (Levisticum officinale)

New growth » Rose, Prairie (Rosa arkansana)

New habits » Red Hot Poker (Kniphofia)

New happiness » Cowslip (Primula veris)

New home » Cornflower (Centaurea cyanus)

New ideas » Indian Paintbrush (Castilleja miniata), Mock Orange (Philadelphus), Water Lily, White (Nymphaea), Alfalfa (Medicago sativa), Paw Paw (Asimina triloba)

New journey » Rose, Prairie (Rosa arkansana)

New life » Bloodroot (Sanguinaria canadensis)

New love » Cornflower (Centaurea cyanus), Water Lily, Red (Nymphaea)

New mother » Lily (Lilium)

New opportunity » Delphinium (Delphinium)

New opportunities » Mangrove, Freshwater (Barringtonia acutangula)

New opportunities, trust » Trilobed Violet (Viola palmata)

New path » Water Ribbons (Triglochin procerum), Rose, Wild (Rosa acicularis)

New possibilities » Scabiosa (Scabiosa)

New relationships » Walnut (Juglans regia)

News, good » Guelder-Rose (Viburnum opulus)

Newborn » American Pasqueflower (Pulsatilla hirsutissima)

Newborn, happy » Daphne (Daphne odora)

Night » Bindweed, Small (Convolvulus minor)

Nightmares, ease » Chamomile, German (Matricaria chamomilla)

Nightmares, protection from » Lemon Verbena (Aloysia triphylla)

No » Chrysanthemum, Yellow (Chrysanthemum), Hemlock (Conium maculatum), Cyclamen (Cyclamen), Nightshade (Solanaceae), Carnation, Striped (Dianthus caryophyllus)

No one could love you more » Cosmos (Cosmos)

N

Nobility » Peony (Paeonia officinalis), Chinese Plum (Prunus mume)

Nourish » Celtic Bean (Vicia faba celtica)

Nourishing » Rosewood (Pterocarpus indicus)

Nourishment » Blue Pimpernel (Lysimachia monelli)

Nourishment, life » Bilberry (Vaccinium myrtillus)

Notice me » Oleander (Nerium oleander)

Noticed you, I have » Gymea Lily (Doryanthes excelsa)

Nothing will separate us » Ivy (Hedera)

Nurture » Lewis Mock Orange (Philadelphus lewisii), Sego Lily (Calochortus nuttallii), Sweet Potato (Ipomoea batatas)

Nurturing » Mock Orange (Philadelphus), Primrose (Primula vulgaris), Chickweed (Stellaria media), Elder (Sambucus nigra), Chenille Plant (Acalypha hispida)

N

O

Objects, material » Woodbine (Lonicera periclymenum)

Obligations » Cotton (Gossypium)

Obstacle » Ox-Eye Daisy (Leucanthemum vulgare)

Obstacles, removal of » Chicory (Cichorium intybus)

Obstinacy » Bindweed, Small (Convolvulus minor)

Offer you all I have, I » Wheat (Triticum)

Offering » Maple (Acer)

Offering, peace » Loosestrife, Purple (Lythrum salicaria)

Old age » Arborvitae (Thuja), Tree of Life (Guaiacum officinale)

Old age, cheerfulness in » Michaelmas Daisy (Aster amellus), Starwort (Stellaria)

Old age, happy » Pine (Pinus sylvestris)

Old flame » Ice Plant (Carpobrotus edulis)

Old lessons » Bear's Breech (Acanthus mollis)

Oneness » Trillium (Trillium)

Only one, you are the » Daffodil (Narcissus pseudonarcissus)

Only you deserve my love » Campion Rose (Silene coronaria)

Opinion, changed » Cooktown Orchid (Vappodes phalaenopsis)

Open attitude » Vervain (Verbena officinalis)

Open mind » Billy Goat Plum (Planchonia careya)

Open your heart » Wild Pansy (Viola tricolor), Basil (Ocimum basilicum)

Open-heartedness » Baby Blue Eyes (Nemophila menziesii)

Opening » Primrose (Primula vulgaris)

Opening channels » Hepatica (Hepatica)

Opening heart » Downy Hawthorn (Crataegus mollis)

Openness » Ice Plant (Carpobrotus edulis), Lime (Tilia x europaea), Trilobed Violet (Viola palmata)

Openness, inner » Bells of Ireland (Moluccella laevis)

Openness to love » Love-in-a-Mist (Nigella damascena)

Opportunities » Germander (Teucrium canadense)

Opportunities, new » Mangrove, Freshwater (Barringtonia acutangula)

Opportunities, new creative » Iris, Fairy (Dietes grandiflora)

Opportunities, trust new » Trilobed Violet (Viola palmata)

Opportunities with equal challenges » Variegated Box (Buxus sempervirens)

Opportunity » Rosella Flower (Hibiscus heterophyllus), Delphinium (Delphinium), Golden Trumpet Tree (Tabebuia alba)

Optimism » Golden Wattle (Acacia pycnantha), Anemone (Anemone), Chrysanthemum, Florist's (Chrysanthemum morifolium), Freesia (Freesia), Hollyhock (Alcea rosea), Jade (Crassula ovata), Golden Trumpet Tree (Tabebuia alba), Starwort (Stellaria), Candle Bush (Cassia alata), Kiwi (Actinidia chinensis)

O

Optimism during difficult times » Willowherb (Epilobium)

Orderliness » Broom (Genisteae)

Orderly » Cosmos (Cosmos)

Origins » Scabiosa (Scabiosa)

Organisation » Carrot (Daucus carota subsp. sativus)

Ornamentation » Hornbeam (Carpinus)

Others, love of » Ithuriel's Spear (Triteleia laxa)

Our love is pure » Rose, Lavender (Rosa)

Our love shall endure » Cactus (Cactaceae)

Our love shall endure after death » Asphodel (Asphodelus)

Our passion will survive » Tropicbird Orchid (Angraecum eburneum)

Outcomes » Bedstraw (Galium verum)

Outlook, positive » Ixora (Ixora coccinea)

Outdoor spaces » Cow Parsley (Anthriscus sylvestris)

Outgoing nature » Lisianthus (Eustoma grandiflorum)

Over-adornment » Musk Thistle (Carduus nutans)

Over-assertiveness » Lupin (Lupinus perennis)

Overcoming » Sturt's Desert Pea (Swainsona formosa), Chinese Plum (Prunus mume)

Overcoming abuse » Chinese Lantern (Physalis heterophylla)

Overcoming difficulties » Mistletoe (Viscum album)

Over-extension » Tree Peony (Paeonia suffruticosa)

Over-enthusiasm » Anemone (Anemone)

Overlooked » Pussytoes (Antennaria)

Overshadowing » Kudzu (Pueraria montana)

Over-thinking » Nasturtium (Tropaeolum majus)

Over-work » Pelargonium (Pelargonium cucullatum)

Own power » Tomato (Solanum lycopersicum)

P

Pain » Nettle (Urtica), Rose, Cherokee (Rosa laevigata), Blackberry (Rubus fruticosus)

Pain, let go of » Crocus (Crocus)

Pain, pleasure mixed with » Dog Rose (Rosa canina)

Painful memories » Pheasant's Eye (Adonis vernalis)

Paradise » Bird of Paradise (Strelitzia reginae)

Paradise, you are my » Bird of Paradise (Strelitzia reginae)

Pardon » Hyssop (Hyssopus officinalis)

Parting, sorrowful » Wormwood (Artemisia absinthium)

Partner?, will you be my » Honey Grevillea (Grevillea eriostachya)

Partnership » Emu Bush (Eremophila duttonii), Lily (Lilium), Tarragon (Artemisia dracunculus)

Partnership, romantic » Peach Blossom (Prunus persica)

Passion » Red Tulip (Tulipa), Waratah (Telopea speciosissima), Tulip, Wild (Tulipa sprengeri), Chrysanthemum, Red (Chrysanthemum), Rose, Red (Rosa), Passion Flower (Passiflora incarnate), Trillium (Trillium), Water Lily, Red (Nymphaea), Hop (Humulus lupulus), Dittany White (Origanum dictamnus), Zedoary (Curcuma zedoaria), Hibiscus, Red (Hibiscus rosa-sinensis)

Passion, fiery » Teuila (Alpinia purpurata)

Passion in love » Puerto Rican Hibiscus (Thespesia grandiflora)

Passion, my heart is full of » Lords and Ladies (Arum maculatum)

Passion will survive, our » Tropicbird Orchid (Angraecum eburneum)

Passionate love » Bleeding Heart (Lamprocapnos spectabilis), Lime, Key West (Citrus aurantifolia)

Past, let go of the » Lilac (Syringa vulgaris)

Past life » Bear's Breech (Acanthus mollis)

Paternal affection » Sorrel (Rumex acetosa)

Paternal error » Cuckoo Flower (Cardamine pratensis)

Path, life » African Daisy (Osteospermum), Plantain (Plantago major), Wand Flower (Sparaxis grandiflora)

Path, spiritual » Jack-in-the-Pulpit (Arisaema triphyllum)

Path, well-trodden » Plantain (Plantago major)

Patience » Scottish Primrose (Primula scotica), Aster (Aster), Flax (Linumusitatissimum), Forsythia (Forsythia), Primrose (Primula vulgaris), Godetia (Clarkia amoena), Chamomile, Roman (Chamaemelum nobile), Wisteria (Wisteria sinensis), Dagger's Log (Agave karatto miller), Linnaea (Linnaea borealis), Red Whortleberry (Vaccinium), Dock (Rumex), Michaelmas Daisy (Aster amellus), Ox-Eye Daisy (Leucanthemum vulgare), Patience Dock (Rumex patientia)

Patience in adversity » Chamomile, German (Matricaria chamomilla)

Patient, be » Flax (Linum usitatissimum)

Path, life » Bee Orchid (Ophrys apifera)

Path, new » Water Ribbons (Triglochin procerum), Rose, Wild (Rosa acicularis)

Paths, find new » Purple Orchid (Cattleya skinneri)

Peace » Billy Buttons (Pycnosorus globosus), Japanese Cherry (Prunus serrulata), California Poppy (Eschscholzia californica), Honesty (Lunaria annua), Apple Blossom (Malus domestica), Camellia, Japanese (Camellia japonica), Holly (Ilex aquifolium), Meadowsweet (Filipendula ulmaria), Cosmos (Cosmos), Hazel (Corylus), Olive (Olea europaea), Basil (Ocimum basilicum), Mustard (Sinapis arvensis), Lime (Tilia x europaea), White Nun Orchid (Lycaste skinneri alba), Rocky Mountain Columbine (Aquilegia caerulea), White Pine (Pinus strobus), Fir (Abies), Lilac, White (Syringa), Loosestrife, Yellow (Lythrum salicaria), Passionfruit (Passiflora edulis), Sweet Potato (Ipomoea batatas), Tea (Camellia sinensis), Vanilla (Vanilla planifolia), Ylang-Ylang (Cananga odorata)

Peace, I wish you » Holly (Ilex aquifolium)

Peace, inner » Snowdrop (Galanthus nivalis), Sage (Salvia officinalis), Corn (Zea mays)

Peace of mind » Daisy (Bellis perennis), Geranium (Geranium), Heartsease (Viola tricolor), Woodbine (Lonicera periclymenum)

Peace offering » Loosestrife, Purple (Lythrum salicaria)

Peace, mental » Rocky Mountain Columbine (Aquilegia caerulea)

Peaceful settlement » Vervain (Verbena officinalis)

Peaceful sleep » Primrose (Primula vulgaris), Elder (Sambucus nigra), Buckbean (Menyanthes)

Pensive beauty » Rose, Burgundy (Rosa)

Perfect loveliness » Camellia, White (Camellia)

Perfect, you are » Hibiscus (Hibiscus), Pineapple (Ananas comosus)

Perfection » Pomegranate Blossom (Punica granatum)

Perfection of female loveliness » Shrimp Plant (Justicia)

Perfume » Cashew (Anacardium occidentale)

Perception » Eyebright (Euphrasia officinalis), Ginger (Zingiber officinale)

Perception, increased » Snapdragon (Antirrhinum majus)

Perception, inner » Clary Sage (Salvia sclarea)

Perception, self- » Venus' Looking Glass (Triodanis perfoliata)

Perplexity » Love-in-a-Mist (Nigella damascena)

Presence, strong » Jade (Crassula ovata)

Perspective » Madia (Madia elegans)

Perspective, clear » Pine Drops (Pterospora andromedea)

Perfection » Pink (Dianthus plumarius)

Perseverance » Hydrangea (Hydrangea), Karee (Rhus pendulina), Larch (Larix decidua), Madder, Wild (Galium mollugo), Sarsaparilla, Wild (Aralia nudicaulis)

Persistence » Cattle Bush (Trichodesma zelanicum), Burdock (Arctium), Bindweed, Great (Convolvulus major), Hickory (Carya), Sand Lily (Leucocrinum montanum)

Personal energies, clear » Purple Saxifrage (Saxifraga oppositifolia)

Personal evolution » Sagebrush (Artemisia tridentate)

P

Personal gifts » Treasure Flower (Gazania rigens)

Personal glory » Hibiscus (Hibiscus)

Personal power » Monkey Flower (Mimulus guttatus)

Personal success » Sassafras (Sassafras variifolium)

Personal transformation » Coriander (Coriandrum sativum)

Personal truth » Monks' Aster (Aster)

Personal value, awareness of » Cloudberry (Rubus chamaemorus)

Personal will » Centaury (Erythraea centaurium)

Personality » Great Maple (Acer pseudoplatanus)

Perspective, broad » Venus Flytrap (Dionaea muscipula)

Perspective, clear » Eyebright (Euphrasia officinalis)

Perspective, higher » Ash (Fraxinus)

Petulance » Barberry (Berberis vulgaris)

Physical attack, protection from » Bitter Root (Lewisia rediviva)

Physical beauty » Jojoba (Simmondsia chinensis)

Physical cleansing » Cedar of Lebanon (Cedrus libani), Luffa (Luffa aegyptiaca)

Physical confidence » Banana Flower (Musa)

Physical healing » Tree Peony (Paeonia suffruticosa)

Physical health » Echinacea (Echinacea purpurea),

Physical heart health » Lily of the Valley (Convallaria majalis)

Physical stamina » Coltsfoot (Tussilago farfara)

Physical strength » Witchhazel (Hamamelis virginiana), Wood of Life (Guaiacum sanctum)

Physical support » Bistort (Polygonum bistorta)

Physical temptation » Tree Peony (Paeonia suffruticosa)

Physical tension, relieve » Sweet Marjoram (Origanum marjorana)

Physical transition » Lily of the Valley (Convallaria majalis)

Pity » Pine (Pinus sylvestris), Spruce (Picea)

P

Plagiarism » Siberian Iris (Iris sibirica), Iris, Fairy (Dietes grandiflora)

Plant alchemy » Hellebore (Helleborus)

Platonic love » Bittersweet (Solanum dulcamara), Acacia (Acacia)

Play » Hyacinth (Hyacinthus)

Play, let's » Daisy (Bellis perennis), Hyacinth (Hyacinthus)

Playfulness » Daisy (Bellis perennis), African Daisy (Osteospermum), Canna (Canna generalis striatus)

Please, desire to » Cranes-Bill (Geranium maculatum), Mezereum (Daphne mezereum)

Please forgive me » Kantuta (Cantua buxifolia)

Please keep this secret » Woodbine (Lonicera periclymenum)

Please me, you » Godetia (Clarkia amoena), Heliotrope (Heliotropium)

Please understand » Hydrangea (Hydrangea)

Please you, I want to » Daphne (Daphne odora)

Pleasing » Godetia (Clarkia amoena)

Pleasing others, stop » Witchhazel (Hamamelis virginiana)

Pleasure » Chocolate Flower (Berlandiera lyrata), Opium Poppy (Papaver somniferum)

Pleasure, dangerous » Tuberose (Polianthes tuberosa)

Pleasure, I am intoxicated with » Heliotrope (Heliotropium)

Pleasure mixed with pain » Dog Rose (Rosa canina)

Pleasure, reviving » Daylily (Hemerocallis)

Pledged to another, I am » Passion Flower (Passiflora incarnate)

Poetry » Hazel (Corylus), Rose, Briar (Rosa rubiginosa)

Politeness » Ageratum (Ageratum), Mimosa (Acacia dealbata)

Positive action » Scotch Thistle (Onopordum acanthium)

Positive change » Edelweiss (Leontopodium alpinum), Dog Rose (Rosa canina), Radish (Raphanus sativus)

Positive choices » African Daisy (Osteospermum)

P

Positive energy » Mastic (Pistacia lentiscus)

Positive outlook » Ixora (Ixora coccinea)

Positive self-image » Hibiscus, Native Yellow (Hibiscus brackenridgei)

Positive thinking » Amaryllis (Amaryllis)

Positive transformation » Trout Lily (Erythronium americanum)

Positivity, increase » Black Cohosh (Cimicifuga racemosa)

Possession cure » Periwinkle (Vinca minor)

Possibilities » Crowea (Crowea exalata), Himalayan Blue Poppy (Meconopsis grandis), Delphinium (Delphinium), Hippeastrum (Hippeastrum), Yellow Elder (Tecoma stans)

Possibilities, new » Scabiosa (Scabiosa)

Potency » Bean (Phaseolus vulgaris)

Potency, sexual » Banana Flower (Musa)

Potential » Himalayan Blue Poppy (Meconopsis grandis), Onion (Allium cepa)

Potential, extended » Rock Rose (Helianthemum)

Poverty » Campion (Silene vulgaris)

Power » Violet Nightshade (Solanum brownii), Queen of the Night (Selenicereus grandiflorus), Dandelion (Taraxacum officinale), Jonquil (Narcissus jonquilla), Ash (Fraxinus), Black Orchid (Trichoglottis brachiata), Rowan (Sorbus aucuparia), Cinnamon (Cinnamomum verum), Ebony (Diospyros crassiflora), Frankincense (Boswellia sacra)

Power, creative » Iris, Black (Iris nigricans)

Power, mystical » Redwood (Sequoiadendron giganteum)

Power, own » Tomato (Solanum lycopersicum)

Power, personal » Monkey Flower (Mimulus guttatus)

Power, sexual » Patchouli (Pogostemon cablin)

Powers, awaken magical » Okra (Abelmoschus esculentus)

Powers, mental » Celery (Apium graveolens), Ginseng (Panax), Horehound (Marrubium vulgare), Savory (Satureja hortensis), Tangerine (Citrus tangerina)

Powers, psychic » Celery (Apium graveolens), Centaury (Erythraea centaurium), Bladder-Fucus (Fucus vesiculosus), Cedar (Cedrus), Grass (Gramineae), Star Anise (Illicium verum)

Powers, shamanic » Peyote (Lophophora williamsii)

Practical magic » Maple (Acer)

Practicality » Maple (Acer)

Praiseworthy » Fennel (Foeniculum vulgare)

Pray » Ratchaphruek (Cassia fistula), Rose, Cherokee (Rosa laevigata)

Prayers answered » Frog Orchid (Coeloglossum)

Precocity » Rose, May (Rosa)

Prefer you, I » Geranium (Geranium)

Preference » Geranium, Scarlet (Pelargonium)

Preparation » Venus Flytrap (Dionaea muscipula)

Present, aware of » Horse-Chestnut (Aesculus hippocastanum)

Preservation » Beech (Fagus)

Pressure, grace under » Snapdragon (Antirrhinum majus)

Pretension » Rosebay Willowherb (Chamerion angustifolium)

Pretty » Rose, Pompon (Rosa)

Pride » Amaryllis (Amaryllis), Lily (Lilium), Heliconia (Heliconia), African Daisy (Osteospermum), Thistle, Scotch (Onopordum acanthium), Hop (Humulus lupulus), Tiger Lily (Lilium tigrinum), Oak (Quercus robur), Pride of Barbados (Poinciana pulcherrima), Rocky Mountain Columbine (Aquilegia caerulea), Texas Bluebonnet (Lupinus texensis), Auricula (Primula auricular)

Priorities » Petunia (Petunia)

Presence revives me, your » Rosemary (Rosmarinus officinalis)

Preservation » Basil (Ocimum basilicum)

Preservation of beauty » Osmanthus (Osmanthus fragrans)

Problem solving » Litchi (Litchi chinensis)

Profit » Cabbage (Brassica oleracea var. capitata)

P

Prohibition » Privet (Ligustrum vulgare)

Proud of you, I am » Tiger Lily (Lilium tigrinum), Lily (Lilium), Heliconia (Heliconia)

Proud spirit » Gloxinia (Gloxinia)

Progress » Maltese Centaury (Paleocyanus crassifoleus)

Progression » Five Corners (Styphelia laeta), Carnation (Dianthus caryophyllus), Rafflesia (Rafflesia arnoldii), Hibiscus, White (Hibiscus arnottianus), Crepe Myrtle (Lagerstroemia indica)

Projects, completed » Stock (Matthiola incana)

Prolific » Fig (Ficus carica)

Prolong life » Elder (Sambucus nigra)

Promiscuity » Pistachio (Pistacia vera)

Promise » Plum (Prunus domestica), Maple (Acer)

Promise, I » Madonna Lily (Lilium candidum), Chrysanthemum, White (Chrysanthemum)

Promise, keep your » Plum (Prunus domestica)

Promises » Rose, Wild (Rosa acicularis), Peanut (Arachis hypogaea)

Promises, broken » Hoya (Hoya australis)

Promotion » Eggplant (Solanum melongena)

Proposition » Chrysanthemum, Red (Chrysanthemum)

Prosperity » Tree Peony (Paeonia suffruticosa), Peruvian Lily (Alstroemeria), Peony (Paeonia officinalis), Alkanet (Alkanna tentoria), Peach Blossom (Prunus persica), Great Rhododendron (Rhododendron maximum), Beech (Fagus), Bryony (Bryonia), Asparagus (Asparagus officinalis), Knotweed (Polygonum aviculare), Kumquat (Citrus japonica), Peanut (Arachis hypogaea), Queen of the Meadow (Filipendula ulmaria), Spinach (Spinacia oleracea), Tea (Camellia sinensis), Wheat (Triticum), Yellow Dock (Rumex crispus)

Prophecy » Mugwort (Artemisia vulgaris)

Prophetic dreams » Mugwort (Artemisia vulgaris), Bracken (Pteridium)

Prosperity » Jade (Crassula ovata), Stargazer Lily, Pink (Lilium orientalis), Baby Blue Eyes (Nemophila menziesii), Ash (Fraxinus), Honesty (Lunaria annua), Pomegranate Blossom (Punica granatum)

Protect you, I will » Rose, White (Rosa)

Protected heart » Gerbera Daisy, Pink (Gerbera jamesonii)

Protection » Antarctic Pearlwort (Colobanthus quitensis), Daisy (Bellis perennis), Lavender (Lavandula stoechas), Sweet Pea (Lathyrus odoratus), Althea (Hibiscus syriacus), Delphinium (Delphinium), Queen Anne's Lace (Daucus carota), Rose, White (Rosa), Tuberose (Polianthes tuberosa), Native Geranium (Geranium solanderi), Sage (Salvia officinalis), Delphinium (Delphinium), Galangal (Alpinia galangal) St John's Wort (Hypericum perforatum), Bittersweet (Solanum dulcamara), Calendula (Calendula officinalis), Holly (Ilex aquifolium), Monkshood (Aconitum), Petunia (Petunia), Garlic (Allium sativum), Juniper (Juniperus), Hellebore (Helleborus), Mugwort (Artemisia vulgaris), Mullein (Verbascum thapsus), Angelica (Angelica archangelica), Lady's Mantle (Alchemilla vulgaris), Sage (Salvia officinalis), Onion (Allium cepa), Marshmallow (Althea officinalis), Rose of Jerico (Anastatica hierochuntica), Burdock (Arctium), Bloodroot (Sanguinaria canadensis), Ginseng (Panax), Solomon's Seal (Polygonatum), Ash (Fraxinus), Honesty (Lunaria annua), Mulberry, Black (Morus nigra), Oak (Quercus robur), Wood Betony (Stachys betonica), Cloves (Eugenia caryophyllata), Chives (Allium schoenoprasum), Clover (Trifolium), Pepper (Piper nigrum), Birch (Betula), Yew (Taxus baccata), Rowan (Sorbus aucuparia), Bladder-Fucus (Fucus vesiculosus), Mountain Laurel (Kalmia latifolia), Mayflower (Epigaea repens), Sagebrush (Artemisia tridentate), African Violet (Saintpaulia), Bean (Phaseolus vulgaris), Caraway (Carum carvi), Cedar (Cedrus), Cauliflower (Brassica oleracea), Chilli (Capsicum), Boneset (Eupatorium perfoliatum), Frankincense (Boswellia sacra), Gorse (Ulex europaeus), Grass (Gramineae), Hens and Chickens (Sempervivum tectorum), Kava-Kava (Piper methysticum), Leek (Allium ampeloprasum), Lettuce (Lactuca sativa), Liquid Amber (Liquidambar styraciflua), Marjoram (Origanum majorana), Papaya (Carica papaya), Soy Bean (Glycine max), Vanilla (Vanilla planifolia)

Protection against evil spirits » Nettle (Urtica)

P

Protection against negativity » Madonna Lily (Lilium candidum)

Protection against witchcraft » Larch (Larix decidua)

Protection, boundary » Chrysanthemum, Yellow (Chrysanthemum)

Protection, energy » Rue (Ruta graveolens)

Protection, female » Purple Pitcher Plant (Sarracenia purpurea)

Protection from bad dreams » Cedar (Cedrus)

Protection from curses » Mullein (Verbascum thapsus), Yucca (Yucca filamentosa)

Protection from danger » Red Clover (Trifolium pratense), Heather, White (Calluna vulgaris)

Protection from deception » Sweet Violet (Viola odorata)

Protection from disease » Wood Anemone (Anemone nemerosa), Larch (Larix decidua), Laurel (Laurus nobilis), Ratchaphruek (Cassia fistula)

Protection from distractions » Thistle, Common (Cirsium vulgare)

Protection from enchantment » Rowan (Sorbus aucuparia)

Protection from evil » Meadowsweet (Filipendula ulmaria), Dill (Anethum graveolens), Centaury (Erythraea centaurium), Cranes-Bill (Geranium maculatum), Larch (Larix decidua), Elder (Sambucus nigra), Vervain (Verbena officinalis), Rowan (Sorbus aucuparia), Sagebrush (Artemisia tridentate), Teasel (Dipsacus)

Protection from evil spirits » Mustard (Sinapis arvensis), Chives (Allium schoenoprasum), Bean (Phaseolus vulgaris), Tormentil (Potentilla erecta)

Protection from inebriation » Sweet Violet (Viola odorata)

Protection from infection » Witchhazel (Hamamelis virginiana)

Protection from lightning » Sweet Marjoram (Origanum marjorana), Oak (Quercus robur)

Protection from negative energy » Okra (Abelmoschus esculentus)

Protection from negative spirits » Mullein (Verbascum thapsus)

Protection from nightmares » Lemon Verbena (Aloysia triphylla)

Protection from outside influences » Walnut (Juglans regia)

Protection from physical attack » Bitter Root (Lewisia rediviva)

Protection from snakes » Lemongrass (Cymbopogon citratus)

Protection from spirits » Tiger Lily (Lilium tigrinum)

Protection from storms » Willowherb (Epilobium)

Protection from supernatural energies » Hazel (Corylus)

Protection from witchcraft » Laurel (Laurus nobilis), Scarlet Pimpernel (Anagallis arvensis)

Protection, hidden » Puti Tai Nobiu (Bougainvillea spectabilis)

Protection of food » Parsley (Petroselinum crispum)

Protection of home » Cornflower (Centaurea cyanus), Chives (Allium schoenoprasum)

Protection of love » Tormentil (Potentilla erecta)

Protection, loyal » Spring Onion (Allium fistulosum)

Protection, magical » Rowan (Sorbus aucuparia)

Protection, psychic » Red Clover (Trifolium pratense), Broom (Genisteae), Sagebrush (Artemisia tridentate)

Protection, spiritual » Angelica (Angelica archangelica), Rue (Ruta graveolens)

Protective boundaries » Broccoli (Brassica oleracea var. italica)

Prosperity » Teuila (Alpinia purpurata)

Proud of you, I am » Lily (Lilium), Heliconia (Heliconia)

Prudence » Lemon (Citrus limon), Service Tree (Sorbus)

Psychic abilities » Mugwort (Artemisia vulgaris)

Psychic abilities, strengthen » Bearberry (Arctostaphylos uva-ursi)

Psychic awareness » Rosemary (Rosmarinus officinalis), Wild Banana Orchid (Schomburgkiathomsoniana),Cauliflower(Brassicaoleracea),Lemongrass (Cymbopogon citratus)

Psychic development » Water Lily, Purple (Nymphaea), Cinnamon (Cinnamomum verum), Frankincense (Boswellia sacra), Galangal (Alpinia galangal), Kava-Kava (Piper methysticum), Purslane (Portulaca oleracea)

P

Psychic healing » Skullcap (Scutellaria)

Psychic inituition » Rowan (Sorbus aucuparia)

Psychic protection » Red Clover (Trifolium pratense), Broom (Genisteae), Sagebrush (Artemisia tridentate)

Psychic powers » Celery (Apium graveolens), Centaury (Erythraea centaurium), Bladder-Fucus (Fucus vesiculosus), Cedar (Cedrus), Grass (Gramineae), Star Anise (Illicium verum)

Psychic skills » Himalayan Blue Poppy (Meconopsis grandis), Aconite (Aconite)

Psychic vision » Sallow (Salix cinerea)

Pure affection » Carnation, White (Dianthus caryophyllus)

Pure, our love is » Rose, Lavender (Rosa)

P

Purification » Hawthorn (Crataegus monogyna), Feverfew (Tanacetum parthenium), Hyssop (Hyssopus officinalis), Sage (Salvia officinalis), Onion (Allium cepa), Lemon Verbena (Aloysia triphylla), Yucca (Yucca filamentosa), Bloodroot (Sanguinaria canadensis), Centaury (Erythraea centaurium), Iris, Blue Flag (Iris versicolor), Wood Betony (Stachys betonica),Pepper(Pipernigrum),Bulrush(Scirpoidesholoschoenus),Yellow Jessamine (Gelsemium sempervirens), Sagebrush (Artemisia tridentate), Cedar (Cedrus), Cinnamon (Cinnamomum verum), Fennel (Foeniculum vulgare), Frankincense (Boswellia sacra), Grapefruit (Citrus paradisi), Guava (Psidium guajava), Lemongrass (Cymbopogon citratus), tobacco (Nicotiana tabacum), Turmeric (Cucurma longa)

Purifying » Swamp Onion (Allium validum)

Purifying spaces » Juniper (Juniperus)

Purity » Antarctic Pearlwort (Colobanthus quitensis), Baby's Breath (Gypsophila paniculata), Carnation White (Dianthus caryophyllus), Chrysanthemum, White (Chrysanthemum), Rose, White (Rosa), Dogwood (Cornus), Star of Bethlehem (Ornithogalum), Easter Lily (Lilium longiflorum), Stargazer Lily, White (Lilium orientalis), Water Lily (Nymphaea), Olive (Olea europaea), Butterfly Jasmine (Mariposa), Melati (Jasminum sambac), Crab Apple Tree (Malus sylvestris), Deer Grass (Trichophorum cespitosum), White Trillium (Trillium grandiflorum),

Camellia, White (Camellia), Lettuce (Lactuca sativa), Lilac, White (Syringa), Mexican Orange Blossom (Choisya ternata), Strawberry (Fragaria x ananassa), Passionfruit (Passiflora edulis), Trumpet Creeper (Campsis radicans)

Purity of emotions » Apple Blossom (Malus domestica)

Purity of heart » Lily of the Valley (Convallaria majalis), Rose, Lavender (Rosa)

Purpose, clarity of » Deer Grass (Trichophorum cespitosum)

Purpose, higher » Sage (Salvia officinalis)

Purpose, life » Five Corners (Styphelia laeta), Wedding Bush (Ricinocarpos pinifolius), Edelweiss (Leontopodium alpinum), Lily of the Valley (Convallaria majalis), Hemp (Cannabis sativa), Jack-in-the-Pulpit (Arisaema triphyllum), Clary Sage (Salvia sclarea), Cloudberry (Rubus chamaemorus), Khat (Catha edulis)

Purpose, sense of » Hemp (Cannabis sativa)

Purpose, soul » Pussytoes (Antennaria)

Purpose, spiritual » Showy Lady Slipper (Cypripedium reginae)

Puzzle me, you » Love-in-a-Mist (Nigella damascena)

Q

Queen of coquettes, you are the » Queen's Rocket (Hesperis matronalis)

Queen's majesty, you possess a » Acacia (Acacia)

Question, gentle » Heath Bell (Erica cinerea)

Quick decision » Iris Croatica (Iris perunika)

Quick thought » Horehound (Marrubium vulgare)

Quickly, leave me » Pennyroyal (Mentha pulegium)

Quiet, be » Belladonna (Atropa belladonna)

Quiet inspiration » Iris, Black (Iris nigricans)

Quiet reflection » Heath Bell (Erica cinerea)

R

Rain » Cotton (Gossypium)

Ranking, high » Red Blossomed Heilala (Garcinia sessilis)

Rare beauty » Hibiscus, Pink (Hibiscus rosa-sinensis)

Rare worth » Violet, Yellow (Viola pubescens)

Rarity » Mandrake (Mandragora officinarum)

Rashness » Hyacinth (Hyacinthus)

Ready for you, I am » Venus Flytrap (Dionaea muscipula)

Ready, I am » Pelargonium (Pelargonium cucullatum), Rosella Flower (Hibiscus heterophyllus)

Ready, I will be » Astilbe (Astilbe)

Realistic goals » Rose, Cecil Brunner (Rosa Mlle. Cecile Brunner)

Reality, see » Eyebright (Euphrasia officinalis)

Realisation of an idea » Heliconia (Heliconia)

Reason » Goat's Rue (Galega officinalis)

Reawakening » Rowan (Sorbus aucuparia)

Rebellion » Butterfly Jasmine (Mariposa)

Rebirth » Crowsfoot (Erodium crinitum), Sacred Blue Lily (Nymphaea caerulea), Dogwood (Cornus), Dagger's Log (Agave karatto miller), Yew (Taxus baccata)

Rebuff » Lobelia, White (Lobelia)

Rebuild » Fireweed (Chamerion angustifolium)

Receptive, I am » Sego Lily (Calochortus nuttallii)

Recognition » Amaryllis (Amaryllis)

Recollection » Mock Orange (Philadelphus)

Reconciliation » Grevillea (Grevillea banksii), Hazel (Corylus), Bean (Phaseolus vulgaris)

Reconnection » Rafflesia (Rafflesia arnoldii), Sacred Blue Lily (Nymphaea caerulea)

Recovery » Mulla Mulla (Ptilotus exaltatus), Arnica (Arnica montana), Elder (Sambucus nigra), Holly (Ilex aquifolium)

Recovery, depression » Mustard (Sinapis arvensis)

Recovery, health » Nettle (Urtica)

Recurrent thoughts, stop » Horse-Chestnut (Aesculus hippocastanum)

Reduce depression » Air Plant (Tillandsia)

Reduce turmoil » Cedar of Lebanon (Cedrus libani)

Refinement » Orchid (Orchidaceae)

Reflection » Sage (Salvia officinalis), Cloudberry (Rubus chamaemorus)

Reflection, quiet » Heath Bell (Erica cinerea)

Refreshment » Peppermint (Mentha piperita)

Refusal » Chrysanthemum, Yellow (Chrysanthemum), Pink, Variegated (Dianthus plumarius)

Regard » Daffodil (Narcissus pseudonarcissus)

Regeneration » Jade Vine (Strongylodon macrobotrys), Aloe (Aloe vera), Yellow Elder (Tecoma stans), Althea (Hibiscus syriacus)

Regret » Swamp Lily (Crinum pedunculatum), Dogwood (Cornus), Loosestrife, Yellow (Lythrum salicaria)

Regret what I have done, I » Dogwood (Cornus)

Regrets will follow you to the grave, my » Asphodel (Asphodelus)

Reincarnation » Lilac, White (Syringa), Celtic Bean (Vicia faba celtica)

Reintegration » Angel's Trumpet (Brugmansia candida)

Rejected love » Bleeding Heart (Lamprocapnos spectabilis)

Rejection » Ice Plant (Carpobrotus edulis)

Rejuvenation » Calla Lily (Zantedeschia aethiopica), Almond (Prunus amygdalus), Hawkweed (Hieracium), Osmanthus (Osmanthus fragrans)

Relationship » Rose, Red (Rosa)

Relationship balance » Gloxinia (Gloxinia), Motherwort (Leonurus cardiaca)

Relationship, beautiful » Gloxinia (Gloxinia)

Relationship harmony » Tiger Lily (Lilium tigrinum)

R

Relationship rescue » Black Cohosh (Cimicifuga racemosa)

Relationship security » Pagoda Flower (Clerodendrum speciosissimum)

Relationship support » Blue-Eyed Grass (Sisyrinchium montanum)

Relationship with me?, will you begin a » Chrysanthemum, Red (Chrysanthemum)

Relationships » Trout Lily (Erythronium americanum)

Relationships, balanced » Breadfruit (Artocarpus altilis)

Relationships, deepen » Pussytoes (Antennaria)

Relationships, ending » Turnip (Brassica rapa subsp. rapa)

Relationships, heal » Ceibo (Erythrina crista-galli)

Relationships, improved » Linnaea (Linnaea borealis)

Relationships, long-lasting » Lily (Lilium)

Relationships, new » Walnut (Juglans regia)

Relationships, sexual » Wild Banana Orchid (Schomburgkia thomsoniana)

Relationships, strengthening » Lime (Tilia x europaea)

Relax » California Poppy (Eschscholzia californica), Chamomile, German (Matricaria chamomilla), Lemon Balm (Melissa officinalis)

Relaxation » Pasqueflower (Pulsatilla vulgaris), Skullcap (Scutellaria), Yarrow (Achillea millefolium):

Relaxation of nerves » Skullcap (Scutellaria)

Release » Lechenaultia (Lechenaultia formas), Henbane (Hyoscyamus niger), Calendula (Calendula officinalis), Skunk Cabbage (Symplocarpus foetidus), Alder (Alnus), Rose, Meadow (Rosa blanda), Butterfly Weed (Asclepias tuberosa), Moneywort (Bacopa monnieri), Melilot (Melilotus officinalis), Air Plant (Tillandsia)

Release anger » Burdock (Arctium), Firethorn (Pyracantha)

Release attachments » Trumpet Creeper (Campsis radicans)

Release barriers » Lady's Mantle (Alchemilla vulgaris)

Release bitter feelings » Harvest Brodiaea (Brodiaea elegans)

Release, blockage » Bearberry (Arctostaphylos uva-ursi)

R

Release blocks » Iris, Blue Flag (Iris versicolor)

Release, emotional » Dutchman's Breeches (Dicentra cucullaria), Yerba Santa(Eriodictyonglutinosum),Blue-EyedGrass(Sisyrinchiummontanum)

Release emotional blocks » Lime (Tilia x europaea)

Release emotional hurt » Cuckoo Flower (Cardamine pratensis)

Release energies » Rose, Meadow (Rosa blanda)

Release fear » Okra (Abelmoschus esculentus)

Release love addiction » Jack-in-the-Pulpit (Arisaema triphyllum)

Release negative patterns » Macadamia (Macadamia integrifolia)

Release of fear » Mountain Avens (Dryas octopetala)

Release of grief » Artichoke, Globe (Cynara scolymus)

Release of hurt » Puti Tai Nobiu (Bougainvillea spectabilis)

Release tension » Chicory (Cichorium intybus), Chamomile, German (Matricaria chamomilla), Showy Lady Slipper (Cypripedium reginae)

Release you, I » Calendula (Calendula officinalis)

Released emotions » Mulberry, Black (Morus nigra)

Releasing » Patchouli (Pogostemon cablin)

Releasing emotional drama » Prairie Crocus (Pulsatilla patens)

Releasing negativity » Fly Orchid (Ophrys insectifera)

Reliability » Tree of Life (Guaiacum officinale)

Reliance, self » Native Violet (Viola papilionacea), Cerato (Ceratostigma willmottianum)

Relief » Purple Saxifrage (Saxifraga oppositifolia), Balm of Gilead (Commiphora gileadensis)

Relief, anxiety » Clary Sage (Salvia sclarea)

Relief of mental anguish » Sweet Alyssum (Alyssum maritimum)

Relief, stress » Geranium, Rose (Pelargonium graveolens), Sweet Chestnut (Castanea sativa), Osmanthus (Osmanthus fragrans)

Relief, tension » Ginger (Zingiber officinale), Hyacinth (Hyacinthus)

Relief of tensions » Peach Blossom (Prunus persica)

R

Religious enthusiasm » Maltese Cross (Lychnis chalcedonica)

Religious superstition » Passion Flower (Passiflora incarnate)

Religious work » Passion Flower (Passiflora incarnate)

Relieve mental tension » Sweet Marjoram (Origanum marjorana)

Relieve physical tension » Sweet Marjoram (Origanum marjorana)

Reluctance in love » Toadflax (Linaria vulgaris)

Remember, I » Mock Orange (Philadelphus), Melilot (Melilotus officinalis)

Remember you, I » Rosemary (Rosmarinus officinalis)

Remembrance » Forget-Me-Not (Myosotis), Pansy (Viola tricolor var. hortensis), Easter Lily (Lilium longiflorum), Rosemary (Rosmarinus officinalis), Statice (Limonium)

Remorse » Blackberry (Rubus fruticosus), Raspberry (Rubus idaeus)

Removal of curses » Yucca (Yucca filamentosa)

Removal of evil spirits » St John's Wort (Hypericum perforatum)

Removal of negative energies » Heather, Lavender (Calluna vulgaris), St John's Wort (Hypericum perforatum)

Removal of obstacles » Chicory (Cichorium intybus)

Rendezvous » Scarlet Pimpernel (Anagallis arvensis)

Rendezvous, romantic » Ranunculus (Ranunculus)

Renewal » Marigold (Tagetes evecta), Snowdrop (Galanthus nivalis), Daffodil (Narcissus pseudonarcissus), Aloe (Aloe vera), Birch (Betula)

Renewal of energy » Elder (Sambucus nigra)

Renewed youth » Lemon Balm (Melissa officinalis)

Repel evil » Fennel (Foeniculum vulgare)

Repels negativity » Rose of Jerico (Anastatica hierochuntica)

Repentance » Hyssop (Hyssopus officinalis), Rue (Ruta graveolens)

Repose, calm » Buckbean (Menyanthes)

Resentment » Petunia (Petunia)

Reserve » Sycamore (Acer pseudoplatanus)

R

Resignation » Cyclamen (Cyclamen), Calamus Root (Acorus calamus), Harebell (Campanula rotundifolia)

Resilience » Dahlia (Dahlia), Elder (Sambucus nigra), Madder, Wild (Galium mollugo), Ragwort (Jacobaea vulgaris)

Resist you, I cannot » Quince (Cydonia oblonga)

Resistance » Saint Barnaby's Thistle (Centaurea solstitialis)

Resolution » Crowea (Crowea exalata), Rose, Musk (Rosa moschata), Artichoke, Globe (Cynara scolymus), Sweet Potato (Ipomoea batatas)

Resolution to win » Columbine (Aquilegia vulgaris)

Resolve » Tree Spider Orchid (Dendrobium tetragonum)

Resolve conflict » Wood Betony (Stachys betonica)

Respect » Oleander (Nerium oleander), Hibiscus, White (Hibiscus arnottianus), Rose, Red (Rosa), Daffodil (Narcissus pseudonarcissus), Purple Orchid (Cattleya skinneri)

Respect for differences » Stephanotis (Stephanotis floribunda)

Respect, self » Thistle, Scotch (Onopordum acanthium)

Respect you, I » Hibiscus, White (Hibiscus arnottianus), Rose, Red (Rosa)

Respect your uniqueness, I » Purple Orchid (Cattleya skinneri)

Repose » Bindweed, Blue (Convolvulus)

Resolution, conflict » White Pine (Pinus strobus)

Resonance » Wild Pansy (Viola tricolor)

Responsibility » Fairy Fan Flower (Scaevola aemula), Violet Nightshade (Solanum brownii)

Responsibility, social » Sweet Pea (Lathyrus odoratus)

Restoration » Aloe (Aloe vera), Peppermint (Mentha piperita), Lime (Tilia x europaea), Persicaria (Persicaria lapathifolia), Fringed Violet (Thysanotus tuberosus)

Restoration of trust » Saffron (Crocus sativus)

Restoration, life » Yerba Santa (Eriodictyon glutinosum)

Restoration of intuition » Althea (Hibiscus syriacus)

R

Restoration of self » Fireweed (Chamerion angustifolium)

Restore health » Lemon Balm (Melissa officinalis)

Restored, trust » Baby Blue Eyes (Nemophila menziesii)

Resurrection » Dogwood (Cornus), Rose of Jerico (Anastatica hierochuntica), Water Lily (Nymphaea), Tiger Lily (Lilium tigrinum), Holly (Ilex aquifolium)

Rest » Henbane (Hyoscyamus niger)

Retaliation » Scotch Thistle (Onopordum acanthium)

Retribution » Bird's Foot Trefoil (Lotus corniculatus)

Return of joy » Prairie Lily (Lilium philadelphicum)

Return, I will » Rose, Yellow (Rosa)

Return, I happily await your » Red Whortleberry (Vaccinium)

Return to me » Japanese Cherry (Prunus serrulata)

Returned desire » Jonquil (Narcissus jonquilla)

Reunion » Tulip, Wild (Tulipa sprengeri)

Revealed, secrets » Opoponax (Commiphora erythraea), Madonna Lily (Lilium candidum),

Revealing » Godetia (Clarkia amoena)

Revelation » Redwood (Sequoiadendron giganteum)

Revelations » Field Poppy (Papaver rhoeas)

Revenge » Bird's Foot Trefoil (Lotus corniculatus), Liquorice (Glycyrrhiza glabra), Scammony (Convolvulus scammonia)

Reverance » Red Blossomed Heilala (Garcinia sessilis)

Revitalisation » Banana Flower (Musa)

Revives me, your presence » Rosemary (Rosmarinus officinalis)

Reviving pleasure » Daylily (Hemerocallis)

Reward » Honey Grevillea (Grevillea eriostachya)

Riches, desire for » Marsh Marigold (Caltha palustris)

Right path, choose the » Lily of the Valley (Convallaria majalis)

R

Rigidity, soften » Lady's Mantle (Alchemilla vulgaris)

Rigour » Lantana (Lantana camara)

Risk » Tamarisk (Tamarix)

Risk, calculated » Oleander (Nerium oleander)

Risky venture, good luck » Goldenrod (Solidago virgaurea)

Ritual cleansing » Vervain (Verbena officinalis)

Rivalry » Rocket (Eruca sativa)

Romance » Carnation (Dianthus caryophyllus), Azalea (Rhododendron Tsutsusi), Peony (Paeonia officinalis), Mistletoe (Viscum album), Peach Blossom (Prunus persica), Guava (Psidium guajava)

Romantic partnership » Peach Blossom (Prunus persica)

Romantic rendezvous » Ranunculus (Ranunculus)

Rough, you are too » Mimosa (Acacia dealbata)

ℝ

Royalty » Bird of Paradise (Strelitzia reginae), Walnut (Juglans regia), Purple Orchid (Cattleya skinneri), Iris, Black (Iris nigricans), Ratchaphruek (Cassia fistula), Alder (Alnus), Angrec (Angraecum), Hibiscus, Purple (Hibiscus rosa-sinensis)

Responsibility » Southern Cross (Xanthosia rotundifolia)

Retaliation » Scotch Thistle (Onopordum acanthium)

Rudeness » Cocklebur (Xanthium), Angrec (Angraecum)

Rural happiness » Tulip Tree (Liriodendron), Violet, Yellow (Viola pubescens)

S

Sacrifice » Field Poppy (Papaver rhoeas), Hyssop (Hyssopus officinalis), Poinciana (Delonix regia)

Sacred union » Hawthorn (Crataegus monogyna)

Sacredness » Sacred Blue Lily (Nymphaea caerulea), Calendula (Calendula officinalis), Champa (Calophyllum)

Sad memories » African Daisy (Osteospermum)

Sadness » Mulberry, Black (Morus nigra)

Sadness, end of » Poke Weed (Phytolacca americana)

Safe home » Heather, White (Calluna vulgaris)

Safe travels » Loveage (Levisticum officinale)

Safe, your are » Queen Anne's Lace (Daucus carota), Evening Primrose (Oenothera)

Safety » Borage (Borago officinalis), Baby Blue Eyes (Nemophila menziesii), Broccoli (Brassica oleracea var. italica), Traveller's Joy (Clematis vitalba)

Sanctuary » Queen Anne's Lace (Daucus carota)

Satire » Pepper (Piper nigrum), Prickly Pear (Opuntia ficus-indica)

Scattered thoughts » Pasqueflower (Pulsatilla vulgaris)

Sea, the » Bladder-Fucus (Fucus vesiculosus)

Second sight » Clover (Trifolium)

Secrecy » Fern (Tracheophyta)

Secret » Tree Spider Orchid (Dendrobium tetragonum), Woodbine (Lonicera periclymenum), Fern (Tracheophyta)

Secrets » Woodbine (Lonicera periclymenum)

Secret love » Gardenia (Gardenia jasminoides), Acacia (Acacia), Toothwort (Lathraea squamaria)

Secret, meaningful » Ranunculus (Ranunculus)

Secret, please keep this » Woodbine (Lonicera periclymenum)

Secrets revealed » Madonna Lily (Lilium candidum), Opoponax (Commiphora erythraea)

Security » Rose, Cecil Brunner (Rosa Mlle. Cecile Brunner) Baby Blue Eyes (Nemophila menziesii), Marsh Marigold (Caltha palustris), Tiger Lily (Lilium tigrinum), Bilberry (Vaccinium myrtillus), Broccoli (Brassica oleracea var. italica)

Security, relationship » Pagoda Flower (Clerodendrum speciosissimum)

Sedation » Motherwort (Leonurus cardiaca)

See, ability to » Clary Sage (Salvia sclarea)

S

See reality » Eyebright (Euphrasia officinalis)

See your beauty, I » Tulip, Variegated (Tulipa)

See you, I can » Eyebright (Euphrasia officinalis)

See you, I cannot wait to » Himalayan Balsam (Impatiens glandulifera)

Seek, to » Parosela (Dalea)

Self-acceptance » Bird of Paradise (Strelitzia reginae)

Self-assured » Orchid (Orchidaceae)

Self-assuredness » Hollyhock (Alcea rosea)

Self-awakening, true » Red Hot Poker (Kniphofia)

Self-awareness » Clubmoss (Lycopodium), Gotu Kola (Hydrocotyle asiatica)

Self-awareness, enhanced » Red Clover (Trifolium pratense)

Self-belief » Lechenaultia (Lechenaultia formas), Star of Bethlehem (Ornithogalum), Gentian (Gentiana)

Self, belief in » Mountain Avens (Dryas octopetala)

Self-care » Apple Blossom (Malus domestica)

Self-confidence » Fairy Fan Flower (Scaevola aemula), Sturt's Desert Rose (Gossypium sturtianum), Sunflower (Helianthus annuus), Artichoke, Jerusalem (Helianthus tuberosus), Larch (Larix decidua), Mountain Avens (Dryas octopetala), Puerto Rican Hibiscus (Thespesia grandiflora), Cerato (Ceratostigma willmottianum), Suncup (Lonicera ovata), Wake Robin (Trillium pendulum)

Self-defense » Saint Barnaby's Thistle (Centaurea solstitialis)

Self-determination » Maltese Centaury (Paleocyanus crassifoleus)

Self-empowerment » Saguaro Cactus Blossom (Carnegiea gigantean)

Self-esteem » Larch (Larix decidua), Elder (Sambucus nigra), Skullcap (Scutellaria), Crab Apple Tree (Malus sylvestris), Milkmaids (Dentaria californica)

Self-expression » Indian Paintbrush (Castilleja miniata), Canterbury Bells (Campanula medium)

Self-forgiveness » Heartsease (Viola tricolor), Heliotrope (Heliotropium), Pine (Pinus sylvestris), Naked Lady (Lycoris squamigera)

S

Self, gentle on » Crown Vetch (Securigera varia)

Self, higher » Rue (Ruta graveolens), Chervil (Anthriscus cerefolium)

Self-image, positive » Hibiscus, Native Yellow (Hibiscus brackenridgei)

Self-improvement » Tulip, Wild (Tulipa sprengeri)

Self-love » Orchid (Orchidaceae), Oregon Grape (Mahonia aquifolium), Poet's Narcissus (Narcissus poeticus),

Self, happy with » Chickweed (Stellaria media)

Self-healing » Fairy Aprons (Utricularia dichotoma)

Self, higher » Echinacea (Echinacea purpurea), Rose, Musk (Rosa moschata),

Self-insight » Rhododendron (Rhododendron)

Self-neglect » Snowdrop (Galanthus nivalis)

Self-nurture » Allspice (Pimenta dioica)

Self-perception » Venus' Looking Glass (Triodanis perfoliata)

Self-reliance » Sweet Marjoram (Origanum marjorana), Tropicbird Orchid (Angraecum eburneum), Native Violet (Viola papilionacea), Cerato (Ceratostigma willmottianum)

Self-respect » Thistle, Scotch (Onopordum acanthium)

Self, restoration of » Fireweed (Chamerion angustifolium)

Self-sabotage, end » Red Hot Poker (Kniphofia)

Self-sacrifice » Andromeda (Andromeda polifolia)

Self, sense of » Linnaea (Linnaea borealis)

Self, shadow » Rhododendron (Rhododendron)

Self-sufficiency » Hawkweed (Hieracium), Ithuriel's Spear (Triteleia laxa)

Self-sustenance » Blue Pimpernel (Lysimachia monelli)

Self, true » Mallow (Malva sylvestris), Ox-Eye Daisy (Leucanthemum vulgare)

Self, understanding » Self-Heal (Prunella vulgaris)

Self-value » Allspice (Pimenta dioica)

Self-worth » Venus' Looking Glass (Triodanis perfoliata), Calla Lily (Zantedeschia aethiopica)

Sense of purpose » Hemp (Cannabis sativa)

Sense of self » Gloxinia (Gloxinia), Linnaea (Linnaea borealis)

Sensitive love » Mimosa (Acacia dealbata)

Sensitivity » Bleeding Heart (Lamprocapnos spectabilis), Centaury (Erythraea centaurium), Aspen (Populus tremula), Ginger (Zingiber officinale), Sego Lily (Calochortus nuttallii)

Sensory awareness » Ginger (Zingiber officinale), Texas Bluebonnet (Lupinus texensis)

Sensuality » Apple Blossom (Malus domestica), Avens (Geum), Strawberry (Fragaria x ananassa)

Sentiment, warmth of » Spearmint (Mentha spicata)

Separate us, nothing will » Ivy (Hedera)

Separation » Water Lily (Nymphaea)

Service » Jack-in-the-Pulpit (Arisaema triphyllum), Showy Lady Slipper (Cypripedium reginae), Texas Bluebonnet (Lupinus texensis), Noble Star Cactus (Stapelia nobilis)

Settlement, peaceful » Vervain (Verbena officinalis)

Sex » Orchid (Orchidaceae), Tuberose (Polianthes tuberosa), Firethorn (Pyracantha), Mango (Mangifera indica), Ylang-Ylang (Cananga odorata)

Sex, changing » Persimmon (Diospyros virginiana)

Sexual potency » Banana Flower (Musa)

Sexual power » Patchouli (Pogostemon cablin)

Sexual relationships » Wild Banana Orchid (Schomburgkia thomsoniana)

Sexual trust » Purple Pitcher Plant (Sarracenia purpurea)

Sexual vitality » Purple Pitcher Plant (Sarracenia purpurea)

Sexuality » Moon Orchid (Phalaenopsis amabilis), Celtic Bean (Vicia faba celtica), Indian Pink (Spigelia marilandica)

Sexuality, balancing » Wild Banana Orchid (Schomburgkia thomsoniana)

Sexuality, male » Coconut (Cocus nucifera)

Sexy, you are » Orchid (Orchidaceae)

S

Shadow and light » Variegated Box (Buxus sempervirens)

Shadow self » Rhododendron (Rhododendron)

Shamanic powers » Peyote (Lophophora williamsii)

Shame » Peony (Paeonia officinalis), Hyssop (Hyssopus officinalis)

Shape-shifting » Yucca (Yucca filamentosa), Arfaj (Rhanterium epapposum), Heath Bell (Erica cinerea), Mandrake (Mandragora officinarum)

Sharing » Tarragon (Artemisia dracunculus)

Sharing knowledge » Water Lily, Blue (Nymphaea)

Sharpen sight » Greater Celandine (Chelidonium majus)

Sharpness » Barberry (Berberis vulgaris), Lantana (Lantana camara)

Shield » Alder (Alnus)

Shield from interference » Native Wood Violet (Viola odorata)

Shelter » Plane Tree (Platanus)

Shy, I am » Marvel of Peru (Mirabilis jalapa), Moving Plant (Mimosa pudica)

Shy love » Moss Rose (Portulaca grandiflora)

Shyness » Sweet Violet (Viola odorata), Vetch (Vicia)

Sight, second » Clover (Trifolium)

Sight, sharpen » Greater Celandine (Chelidonium majus)

Silence » Belladonna (Atropa belladonna)

Silliness » Fool's Parsley (Aethusa cynapium)

Simplicity » Godetia (Clarkia amoena), Stargazer Lily, White (Lilium orientalis), Marguerite Daisy (Argyranthemum frutescens), Melati (Jasminum sambac), Rose, Briar (Rosa rubiginosa), Tea (Camellia sinensis), Rose, Burgundy (Rosa)

Sincere, I am » Rose, Dark Pink (Rosa)

Sincerity » Rose, Dark Pink (Rosa), Honesty (Lunaria annua), Fern (Tracheophyta), Chervil (Anthriscus cerefolium), Satin Flower (Olsynium douglasii)

Sincerity of motive » Deer Grass (Trichophorum cespitosum)

Singularity » Celosia (Celosia)

S

Sisterhood » Pride of Barbados (Poinciana pulcherrima)

Situation, dangerous » Bindweed, Great (Convolvulus major)

Scepticism » Nightshade (Solanaceae)

Skill » Spider Orchid (Caladenia)

Skill with words » Hazel (Corylus)

Slander » Nettle (Urtica), Madder (Rubia tinctorum), Snake's Tongue (Sansevieria)

Sleep » Celery (Apium graveolens), Hop (Humulus lupulus), Heal-All (Pedicularis canadensis), Lettuce (Lactuca sativa)

Sleep attend you, may sweet » Buckbean (Menyanthes)

Sleep-inducing » Clary Sage (Salvia sclarea)

Sleep, peaceful » Primrose (Primula vulgaris), Elder (Sambucus nigra), Buckbean (Menyanthes)

Slow down » Stock (Matthiola incana), Speedwell (Veronica officinalis)

Slowing of pace » Stock (Matthiola incana)

Smile » Eggplant (Solanum melongena)

Snakes, protection from » Lemongrass (Cymbopogon citratus)

Social responsibility » Sweet Pea (Lathyrus odoratus)

Social situations, comfort in » White Flag (Spathiphyllum)

Soften rigidity » Lady's Mantle (Alchemilla vulgaris)

Softens my pain, your presence » Milkvetch (Astragalus)

Solace » Lady's Mantle (Alchemilla vulgaris)

Solace in adversity » Firethorn (Pyracantha)

Solitude » Heather, Lavender (Calluna vulgaris)

Solutions » Snowdrop (Galanthus nivalis), Venus Flytrap (Dionaea muscipula)

Solving, problem » Litchi (Litchi chinensis)

Soothe » Showy Lady Slipper (Cypripedium reginae)

Soothes me, your presence » Petunia (Petunia)

S

Soothing » Evening Primrose (Oenothera), Chamomile, German (Matricaria chamomilla), Jojoba (Simmondsia chinensis)

Sorcery » Nightshade (Solanaceae)

Sorcery, anti- » Boneset (Eupatorium perfoliatum)

Sorrow » Calendula (Calendula officinalis), Jonquil (Narcissus jonquilla)

Sorrowful parting » Wormwood (Artemisia absinthium)

Sorrowful remembrance » Pheasant's Eye (Adonis vernalis)

Sorry » Snapdragon (Antirrhinum majus)

Sorry, I am » Flannel Flower (Actinotus helianthi), Scottish Primrose (Primula scotica), Rose, Pale Pink (Rosa), Rose, Musk (Rosa moschata), Calendula (Calendula officinalis), Snapdragon (Antirrhinum majus), Kantuta (Cantua buxifolia), Loosestrife, Yellow (Lythrum salicaria), Clarkia (Clarkia purpurea), Dagger Hakea (Hakea teretifolia)

Sorry I cannot be with you » Carnation, Striped (Dianthus caryophyllus)

Sorry you are hurt, I am » Iris, Fairy (Dietes grandiflora)

Soul » Sego Lily (Calochortus nuttallii)

Soul purpose » Pussytoes (Antennaria)

Souls, united » Phlox (Phlox)

Space » Lechenaultia (Lechenaultia formas)

Space cleansing » Alkanet (Alkanna tentoria)

Space clearing » Lilac (Syringa vulgaris)

Space, I need » Cow Parsley (Anthriscus sylvestris)

Space, I need some » Lechenaultia (Lechenaultia formas)

Spaces, outdoor » Cow Parsley (Anthriscus sylvestris)

Spaces, purifying » Juniper (Juniperus)

Spatial awareness » Pink Knotweed (Persicaria capitata)

Speak up » Siberian Iris (Iris sibirica), Forget-Me-Not (Myosotis)

Special talents » African Daisy (Osteospermum)

Spell breaker » Snapdragon (Antirrhinum majus)

Spellcasting » Vervain (Verbena officinalis)

S

Spells, love » Dutchman's Breeches (Dicentra cucullaria)

Spell strengthener » Calamus Root (Acorus calamus)

Spirit messages » Iris, Blue Flag (Iris versicolor)

Spirit, proud » Gloxinia (Gloxinia)

Spirits, banish evil » Soy Bean (Glycine max)

Spirits, banishing unwanted » Solomon's Seal (Polygonatum)

Spirits, calling » Ginkgo (Ginkgo biloba)

Spirits, expel evil » Wood Betony (Stachys betonica)

Spirits, lift » Cranes-Bill (Geranium maculatum), Lemon Balm (Melissa officinalis), Red Bud (Cercis siliquastrum)

Spirits, protection from » Tiger Lily (Lilium tigrinum)

Spirits, protection from evil » Mustard (Sinapis arvensis)

Spirits, protection from negative » Mullein (Verbascum thapsus)

Spirits, summon » Solomon's Seal (Polygonatum)

Spiritual balance » Passion Flower (Passiflora incarnate)

Spiritual desires » Thistle, Common (Cirsium vulgare)

Spiritual growth » Sacred Lotus (Nelumbo nucifera), Angel's Trumpet (Brugmansia candida), Frankincense (Boswellia sacra)

Spiritual healing » Motherwort (Leonurus cardiaca)

Spiritual knowledge » Silversword (Argyroxiphium sandwicense)

Spiritual path » Jack-in-the-Pulpit (Arisaema triphyllum)

Spiritual protection » Angelica (Angelica archangelica), Rue (Ruta graveolens)

Spiritual purpose » Showy Lady Slipper (Cypripedium reginae)

Spritual strength » Rowan (Sorbus aucuparia)

Spirituality » Basil (Ocimum basilicum), Champa (Calophyllum), Rosewood (Pterocarpus indicus), African Violet (Saintpaulia), Cinnamon (Cinnamomum verum), Eggplant (Solanum melongena), Frankincense (Boswellia sacra), Maltese Cross (Lychnis chalcedonica), Sandalwood (Santalum album), Penstemon (Penstemon x mexicali), Coriander (Coriandrum sativum), Mahogany (Swietenia macrophylla)

Spirituality, a tribute to your beauty and » Lilac, White (Syringa)

Spirituality, authentic » Jack-in-the-Pulpit (Arisaema triphyllum)

Splendour » Sumac (Rhus)

Spontaneity » Stargazer Lily, Pink (Lilium orientalis)

Sport » Hyacinth (Hyacinthus)

Spring » American Pasqueflower (Pulsatilla hirsutissima), Apricot (Prunus armeniaca)

Stability » Shasta Daisy (Leucanthemum maximum), Hippeastrum (Hippeastrum), Passion Flower (Passiflora incarnate), Walnut (Juglans regia), Elm (Ulmus), Sky Vine (Thunbergia alata)

Stability, inner » Mustard (Sinapis arvensis)

Stability, mental » Ranunculus (Ranunculus), Walnut (Juglans regia)

Stabilises emotions » Blackthorn (Prunus spinosa)

Stabilising inner energy » Elder (Sambucus nigra)

Stabilisation, mood » Artichoke, Jerusalem (Helianthus tuberosus)

Stages of life » Primrose (Primula vulgaris)

Stagnant energy, clear » Skunk Cabbage (Symplocarpus foetidus)

Stamina, male » Asparagus (Asparagus officinalis)

Stamina, physical » Coltsfoot (Tussilago farfara)

Stand firm » Pennyroyal (Mentha pulegium)

Stand strong » Sacred Lotus (Nelumbo nucifera)

Standing tall » Pink Knotweed (Persicaria capitata)

Start again, let's » Kantuta (Cantua buxifolia)

Stateliness » Foxglove (Digitalis purpurea)

Stay strong » Sundew (Drosera auriculata), Mullein (Verbascum thapsus)

Stay true » Azalea (Rhododendron Tsutsusi)

Stay with you in good times and bad, I will » Virginia Creeper (Parthenocissus quinquefolia)

Staying with you, I am » Pohutukawa (Metrosideros excelsa)

Steadfastness » Oak (Quercus robur), Sweet Violet (Viola odorata)

Steadfastness in faith » Oak (Quercus robur)

Sternness » Sea Holly (Eryngium maritimum)

Still, be » Belladonna (Atropa belladonna), Aconite (Aconite)

Stills fears » Aspen (Populus tremula)

Stillness » Statice (Limonium)

Stimulating » Blackthorn (Prunus spinosa)

Stimulation » Cayenne (Capsicum frutescens)

Stimulation of intellect » Artichoke, Jerusalem (Helianthus tuberosus)

Stoicism » Boxwood (Buxus)

Stop » Hemlock (Conium maculatum)

Stop gossip » Slippery Elm (Ulmus rubra)

Stop pleasing others » Witchhazel (Hamamelis virginiana)

Stop recurrent thoughts » Horse-Chestnut (Aesculus hippocastanum)

Storm » Lobelia (Lobelia inflata)

Storms, protection from » Willowherb (Epilobium)

Strength » Thyme (Thymus vulgaris), Lantern Bush (Abutilon halophilum), Rosella Flower (Hibiscus heterophyllus), Magnolia (Magnolia campbellii), Pohutukawa (Metrosideros excelsa), Peruvian Lily (Alstroemeria), Sunflower (Helianthus annuus), Tuberose (Polianthes tuberosa), Feverfew (Tanacetum parthenium), Garlic (Allium sativum), Mugwort (Artemisia vulgaris), Tree Houseleek (Aeonium), Blue Pimpernel (Lysimachia monelli), Echinacea (Echinacea purpurea), Bloodroot (Sanguinaria canadensis), Woodbine (Lonicera periclymenum), Mulberry, Black (Morus Nigra), Oak (Quercus robur), Dagger's Log (Agave karatto miller), Melati (Jasminum sambac), Teuila (Alpinia purpurata), Prairie Lily (Lilium philadelphicum), Fennel (Foeniculum vulgare), Frankincense (Boswellia sacra), Hickory (Carya), Masterwort (Peucedanum ostruthium), Plantain (Plantago major), Psyllium (Plantago ovata), Saffron (Crocus sativus), Spinach (Spinacia oleracea), Tea (Camellia sinensis), Poison Ivy (Rhus toxicodendron)

S

Strength, emotional » Artichoke, Globe (Cynara scolymus), Gerbera Daisy, Red (Gerbera jamesonii)

Strength, gentle » Wooly Sunflower (Eriophyllum lanatum)

Strength, family » Woodbine (Lonicera periclymenum)

Strength, female » Rose, Cherokee (Rosa laevigata)

Strength, feminine » Lady's Mantle (Alchemilla vulgaris)

Strength for challenges » Mint (Mentha)

Strength, immune-system » Self-Heal (Prunella vulgaris)

Strength, inner » Arfaj (Rhanterium epapposum), Suncup (Lonicera ovata), Flame Tree (Brachychiton acerifolius), Dahlia (Dahlia), Wild Pansy (Viola tricolor), Snapdragon (Antirrhinum majus), Scotch Thistle (Onopordum acanthium), Thistle, Common (Cirsium vulgare), Walnut (Juglans regia), Olive (Olea europaea), Lemon Balm (Melissa officinalis), Aspen (Populus tremula), Elder (Sambucus nigra)

Strength in adversity » Walnut (Juglans regia)

Strength in love » Quince (Cydonia oblonga)

Strength, male » Spirulina (Arthrospira)

Strength, masculine » Oak (Quercus robur)

Strength, mental » Rosemary (Rosmarinus officinalis), Caraway (Carum carvi)

Strength, physical » Witchhazel (Hamamelis virginiana), Wood of Life (Guaiacum sanctum)

Strength of character » Gladiola (Gladiolus), Pine (Pinus sylvestris)

Strength, magical » Wood of Life (Guaiacum sanctum)

Strength, physical » Echinacea (Echinacea purpurea)

Strength, spiritual » Rowan (Sorbus aucuparia)

Strengthen desire » Purple Orchid (Cattleya skinneri)

Strengthen energy » Pepper (Piper nigrum)

Strengthen faith » Basil (Ocimum basilicum)

Strengthen friendship » Macadamia (Macadamia integrifolia)

Strengthen mind » Lemon Balm (Melissa officinalis)

S

Strengthen psychic abilities » Bearberry (Arctostaphylos uva-ursi)

Strengthen relationships » Lime (Tilia x europaea)

Strengthener, spell » Calamus Root (Acorus calamus)

Stress relief » Geranium, Rose (Pelargonium graveolens), Sweet Chestnut (Castanea sativa), Osmanthus (Osmanthus fragrans)

Strong, be » Sunflower (Helianthus annuus)

Strong heart » Wild Pansy (Viola tricolor)

Strong presence » Jade (Crassula ovata)

Strong voice » Blue Pimpernel (Lysimachia monelli)

Stubbornness » Cattle Bush (Trichodesma zelanicum)

Studies, I wish you success in your » Clematis (Clematis)

Study » Clematis (Clematis), Mulberry, White (Morus alba)

Study support » Peppermint (Mentha piperita)

Stupidity » Geranium, Scarlet (Pelargonium)

Subconscious » Violet, Blue (Viola sororia)

Submission » Black Orchid (Trichoglottis brachiata), Grass (Gramineae), Harebell (Campanula rotundifolia)

Substance » Tree of Life (Guaiacum officinale)

Succeed, I believe you can » Nasturtium (Tropaeolum majus)

Succeed, I will » Hollyhock (Alcea rosea)

Success » Acacia (Acacia), Maple (Acer), Cinnamon (Cinnamomum verum), Melissa (Melissa officinalis), Peyote (Lophophora williamsii)

Success » Baby Blue Eyes (Nemophila menziesii), Flame Lily (Gloriosa rothschildiana), Frankincense (Boswellia sacra), Shamrock (Trifolium dubium)

Success » Lechenaultia (Lechenaultia formas)

Success, independent » Cranberry Heath (Astroloma humifusum)

Success in your studies, I wish you » Clematis (Clematis)

Success, I wish you » Peruvian Lily (Alstroemeria), Mullein (Verbascum thapsus)

Success, personal » Sassafras (Sassafras variifolium)

Success with creative ideas » Iris, Fairy (Dietes grandiflora)

Suffering » Fir (Abies), Rose, Cherokee (Rosa laevigata)

Summer » Prairie Lily (Lilium philadelphicum)

Summon spirits » Solomon's Seal (Polygonatum)

Summon the devil » Heath Bell (Erica cinerea)

Sunshine » Heliconia (Heliconia)

Sun shines when I am with you, the » Daffodil (Narcissus pseudonarcissus)

Supernatural energies, protection from » Hazel (Corylus)

Superstition » Aloe (Aloe vera)

Superstition » St John's Wort (Hypericum perforatum)

Superstition, religious » Passion Flower (Passiflora incarnate)

Support » Fairy Fan Flower (Scaevola aemula), Daisy (Bellis perennis), Mountain Laurel (Kalmia latifolia)

Support, be my » Bryony, Black (Dioscorea communis)

Support birth » Trillium (Trillium)

Support during change » Walnut (Juglans regia)

Support, exam » Larch (Larix decidua)

Support, physical » Bistort (Polygonum bistorta)

Support, relationship » Blue-Eyed Grass (Sisyrinchium montanum)

Support, study » Peppermint (Mentha piperita)

Support you, I » Nasturtium (Tropaeolum majus)

Suppressed emotions » Firethorn (Pyracantha)

Surrender, I » Crown Vetch (Securigera varia)

Surprise » Betony (Stachys officinalis)

Surround me in natural beauty » Persimmon (Diospyros virginiana)

Survival » Waratah (Telopea speciosissima), Dandelion (Taraxacum officinale), Tropicbird Orchid (Angraecum eburneum), Texas Bluebonnet (Lupinus texensis), Kapok (Bomliax ceilia)

Survival, ensure » Goosegrass (Galium aparine)

Survive you, I will not » Mulberry, Black (Morus nigra)

Sustenance » Peyote (Lophophora williamsii)

Sweet » Carnation, White (Dianthus caryophyllus)

Sweet dreams » Lemon Verbena (Aloysia triphylla)

Sweet life » Honeysuckle (Lonicera)

Sweet memories » Evening Primrose (Oenothera), Periwinkle (Vinca minor)

Sweet words » Rose, Briar (Rosa rubiginosa)

Sweet, you are » Chrysanthemum, White (Chrysanthemum)

Sweet you are, how » Pink, Clove-Scented (Dianthus caryophyllus)

Sweetheart, it hurts not to have a » Puti Tai Nobiu (Bougainvillea spectabilis)

Sweetness » Lily of the Valley (Convallaria majalis), Daphne (Daphne odora), Lime (Tilia x europaea)

Sympathy » Shasta Daisy (Leucanthemum maximum), Statice (Limonium), Thrift (Armeria maritima)

S

T

Take care of yourself » Azalea (Rhododendron Tsutsusi)

Take courage » Mullein (Verbascum thapsus)

Talents, special » African Daisy (Osteospermum)

Tall, standing » Pink Knotweed (Persicaria capitata)

Tartness » Barberry (Berberis vulgaris)

Taste, good » Fuchsia (Fuchsia magellanica)

Teaching » Water Lily, Pink (Nymphaea)

Teasing, I was only » Sweet William (Dianthus barbatus)

Telepathic communication » Greater Celandine (Chelidonium majus)

Tell me the truth » Chrysanthemum, White (Chrysanthemum), Bittersweet (Solanum dulcamara)

Telling the truth, I am » Rose, White (Rosa)

Temper, hot » Barberry (Berberis vulgaris)

Tempering » Godetia (Clarkia amoena)

Temptation » Quince (Cydonia oblonga)

Temptation, victory over » Sweet Chestnut (Castanea sativa)

Tenacity » Feverfew (Tanacetum parthenium), Ivy (Hedera), Hound's Tongue (Cynoglossum officinalis):

Tenderness » Crown Vetch (Securigera varia)

Tension » Bee Balm (Monarda)

Tension, release » Chicory (Cichorium intybus), Chamomile, German (Matricaria chamomilla), Showy Lady Slipper (Cypripedium reginae)

Tension relief » Hyacinth (Hyacinthus), Ginger (Zingiber officinale)

Tensions, relief of » Peach Blossom (Prunus persica)

Thank you » Poinsettia (Euphorbia pulcherrima), Bluebell, Common (Hyacinthoides non-scripta), Rose, Dark Pink (Rosa), Canterbury Bells (Campanula medium), Ageratum (Ageratum)

Thankfulness » Harebell (Campanula rotundifolia)

The devil » Firethorn (Pyracantha)

The halcyon days of our love are at hand » Beech (Fagus)

The sea » Bladder-Fucus (Fucus vesiculosus)

The sun shines when I'm with you » Daffodil (Narcissus pseudonarcissus)

The world » Pumpkin (Cucurbita pepo)

Theft, anti- » Juniper (Juniperus), Caraway (Carum carvi)

Think again » Sacred Lotus (Nelumbo nucifera)

Think of me » Flamingo Flower (Anthurium)

Thinking, clear » Chickweed (Stellaria media), Peppermint (Mentha piperita)

Thinking, expansive » Banana Flower (Musa)

Thinking of you » Purple Violet (Viola), Fairy Aprons (Utricularia dichotoma)

Thinking of you, I am » Heartsease (Viola tricolor)

This must end » Hemlock (Conium maculatum), Angel's Trumpet (Brugmansia candida), Begonia (Begonia)

Time » Fir (Abies)

Time to love again » Crocus (Crocus)

Time, wasting » Blue Pimpernel (Lysimachia monelli)

Times, better » Kumquat (Citrus japonica)

Timidity » Marvel of Peru (Mirabilis jalapa)

Thought, creative » Great Maple (Acer pseudoplatanus)

Thought, free » Ragwort (Jacobaea vulgaris)

Thoughtfulness » Freesia (Freesia)

Thought, quick » Horehound (Marrubium vulgare)

Thoughts, banish negative » Lemon (Citrus limon)

Thoughts, dark » Nightshade (Solanaceae)

Thoughts, inspirational » Iris, Black (Iris nigricans)

Thoughts, loving » Pansy (Viola tricolor var. hortensis)

Thoughts, scattered » Pasqueflower (Pulsatilla vulgaris)

Thrive » Speedwell (Veronica officinalis)

To cure » Marshmallow (Althea officinalis)

To increase » Pumpkin (Cucurbita pepo)

To laugh » Scarlet Pimpernel (Anagallis arvensis)

To seek » Parosela (Dalea)

To win » Parsley (Petroselinum crispum)

Together, coming » Pot of Gold (Winteria aureispina)

Togetherness » Love Seed (Adenanthera pavonina), Chain of Love (Antigonon leptopus)

Token, a » Laurustinus (Viburnum tinus)

Tolerance » Impatiens (Impatiens walleriana)

Too good to be true » Variegated Box (Buxus sempervirens)

T

Touch me, do not » Burdock (Arctium)

Toxin clearer » Centaury (Erythraea centaurium)

Transcendence » Yew (Taxus baccata), Meadow Saffron (Colchicum autumnale)

Transient brilliance » Rose, China (Rosa chinensis)

Transition » Water Hyacinth (Eichbornia crassipes), Turk's Cap (Lilium superbum)

Transform darkness » Mustard (Sinapis arvensis)

Transform emotions » Rose, Prairie (Rosa arkansana)

Transformation » Pohutukawa (Metrosideros excelsa), Evening Primrose (Oenothera), Mistletoe (Viscum album), Yucca (Yucca filamentosa), Persimmon (Diospyros virginiana)

Transformation, healing » Yesterday, Today and Tomorrow (Brunfelsia)

Transformation, inner » Sweet Chestnut (Castanea sativa), Fireweed (Chamerion angustifolium)

Transformation, personal » Coriander (Coriandrum sativum)

Transformation, positive » Trout Lily (Erythronium americanum)

Transient beauty » Cereus (Cereus)

Transient happiness » Spiderwort (Tradescantia)

Transition » Hemlock (Conium maculatum), Angel's Trumpet (Brugmansia candida), Mayflower (Epigaea repens)

Transition, calm » Bee Balm (Monarda)

Transition, physical » Lily of the Valley (Convallaria majalis)

Tranquility » Heath (Erica), Cosmos (Cosmos), Stonecrop (Sedum)

Trauma » Bee Balm (Monarda)

Trauma, healing » Arnica (Arnica montana)

Travel » Lechenaultia (Lechenaultia formas), Pink Heath (Epacris impressa), Rose, Prairie (Rosa arkansana), Lucky Hand (Orchis)

Travel, astral » Broom (Genisteae)

Travel, desire to » Stephanotis (Stephanotis floribunda)

Travel, let's » Stephanotis (Stephanotis floribunda)

Travel opportunities » Jade Vine (Strongylodon macrobotrys)

Travel well » Basil (Ocimum basilicum)

Travels, safe » Loveage (Levisticum officinale)

Treachery » Bilberry (Vaccinium myrtillus), Spoonwood (Kalmia latifolia)

Treasure » Achimenes (Achimenes)

Tribute to your beauty and spirituality, a » Lilac, White (Syringa)

Trickery » Clematis (Clematis)

Truce » Kangaroo Paw (Anigozanthos manglesii)

True affection » Cereus (Cereus)

True feelings » Poinsettia (Euphorbia pulcherrima), Fuchsia (Fuchsia magellanica)

True friendship » Geranium, Oak Leaf (Pelargonium quercifolium)

True, I promise to be » Lemon (Citrus limon)

True love » Forget-Me-Not (Myosotis), Teuila (Alpinia purpurata)

True self » Mallow (Malva sylvestris), Ox-Eye Daisy (Leucanthemum vulgare)

True self-awakening » Red Hot Poker (Kniphofia)

True to yourself, be » Aster (Aster)

True voice » Delphinium (Delphinium)

Trust » Royal Bluebell (Wahlenbergia gloriosa), Water Ribbons (Triglochin procerum), Lavender (Lavandula stoechas), Rose, Wild (Rosa acicularis), Freesia (Freesia), Heather, White (Calluna vulgaris), Ithuriel's Spear (Triteleia laxa), Tomato (Solanum lycopersicum), Gentian (Gentiana), Oregon Grape (Mahonia aquifolium), Maltese Centaury (Paleocyanus crassifoleus), Princess Flower Tree (Tibouchina semidecandra)

Trust, encourage » Fennel (Foeniculum vulgare)

Trust in love » Aspen (Populus tremula), Ceibo (Erythrina crista-galli)

Trust, increased » Ithuriel's Spear (Triteleia laxa)

Trust, inner » Motherwort (Leonurus cardiaca)

Trust new opportunities » Trilobed Violet (Viola palmata)

T

Trust personal judgement » Ceibo (Erythrina crista-galli)

Trust me » Fairy Aprons (Utricularia dichotoma), Royal Bluebell (Wahlenbergia gloriosa), Chrysanthemum, White (Chrysanthemum)

Trust, restoration of » Saffron (Crocus sativus)

Trust restored » Baby Blue Eyes (Nemophila menziesii)

Trust, sexual » Purple Pitcher Plant (Sarracenia purpurea)

Trust you, I » Flannel Flower (Actinotus helianthi), Rose, Wild (Rosa acicularis),

Royal Bluebell (Wahlenbergia gloriosa)

Trust you, I do not » Geranium, Scarlet (Pelargonium)

Truth » Antarctic Pearlwort (Colobanthus quitensis), Lily (Lilium), Rose, White (Rosa), Thistle, Scotch (Onopordum acanthium), Oak (Quercus robur), Iris Croatica (Iris perunika)

Truth, inner » Betony (Stachys officinalis)

Truth, personal » Monks' Aster (Aster)

Truth, tell me the » Chrysanthemum, White (Chrysanthemum), Bittersweet (Solanum dulcamara)

Truth-telling » Snapdragon (Antirrhinum majus)

Tryst, I long for a » Pea (Pisum sativum)

Turmoil, reduce » Cedar of Lebanon (Cedrus libani)

U

Ultimate joy » Great Rhododendron (Rhododendron maximum)

Unanimity » Phlox (Phlox)

Uncertainty » Bindweed, Field (Convolvulus arvensis)

Unchanging friendship » Arborvitae (Thuja)

Unchecked ego » Madder (Rubia tinctorum)

Unconditional love » Scottish Primrose (Primula scotica), Straw Flower (Xerochrysum bracteatum), Chicory (Cichorium intybus), Hawkweed (Hieracium)

Unconscious beauty » Rose, Burgundy (Rosa)

Uncrossing » Boneset (Eupatorium perfoliatum), Fennel (Foeniculum vulgare)

Understand, I » Jade Vine (Strongylodon macrobotrys), Sacred Blue Lily (Nymphaea caerulea), Sweet Alyssum (Alyssum maritimum), Poinciana (Delonix regia)

Understanding » Boronia (Boronia ledifolia), Grass Tree (Xanthorrhoea resinosa), Camellia, Japanese (Camellia japonica), Hydrangea (Hydrangea), Calendula (Calendula officinalis), Trout Lily (Erythronium americanum), Beech (Fagus), Yellow Dock (Rumex crispus), Soaproot (Chlorogalum pomeridianum)

Understand, please » Hydrangea (Hydrangea)

Understand you, I » Trout Lily (Erythronium americanum)

Understand dreams » Greater Celandine (Chelidonium majus)

Understanding, human » Artichoke, Globe (Cynara scolymus)

Understanding, self » Self-Heal (Prunella vulgaris)

Understanding unknown » Rocky Mountain Columbine (Aquilegia caerulea)

Undying love » Purple Tulip (Tulipa)

Unfaded feelings » Amaranthus (Amaranth)

Unforgettable, you are » Carnation, Pink (Dianthus caryophyllus)

Unfortunate attachments » Mournful Widow (Scabiosa atropurpurea)

Unfortunate love » Devil's Bit (Succisa pratensis)

Unfeeling, you are » Hydrangea (Hydrangea)

Ungrounded energy » Sweet Pea (Lathyrus odoratus)

Union » Lily (Lilium), Rose, Dark Pink (Rosa)

Union, sacred » Mistletoe (Viscum album), Hawthorn (Crataegus monogyna)

Uniqueness » Orchid (Orchidaceae), Ceibo (Erythrina crista-galli)

Uniqueness, I respect your » Purple Orchid (Cattleya skinneri)

U

United souls » Phlox (Phlox)

Unity » Water Lily (Nymphaea), Honeysuckle (Lonicera), Tiger Lily (Lilium tigrinum), Kantuta (Cantua buxifolia), Pyramidal Orchid (Anacamptis pyramidalis)

Unjust, you are » Gentian (Gentiana)

Unknown, facing the » Angelica (Angelica archangelica)

Unknown, understanding » Rocky Mountain Columbine (Aquilegia caerulea)

Unpretending excellence » Camellia, Red (Camellia), Camellia, White (Camellia)

Unresolved grief » Yerba Santa (Eriodictyon glutinosum)

Unresolved issues, Almond (Prunus amygdalus)

Unrequited love » Daffodil (Narcissus pseudonarcissus), Dogwood (Cornus)

Useful knowledge » Parsley (Petroselinum crispum)

Untie bonds » Rose, Meadow (Rosa blanda)

Uprightness » Pine (Pinus sylvestris)

Uselessness » Diosma (Coleonema)

Utility » Grass (Gramineae)

V

Valour » Iris, Blue Flag (Iris versicolor), Iris, Black (Iris nigricans), Iris, German (Iris germanica)

Value » Achimenes (Achimenes)

Variety » Aster (Aster), Virginia Creeper (Parthenocissus quinquefolia), Rosa Mundi (Rosa)

Very lovely » Rose, Austrian (Rosa)

Victory » Jasmine (Jasminum officinale), Olive (Olea europaea), Laurel (Laurus nobilis), Leek (Allium ampeloprasum)

Victory over temptation » Sweet Chestnut (Castanea sativa)

Victory through adversity » Spurge Laurel (Daphne laureola)

Vigour » Marigold, Mexican (Tagetes evecta), Nasturtium (Tropaeolum majus), Lemon Balm (Melissa officinalis), Elder (Sambucus nigra)

Virginity » Lilac, White (Syringa)

Virility » Celery (Apium graveolens), Geranium (Geranium), Sarsaparilla (Smilax ornata)

Virtue » Mint (Mentha), Sweet Chestnut (Castanea sativa), Basil (Ocimum basilicum), Oak (Quercus robur), Clover (Trifolium)

Virtue, domestic » Sage (Salvia officinalis)

Virtues, dull » Mignonette (Reseda odorata)

Vision » Rue (Ruta graveolens), Greater Celandine (Chelidonium majus)

Vision, clear » Carrot (Daucus carota subsp. sativus)

Vision, psychic » Sallow (Salix cinerea)

Visions » Mugwort (Artemisia vulgaris), Bee Balm (Monarda), Columbine (Aquilegia vulgaris), Rowan (Sorbus aucuparia), Frankincense (Boswellia sacra), Kava-Kava (Piper methysticum), Tobacco (Nicotiana tabacum)

Visual clarity » Ox-Eye Daisy (Leucanthemum vulgare)

Visualisation, creative » Mugwort (Artemisia vulgaris)

Vitality » Marigold (Tagetes evecta), Dahlia (Dahlia), Lilac (Syringa vulgaris), Daffodil (narcissus pseudonarcissus), Nasturtium (Tropaeolum majus), Hippeastrum (Hippeastrum), Avens (Geum), Morning Glory (Ipomoea purpurea), Coltsfoot (Tussilago farfara), Opium Poppy (Papaver somniferum), Pine (Pinus sylvestris), Castor Oil Plant (Ricinus communis), Broom (Genisteae), Rowan (Sorbus aucuparia), Alfalfa (Medicago sativa), Tangerine (Citrus tangerina), Gazania (Gazania), Robina (Pseudoacacia), Rose, Green (Rosa chinensis viridiflora)

Vitality, sexual » Purple Pitcher Plant (Sarracenia purpurea)

Voice, inner » Native Violet (Viola papilionacea), Wake Robin (Trillium pendulum)

Voice is beautiful, your » Oats (Avena sativa)

Voice, new » Delphinium (Delphinium)

V

Voice, strong » Blue Pimpernel (Lysimachia monelli)

Voluptuous love » Moss Rose (Portulaca grandiflora)

W

Wait for me » Lantern Bush (Abutilon halophilum)

Wait, I will » Astilbe (Astilbe), Ageratum (Ageratum), Patience Dock (Rumex patientia)

Waiting, I am » Zephyr Lily (Zephyranthes)

Want you, I » Tulip, Wild (Tulipa sprengeri)

Want you, I only » Quince (Cydonia oblonga)

War » Yarrow (Achillea millefolium), Greek Valerian (Polemonium caeruleum), Tansy, (Tanacetum vulgare)

Ward off evil » Xu Duan (Dipsacus japonica)

Ward off ill-health » Cranes-Bill (Geranium maculatum), Oak (Quercus robur)

Warm feelings » Ginger (Zingiber officinale)

Warming of feelings » Mulberry, Red (Morus rubra)

Warmth » Dandelion (Taraxacum officinale), Cayenne (Capsicum frutescens), Lime (Tilia x europaea), Teuila (Alpinia purpurata), Cactus (Cactaceae), Mesquite (Prosopis), Prickly Pear (Opuntia ficus-indica), Turmeric (Cucurma longa)

Warmth of feeling » Mint (Mentha)

Warmth of sentiment » Spearmint (Mentha spicata)

Warning » Lantern Bush (Abutilon halophilum), Canterbury Bells (Campanula medium), Firethorn (Pyracantha), Begonia (Begonia), Snakesfoot (Rauvolfia serpentina)

Warrior energy » Astilbe (Astilbe)

Wasting time » Blue Pimpernel (Lysimachia monelli)

Watched, we are being » Begonia (Begonia)

Water magic » Cauliflower (Brassica oleracea)

Weakness » Moschatel (Adoxa moschatellina)

Wealth » Peruvian Lily (Alstroemeria), Peony (Paeonia officinalis), Stargazer Lily, Pink (Lilium orientalis), Marsh Marigold (Caltha palustris), Woodbine (Lonicera periclymenum), Mulberry, White (Morus alba), Bamboo (Bambusoideae), Bok Choy (Brassica rapa subsp. chinensis), Cinnamon (Cinnamomum verum), Patchouli (Pogostemon cablin), Hibiscus, Purple (Hibiscus rosa-sinensis), Corn (Zea mays)

Wealth, attract » Chamomile, Roman (Chamaemelum nobile)

Wealth does not always indicate happiness » Auricula (Primula auricular)

Weariness » Blackberry (Rubus fruticosus)

Wedding » Lisianthus (Eustoma grandiflorum)

Wedding anniversary, happy » Peony (Paeonia officinalis)

Wedding blessings » Sweet Bugle (Lycopus virginicus)

Weight loss » Chives (Allium schoenoprasum)

Welcome » Tiare (Gardenia taitensis), Flamingo Flower (Anthurium), Globe Flower (Trollius), Pineapple (Ananas comosus)

Welcome back » Rose, Yellow (Rosa)

Welcome home » Native Geranium (Geranium solanderi)

Well, get » Sunflower (Helianthus annuus), Self-Heal (Prunella vulgaris)

Well-trodden path » Plantain (Plantago major)

Wellbeing » Petra Vine (Petra valubilis), Corn (Zea mays)

Wellbeing, emotional » Wood Betony (Stachys betonica)

Wellness » Self-Heal (Prunella vulgaris)

Wholeness » Shasta Daisy (Leucanthemum maximum), Hydrangea (Hydrangea), Garlic (Allium sativum), Echinacea (Echinacea purpurea)

Wickedness » Blackberry (Rubus fruticosus)

Will, personal » Centaury (Erythraea centaurium)

Will to live » Self-Heal (Prunella vulgaris), Saguaro Cactus Blossom (Carnegiea gigantean), Prairie Crocus (Pulsatilla patens)

Will you begin a relationship with me? » Chrysanthemum, Red (Chrysanthemum)

Will you marry me? » Wedding Bush (Ricinocarpos pinifolius)), Honey Grevillea (Grevillea eriostachya), Rose, Wild (Rosa acicularis), Lisianthus (Eustoma grandiflorum), Blushing Bride (Tillandsia ionantha), Mistletoe (Viscum album), Orange Blossom (Citrus x sinensis), Myrtle (Myrtus), Queen of the Meadow (Filipendula ulmaria)

Will you meet me? » Scarlet Pimpernel (Anagallis arvensis)

Willpower » Scotch Thistle (Onopordum acanthium), Oak (Quercus robur), Wild Yam (Dioscorea villosa)

Win, I will » Columbine (Aquilegia vulgaris)

Win, to » Parsley (Petroselinum crispum)

Winter » Guelder-Rose (Viburnum opulus)

Wisdom » Magnolia (Magnolia campbellii), Sage (Salvia officinalis), Water Lily, Blue (Nymphaea), Hazel (Corylus), Mulberry, White (Morus alba), Iris, Blue Flag (Iris versicolor), Walnut (Juglans regia), Olive (Olea europaea), Lime (Tilia x europaea), Dagger's Log (Agave karatto miller), Yew (Taxus baccata), Chervil (Anthriscus cerefolium), Fir (Abies), Mulberry, Red (Morus rubra), Redwood (Sequoiadendron giganteum), Jacaranda (Jacaranda acutifolia)

Wisdom from experience » Clary Sage (Salvia sclarea)

Wisdom, higher » Iris Croatica (Iris perunika)

Wisdom, increased » Solomon's Seal (Polygonatum)

Wisdom, inner » Rhododendron (Rhododendron), Saguaro Cactus Blossom (Carnegiea gigantean)

Wish is granted, I hope your » Heather, White (Calluna vulgaris)

Wishes » Ginseng (Panax), Guarana (Paullinia cupana), Job's Tears (Coix lacryma-jobi), Lucky Hand (Orchis), Sandalwood (Santalum album)

Wishes are heard, I hope your » Iris, Fairy (Dietes grandiflora)

Wishes granted » Dandelion (Taraxacum officinale)

Wit » Ragged Robin (Lychnis flos-cuculi), Sorrel, Wild (Rumex acetosella)

Witchcraft » Nightshade (Solanaceae)

Witchcraft, protection from » Scarlet Pimpernel (Anagallis arvensis), Laurel (Laurus nobilis)

With you, I want to be » Rose, Dark Pink (Rosa), Petunia (Petunia), Comfrey (Symphytum officinale)

With you, sorry I cannot be » Carnation, Striped (Dianthus caryophyllus)

Withdrawal » Red Hot Poker (Kniphofia), Moving Plant (Mimosa pudica)

Within, answers » Violet, Blue (Viola sororia)

Withholding » Kudzu (Pueraria montana)

Womanhood » Azalea (Rhododendron Tsutsusi), Pride of Barbados (Poinciana pulcherrima)

Woman's love » Carnation, White (Dianthus caryophyllus), Pink (Dianthus plumarius)

Won, you have » Olive (Olea europaea)

Wonderful » Marvel of Peru (Mirabilis jalapa)

Words, skill with » Hazel (Corylus)

Words, sweet » Rose, Briar (Rosa rubiginosa)

Work, happy » Wand Flower (Sparaxis grandiflora)

Work this out, let's » Almond (Prunus amygdalus)

Work, religious » Passion Flower (Passiflora incarnate)

Work, mental » Mace (Myristica fragrans)

Working, hard » Flamingo Flower (Anthurium)

Working with the fae » Iris, Fairy (Dietes grandiflora)

World, the » Pumpkin (Cucurbita pepo)

Worlds, bond between » tabacco (Nicotiana tabacum)

Worry, do not » Loquat (Eriobotrya japonica), Crowea (Crowea exalata), Agrimony (Agrimonia eupatoria)

Worry, ease of » Jonquil (Narcissus jonquilla)

Worship » Champa (Calophyllum)

Worries, inner » Agrimony (Agrimonia eupatoria)

Worth is rare, such » Achimenes (Achimenes)

Worth, modest » Woodruff (Galium odoratum)

Worth, rare » Violet, Yellow (Viola pubescens)

Worth, self- » Venus' Looking Glass (Triodanis perfoliata)

Worthwhile, life is » Freesia (Freesia)

Worthy » Mandevilla (Mandevilla splendens)

Worthy, you are » Allspice (Pimenta dioica)

Y

Yes » Golden Wattle (Acacia pycnantha), Lechenaultia (Lechenaultia formas), Carnation, Red (Dianthus caryophyllus), Geranium, Ivy-Leafed (Pelargonium peltatum), Clubmoss (Lycopodium)

Yin and yang » Aspen (Populus tremula)

You are adorable » Camellia, White (Camellia)

You are always in my memory » Field Poppy (Papaver rhoeas)

You are beautiful » Frangipani (Plumeria alba), Sweet Pea (Lathyrus odoratus), Rose, Red (Rosa), Heather, Lavender (Calluna vulgaris), Apricot (Prunus armeniaca)

You are clever » Clematis (Clematis)

You are cruel » Nettle (Urtica)

You are loved » Sydney Rock Rose (Boronia serrulata), Ginger (Zingiber officinale)

You are not alone » Sydney Rock Rose (Boronia serrulata)

You are magnificent » Bird of Paradise (Strelitzia reginae)

You are my paradise » Bird of Paradise (Strelitzia reginae)

You are perfect » Hibiscus (Hibiscus), Pineapple (Ananas comosus)

You are the only one » Daffodil (Narcissus pseudonarcissus)

You are the flame in my heart » Camellia, Red (Camellia)

You are safe » Queen Anne's Lace (Daucus carota), Evening Primrose (Oenothera)

You are sexy » Orchid (Orchidaceae)

You are supported » Bluebell, Common (Hyacinthoides non-scripta)

You are sweet » Chrysanthemum, White (Chrysanthemum)

You are too rough » Mimosa (Acacia dealbata)

You are unfeeling » Hydrangea (Hydrangea)

You are unforgettable » Carnation, Pink (Dianthus caryophyllus)

You are unjust » Gentian (Gentiana)

You are worthy » Allspice (Pimenta dioica)

You ask too much of me » Marigold (Tagetes evecta)

You belong here » Hibiscus, White (Hibiscus arnottianus)

You bring me joy » Orange Blossom (Citrus x sinensis)

You can do this » Tree Spider Orchid (Dendrobium tetragonum), Amaryllis (Amaryllis), Dahlia (Dahlia), Black-Eyed Susan (Rudbeckia hirta), Vanilla (Vanilla planifolia)

You delight me » Chocolate Flower (Berlandiera lyrata)

You enchant me » Rose, Mauve (Rosa)

You enthral me » Bracken (Pteridium)

You excite me » Orange Banksia (Banksia ashbyi)

You fascinate me » Rose, Orange (Rosa), Honesty (Lunaria annua)

You freeze me » Ice Plant (Carpobrotus edulis)

You have hurt me » Sturt's Desert Pea (Swainsona formosa)

You have won » Olive (Olea europaea)

You inspire me » Siberian Iris (Iris sibirica)

You lie » Nightshade (Solanaceae)

You, longing for » Camellia, Pink (Camellia)

You make me blush » Marjoram (Origanum majorana)

Y

You must let go » Pasqueflower (Pulsatilla vulgaris)

You need to choose » Pyramidal Orchid (Anacamptis pyramidalis)

You please me » Godetia (Clarkia amoena), Heliotrope (Heliotropium)

You possess a queen's majesty » Acacia (Acacia)

You puzzle me » Love-in-a-Mist (Nigella damascena)

You will be my death » Hemlock (Conium maculatum)

Your grace and beauty have charmed me » Cowslip (Primula veris)

Your love is reciprocated » Ambrosia (Ambrosia)

Your love makes me happy » Hepatica (Hepatica)

Your presence revives me » Rosemary (Rosmarinus officinalis)

Your presence softens my pain » Milkvetch (Astragalus)

Your presence soothes me » Petunia (Petunia)

Your qualities surpass your charms » Mignonette (Reseda odorata)

Your voice is beautiful » Oats (Avena sativa)

Youth » Frangipani (Plumeria alba), Foxglove (Digitalis purpurea), Hibiscus (Hibiscus), Primrose (Primula vulgaris), Marguerite Daisy (Argyranthemum frutescens), Lilac, White (Syringa), Hibiscus, Red (Hibiscus rosa-sinensis)

Youth, renewed » Lemon Balm (Melissa officinalis)

Youthful beauty » Tiare (Gardenia taitensis)

Youthful innocence » Lilac, White (Syringa)

Youthfulness » Crocus (Crocus), Cowslip (Primula veris)

Z

Zeal » Lords and Ladies (Arum maculatum)

Zest » Lemon (Citrus limon)

SECTION TWO

FLOWERS

A

Acacia (Acacia) » you possess a queen's majesty, friendships, joy, secret love, platonic love, success

Acanthus (Acanthus mollis) » arts

Aconite (Aconite) » be still, deep inner quiet, psychic skills

Acorn » see Oak

Achimenes (Achimenes) » such worth is rare, value, treasure, appreciate

Adonis » see Pheasant's Eye

African Daisy (Osteospermum) » positive choices, sad memories, pride, playfulness, life path, special talents, joyful humility

African Violet (Saintpaulia) » spirituality, protection, higher learning

Agapanthus (Agapanthus praecox) » love letters, magical love, my love has not faded, never-fading love

Ageratum (Ageratum) » I will wait, thank you, politeness, delay, assistance

Agrimony (Agrimonia eupatoria) » do not worry, inner fears and worries

Air Plant (Tillandsia) » reduce depression, compassion, release

Alder (Alnus) » release, shield, determination, discrimination, inner confidence, royalty, foundation

Allspice (Pimenta dioica) » you are worthy, self-value, self-nurture

Alkanet (Alkanna tinctoria) » prosperity, space cleansing, falsehood, mendacity, let down, disguise

Althea (Hibiscus syriacus) » I am consumed by love, to cure, desire, protection, life force, resoration of intuition, regeneration, joy, anger dissipated, consumed by love

Alfalfa (Medicago sativa) » life, vitality, new ideas

Almond (Prunus amygdalus) » let's work this out, rejuvenation, unresolved issues

Aloalo » see Hibiscus, Native Yellow

Aloe (Aloe vera) » superstition, grief, restoration, renewal, regeneration

Alyssum, Sweet » see Sweet Alyssum

Amaranthus (Amaranth) » I have not stopped loving you, I have not forgotten you, immortality, unfading feelings

Amaryllis (Amaryllis) » you can do this, congratulations, recognition, long-held goals achieved, determination, discovery, positive thinking, splendid beauty, pride

Ambrosia (Ambrosia) » your love is reciprocated, love returned, mutual love, immortality, courage, fairies, elves

American Pasqueflower (Pulsatilla hirsutissima) » newborn, spring, awaken, anxiety

Andromeda (Andromeda polifolia) » self-sacrifice

Anemone (Anemone) » I cannot wait to see you, anticipation, expectation, light-heartedness, joy, optimism, over-enthusiasm

Angelica (Angelica archangelica) » inspiration, spiritual protection, facing the unknown, protection

Angel's Trumpet (Brugmansia candida) » this must end, I know, letting go, spiritual growth, clarity, transition, reintegration, intuition

Angrec (Angraecum) » royalty, rudeness

Antarctic Pearlwort (Colobanthus quitensis) » purity, truth, authenticity, protection, I believe in you

Anthurium » see Flamingo Flower

Apocynum » see Dogbane

Apple Blossom (Malus domestica) » I love you, love, sensuality, fertility, purity of emotions, inner health, self-care

Apricot (Prunus armeniaca) » beauty, you are beautiful, distrust, doubt, spring, good fortune

Arborvitae (Thuja) » live for me, old age, unchanging friendship

Arfaj (Rhanterium epapposum) » adaptability, inner strength, shape-shifting

Arnica (Arnica montana) » get well, recovery, first aid, trauma healing

Artichoke, Globe (Cynara scolymus) » human understanding, release of grief, emotional strength, resolution, closure

A

Artichoke, Jerusalem (Helianthus tuberosus) » confidence, decisive action, self-confidence, stimulation of intellect, mood stabilisation

Arum Lily » see Calla Lily

Ash (Fraxinus) » I place you above all else, protection, expansion, higher perspective, prosperity, power, grandeur

Ash, Mountain » see Rowan

Asclepias » see Milkweed

Asparagus (Asparagus officinalis) » love, lust, prosperity, fertility, male stamina, male fertility

Aspen (Populus tremula) » sensitivity, yin and yang, duality, confidence, divination, attract money, still fears, trust in love, awareness of the divine

Asphodel (Asphodelus) » mourning, my regrets will follow you to the grave, our love will endure after death

Aster (Aster) » be true to yourself, I wish this had not happened, patience, variety, elegance, afterthought, increase in magical powers

Astilbe (Astilbe) » I will wait, I will be ready, warrior energy, balanced aggression, discipline

Auricula (Primula auricular) » pride, wealth does not always indicate happiness, art, creativity

Auricula, Scarlet (Primula auricular) » avarice

Avens (Geum) » distraction, sensuality, vitality

Avens, Mountain » see Mountain Avens

Avocado (Persea americana) » emotional maturity, love

Azalea (Rhododendron Tsutsusi) » take care of yourself, romance, womanhood, temperance, stay true

A

B

Baby Blue Eyes (Nemophila menziesii) » success, prosperity, trust restored, safety, security, open-heartedness

Baby's Breath (Gypsophila paniculata) » be present in this moment, everlasting love, innocence, purity, breathe, love

Bachelor's Buttons » see Cornflower

Balm » see Lemon Balm

Balm of Gilead (Commiphora gileadensis) » healing, cure, relief

Balsam, Himalayan » see Himalayan Balsam

Bamboo (Bambusoideae) » happiness, longevity, wealth

Banana Flower (Musa) » revitalisation, male confidence, masculine energies, sexual potency, expansive thinking, physical confidence

Barberry (Berberis vulgaris) » hot temper, petulance, sharpness, tartness

Basil (Ocimum basilicum) » travel well, open heart, compassion, strengthen faith, spirituality, peace, love, fidelity, virtue, preservation, mourning, courage in difficulties, harmony

Bayberry (Myrica) » encouragement

Bean (Phaseolus vulgaris) » protection, exorcism, reconciliation, potency, love, protection from evil spirits

Bearberry (Arctostaphylos uva-ursi) » awakening, intuition, strengthen psychic abilities, blockage release

Bear's Breech (Acanthus mollis) » past life, old lessons, memory

Bedstraw (Galium verum) » focus, outcomes, paternal love

Bee Balm (Monarda) » guidance, change, compassion, tension, visions, co-dependency, hop, light-heartedness, heartache, trauma, calm transition

Bee Orchid (Ophrys apifera) » error, life path, inspiration, confidence

Beech (Fagus) » grandeur, prosperity, the halcyon days of our love are at hand, learning, knowledge, understanding, preservation

Beet » see Beetroot

Beetroot (Beta vulgaris) » love, blood

Begonia (Begonia) » warning, we are being watched, this must end

Belladonna (Atropa belladonna) » listen to me, be quiet, be still, silence, emotional breakthroughs, negative imbalances shifted

B

Bellflower (Campanula) » constancy, mourning

Bells of Ireland (Moluccella laevis) » may luck be with you always, good luck, inner openness, awareness

Bergamont » see Bee Balm

Betony (Stachys officinalis) » surprise, hidden fears, inner truth, magic

Betony, Wood » see Wood Betony, Herb Christophe

Bilberry (Vaccinium myrtillus) » treachery, life nourishment, security, grounding

Billy Buttons (Pycnosorus globosus) » peace

Billy Goat Plum (Planchonia careya) » open mind

Bindweed, Blue (Convolvulus) » repose

Bindweed, Field (Convolvulus arvensis) » bonds, uncertainty

Bindweed, Great (Convolvulus major) » dangerous situation, extinguish hopes, insinuation, persistence

Bindweed, Small (Convolvulus minor) » humility, obstinacy, night

Birch (Betula) » renewal, protection, build courage, banish fear

Bird of Paradise (Strelitzia reginae) » you are my paradise, you are magnificent, self-acceptance, inner beauty, paradise, royalty, excellence, magnificent

Bird's Foot Trefoil (Lotus corniculatus) » retribution, revenge

Bistort (Polygonum bistorta) » physical support

Bitter Root (Lewisia rediviva) » protection from physical attack, lift mood

Bittersweet (Solanum dulcamara) » tell me the truth, cleansing, protection, platonic love, enchantment, honesty, caution, facts

Blanket Flower (Gaillardia grandiflora) » competence

Blackberry (Rubus fruticosus) » forgive me for my hastiness, death, envy, grief, injustice, pain, remorse, weariness, wickedness

Black Mulberry » see Mulberry, Black

Black Cohosh (Cimicifuga racemosa) » female healing, nerve calmative, depression support, relationship rescue, increase positivity, lift negativity

Black-Eyed Susan (Rudbeckia hirta) » you can do this, encouragement, justice, motivation, impartiality

Black Iris » see Iris, Black

Black Orchid (Trichoglottis brachiata) » power, absolute authority, submission, control, leadership, mastery

Blackthorn (Prunus spinosa) » crone, stabilises emotions, stimulating, hope, joy, dark arts

Bladder-Fucus (Fucus vesiculosus) » protection, money, psychic powers, the sea, dark emotions

Bladder Senna (Colutea arborescens) » fun, frivolous amusements

Bleeding Heart (Lamprocapnos spectabilis) » I want to tell you how I feel, expressing emotions, passionate love, rejection of love, sensitivity, compassion, detachment, breakup healing, letting go

Bloodroot (Sanguinaria canadensis) » I love you, protection, purification, healing, strength, growth, love, new beginning, new life, hope

Blue-Eyed Grass (Sisyrinchium montanum) » male healing, relationship support, emotional release

Blue Gum Flower (Eucalyptus globulus) » healing, get well

Blue Flag Iris » see Iris, Blue Flag

Blue Pimpernel (Lysimachia monelli) » confidence, strong voice, legacy, wasting time, nourishment, self-sustenance, strength

Bluebell, Common (Hyacinthoides non-scripta) » thank you, you are supported, constancy, gratitude

Bluebell, Royal (Wahlenbergia gloriosa) » generosity, trust, integrity, I trust you

Bluebonnet, Texas » see Texas Bluebonnet

Blushing Bride (Tillandsia ionantha) » will you marry me?, I will marry you, my intentions are serious, bashfulness

Bok Choy (Brassica rapa subsp. chinensis) » wealth, good fortune, good luck

Boneset (Eupatorium perfoliatum) » delay, anti-sorcery, exorcism, protection, uncrossing

B

Borage (Borago officinalis) » bluntness, brusqueness, energy, man of courage, you are loved, feeling loved, grounded joyfulness, optimism, courage, safety

Boronia (Boronia ledifolia) » clarity, I understand, understanding

Bottlebrush (Callistemon linearis) » cleansing, balance

Bouvardia (Bouvardia) » I wish you longevity, congratulations, I am happy for you, enthusiasm, long life, cure

Boxwood (Buxus) » stoicism, goodness, manifestation

Bracken (Pteridium) » you enthral me, enchantment, healing, prophetic dreams

Bramble » see Blackberry

Breadfruit (Artocarpus altilis) » creativity, balanced relationships

Briar Rose » see Rose, Briar

Broccoli (Brassica oleracea var. italica) » safety, security, protective boundaries

Brooklime (Veronica beccabunga) » fidelity

Broom (Genisteae) » humility, vitality, orderliness, healing, cleansing, psychic protection, astral travel, ardour, devotion, humility

Brussels Sprout (Brassica oleracea) » bravery

Bryony (Bryonia) » prosperity

Bryony, Black (Dioscorea communis) » be my support

Buckbean (Menyanthes) » calm repose, may sweet sleep attend you, peaceful sleep

Bulrush (Scirpoides holoschoenus) » humility, faithfulness, docility, purification, communication

Burdock (Arctium) » do not touch me, protection, healing, persistence, importunity, core issues, release anger

Bush Fuchsia (Epacris longiflora) » communication

Buttercup (Ranunculus acris) » cheer up, ingratitude, humility, sweetness, inner child, cheerfulness, financial gain

Butterfly Jasmine (Mariposa) » message, purity, rebellion, independence

Butterfly Lily (Hedychium coronarium) » encouragement

Butterfly Orchid (Psychopsis) » gaiety, expanding awareness

Butterfly Weed (Asclepias tuberosa) » let me go, release

C

Cabbage (Brassica oleracea var. capitata) » gain, profit, devotion, enthusiasum boost

Cactus (Cactaceae) » ardour, endurance, I burn, our love shall endure, warmth

Caladium (Caladium) » great joy, delight

Calamus Root (Acorus calamus) » resignation, fitness, good luck, spell strengthener, encourage healing

Calendula (Calendula officinalis) » I release you, I am grateful, I am sorry, cleansing, protection, contentment, excellence, gratitude, love of nature, grief, sacredness, sorrow, understanding, release

California Poppy (Eschscholzia californica) » I dream of you, relax, peace, death, dreams

California Pitcher Plant (Darlingtonia californica) » insight, denial

Calla Lily (Zantedeschia aethiopica) » magnificent beauty, rejuvenation, dignity, self-worth, forgiveness

Camellia, Japanese (Camellia japonica) » my destiny is in your hands, excellence, concentration, peace, calm

Camellia, Pink (Camellia) » longing for you

Camellia, Red (Camellia) » unpretending excellence, you are the flame in my heart

Camellia, White (Camellia) » perfect loveliness, purity, unpretending excellence, you are adorable

Camphor (Cinnamomum camphora) » chastity, fragrance, health, divination

Campion (Silene vulgaris) » poverty

Campion, Red (Silene) » encouragement

Campion Rose (Silene coronaria) » only you deserve my love

Campion, White (Silene) » night

Candle Bush (Cassia alata) » optimisum

Canna (Canna generalis striatus) » playfulness, gratitude

Candytuft (Iberis) » indifference

Cantaloupe » see Rockmelon

Canterbury Bells (Campanula medium) » I have faith in you, thank you, warning, acknowledgement, self-expression, constancy, faith, gratitude

Capsicum (Capsicum annuum) » fidelity, love, breaking hexes

Caraway (Carum carvi) » protection, lust, health, anti-theft, memory, mental strength

Cardamon (Elettario caramomum) » love, lust

Cardinal Flower (Lobelia cardinalis) » distinction

Cardinal Vine (Ipomoea quamoclit) » busybody

Carnation, Pink (Dianthus caryophyllus) » you are unforgettable, motherly love, encouragement, gratitude

Carnation, Red (Dianthus caryophyllus) » love, compassion, romance, be mine, abundance, progression, life-force, yes

Carnation, Striped (Dianthus caryophyllus) » sorry I cannot be with you, no

Carnation, White (Dianthus caryophyllus) » good luck, purity, devotion, lovely, pure affection, ardent love, sweet, woman's love

Carnation, Yellow (Dianthus caryophyllus) » you have disappointed me, rejection

Carrot (Daucus carota subsp. sativus) » organisation, goal setting, creative freedom, clarity, clear vision, fertility

Cashew (Anacardium occidentale) » money, perfume

Castor Oil Plant (Ricinus communis) » vitality, energy, increase activity

Catchfly » see Campion Rose

C

Catnip (Nepeta cataria) » calm hysteria, clarity, focus, female healing

Cat's Tail Grass (Phleum pratense) » emotional balance, calm

Cattle Bush (Trichodesma zelanicum) » persistence, determination, don't give up, stubbornness

Cauliflower (Brassica oleracea) » moon, protection, psychic awareness, water magic, female energies

Cayenne (Capsicum frutescens) » I challenge you, stimulation, warmth, movement, challenges, creative energy, blockage clearer, energy to action

Cedar (Cedrus) » I live for thee, psychic powers, healing, purification, money, protection, encourage love, protection from bad dreams

Cedar of Lebanon (Cedrus libani) » Christianity, incorruptible, reduce turmoil, physical cleansing

Ceibo (Erythrina crista-galli) » heal relationships, trust personal judgement, trust love, embrace challenges, uniqueness

Celandine (Ficaria verna) » future joy, articulation, confidence in communication, confidence in challenges

Celandine, Greater » see Greater Celandine

Celery (Apium graveolens) » vitality, lust, mental powers, psychic powers, concentration, sleep, aphrodisiac

Celosia (Celosia) » I jest, affection, singularity, foolishness

Celtic Bean (Vicia faba celtica) » nourish, fertility, reincarnation, sexuality

Centaury (Erythraea centaurium) » good luck, protection from evil, purification, toxin clearer, sensitivity, personal will, psychic powers

Cerato (Ceratostigma willmottianum) » self-confidence, self-reliance

Cereus (Cereus) » transient beauty, true affection

Chaconia (Warszewlczia coccinea) » continuity, imperishability

Chain of Love (Antigonon leptopus) » togetherness

Chamomile, English » see Chamomile, Roman

Chamomile, German (Matricaria chamomilla) » equilibrium, relax, calm down, release tension, soothing, ease nightmares, energy, patience in adversity, nervous-system support, love, attract love

C

Chamomile, Roman » (Chamaemelum nobile) » I admire your courage, do not despair, austerity in love, patience, abundance, attract wealth, fortitude, calm

Champa (Calophyllum) » sacredness, worship, meditation, spirituality

Chenille Plant (Acalypha hispida) » nurturing

Cherokee Rose » see Rose, Cherokee

Cherry Blossom » see Sakura

Chervil (Anthriscus cerefolium) » sincerity, love, immortality, higher self, wisdom

Chestnut, Sweet » see Sweet Chestnut

Chickweed (Stellaria media) » free expression, clear thinking, happy with self, joy, clear expression, confidence, nuturing

Chicory (Cichorium intybus) » I love you unconditionally, removal of obstacles, invisibility, momentum, release of tension, favours, frigidity, unconditional love

Chilli (Capsicum) » break hexes, ending unwanted friendships, protection, go away

Chinese Lantern (Physalis heterophylla) » overcoming abuse

Chinese Plum (Prunus mume) » endurance, overcoming, intergrity, nobility, hope

Chives (Allium schoenoprasum) » protection from evil spirits, protection of house, weight loss, protection, long life

Chocolate Flower (Berlandiera lyrata) » you delight me, pleasure, enjoyment, complication, energy, light-heartedness, cheerfulness

Christmas Orchid (Cattleya trianae) » confidence, lightness of being, female healing, female confidence

Christmas Plant (Euphorbia) » determination

Chrysanthemum, Bronze (Chrysanthemum) » friendship

Chrysanthemum, Florist's (Chrysanthemum morifolium) » optimism, joy, longevity, cheerfulness

Chrysanthemum, Red (Chrysanthemum) » will you begin a relationship with me?, I love you, love, passion, invitation, proposition

Chrysanthemum, White (Chrysanthemum) » tell me the truth, trust me, I promise, you are sweet, innocence, purity, honesty

Chrysanthemum, Yellow (Chrysanthemum) » I cannot be with you, no, refusal, boundary protection

Cineraria (Cineraria) » delight, ever bright

Cinnamon (Cinnamomum verum) » forgiveness of hurt, clairvoyance, creativity, defense, divination, dreams, healing, love, mediation, psychic development, purification, spirituality, success, wealth, power

Clarkia (Clarkia purpurea) » I am sorry, forgiveness

Clary Sage (Salvia sclarea) » life purpose, wisdom from experience, elation, abilitiy to see, inner perception, meditation, clarity, euphoria, sleep-induction, anxiety relief

Clematis (Clematis) » You are clever, I wish you success in your studies, good luck with your exams, study, concentration, trickery, ingenuity

Cloudberry (Rubus chamaemorus) » reflection, insight, awareness of personal value, life purpose

Clover (Trifolium) » good luck, fertility, domestic virtue, fortune, luck, long and happy marriage, second sight, protection

Clover, Red » see Red Clover

Cloves (Eugenia caryophyllata) » protection, dignity, exorcism, love, money

Clubmoss (Lycopodium) » grounding, self-awareness, yes

Coast Rhododendron (Rhododendron macrophyllum) » limits, joy, expression

Cocklebur (Xanthium) » rudeness

Cockscomb » see Celosia

Coconut (Cocus nucifera) » male sexuality, balanced emotions

Coffee (Coffea arabica) » decisions, clarity, insight

Coltsfoot (Tussilago farfara) » I am concerned for you, maternal love, concern, children, new challenges, vitality, physical stamina, immunity

C

Columbine (Aquilegia vulgaris) » I will win, constancy, dreams, vision, faith, hope, folly, love, resolution to win

Comfrey (Symphytum officinale) » healing, fusion

Cooktown Orchid (Vappodes phalaenopsis) » attitude, answers, changed opinion

Copihue (Lapageria rosea) » happiness, friendship, gratitude, courage, liberty, guardian of love

Coreopsis (Coreopsis grandiflora) » foresight

Coriander (Coriandrum sativum) » personal transformation, spirituality

Corn (Zea mays) » wellbeing, inner peace, wealth

Cornflower (Centaurea cyanus) » knowledge, protection of home, new friends, friendship, new love, new home blessings, delicacy

Cosmos (Cosmos) » no-one could love you more, peace, tranquility, orderly, beauty, love, coherency, communication

Cotton (Gossypium) » obligations, rain, luck, female healing

Cow Parsley (Anthriscus sylvestris) » I need space, elemental energies, faeries, outdoor spaces

Cowslip (Primula veris) » your grace and beauty have charmed me completely, new happiness, charm, divine beauty, happiness, youthfulness

Crab Apple Tree (Malus sylvestris) » love, marriage, fertility, cleansing, purity, self-esteem

Cranberry Heath (Astroloma humifusum) » independent success

Cranes-Bill (Geranium maculatum) » I am available, my interest has changed, constancy, availability, comfort the heart, lift spirits, love, desire to please, protection from evil, wards off ill health

Crepe Myrtle (Lagerstroemia indica) » eloquence, progression, balanced male and female energies

Crowea (Crowea exalata) » possibilities, don't worry, resolution

Crowsfoot (Erodium crinitum) » rebirth, changes, let's start again, begin again

Crocus (Crocus) » time to love again, let go of pain, breath, breathe, glee, mirth, youthfulness, gladness, cheerfulness, protection, calm, peace of mind, support, happiness, let's play

C

Crocus, Prairie » see Prairie Crocus

Crown Vetch (Securigera varia) » I surrender, affection, tenderness, gentle on self, acceptance, devotion, grounding, calm

Cuckoo Flower (Cardamine pratensis) » paternal error, release emotional hurt

Cucumber (Cucumis sativus) » chastity, fertility, healing

Cyclamen (Cyclamen) » resignation, no, goodbye, childhood healing

D

Dancing Lady Orchid (Oncidium) » light heart

Daffodil (Narcissus pseudonarcissus) » the sun shines when I'm with you, you are the only one, I am hoping for you, hope, regard, unrequited love, respect, inspiration, renewal, vitality

Dagger Hakea (Hakea teretifolia) » I am sorry, forgiveness

Dagger's Log (Agave karatto miller) » focus on life goals, maturity, fortitude, strength, rebirth, breakthroughs, wisdom, patience

Dahlia (Dahlia) » you can do this, encouragement, dignity, confidence, vitality, inner strength, creativity, generosity, faith, resiliency, instability

Daisy (Bellis perennis) » let's play, playfulness, protection, happiness, calm, support, peace of mind

Daisy, Florist's » see Chrysanthemum, Florist's

Daisy, Marguerite » see Marguerite Daisy

Daisy, Michaelmas » see Michaelmas Daisy

Daisy, Ox-Eye » see Ox-Eye Daisy

Daisy, Shasta » see Shasta Daisy

Dandelion (Taraxacum officinale) » I am faithful to you, your wish is granted, long-lasting happiness, healing, intelligence, warmth, power, clarity, survival

Daphne (Daphne odora) » I want to please you, sweetness, honesty, love, innocence, happy newborn, joy

Dayflower (Commelina) » attunement

Daylily (Hemerocallis) » forgetfulness, reviving pleasure, coquetry, flirtation, motherhood, loss of memory

Deer Grass (Trichophorum cespitosum) » motives, purity, clarity of purpose, sincerity of motive

Delphinium (Delphinium) » anything is possible, I have new feelings for you, possibility, new opportunity, protection, new feelings, leadership, communication, true voice

Desert Marigold (Baileya) » cheerfulness

Devil's Bit (Succisa pratensis) » unfortunate love

Dew Plant » see Sundew

Dill (Anethum graveolens) » lust, luck, protection from evil, finances

Diosma (Coleonema) » inutility, uselessness

D Dittany (Origanum dictamnus) » birth

Dittany, White (Origanum dictamnus) » passion

Dock (Rumex) » patience

Dog Rose (Rosa canina) » pleasure mixed with pain, positive change, enthusiasm

Dog Violet (Viola riviniana) » first love

Dog's Mercury (Mercurialis perennis) » goodness

Dogbane (Apocynum cannabinum) » deceit, falsehood

Dogwood (Cornus) » I regret what I have done, rebirth, resurrection, Christianity, regret, purity, unrequited love

Downy Hawthorn (Crataegus mollis) » heart healing, emotional care, opening heart

Dutchman's Breeches (Dicentra cucullaria) » I want you to love me, love spells, etheric cleansing, negative-environment clearing, emotional release

E

Easter Lily (Lilium longiflorum) » female alignment, remembrance, hope, life, innocence, purity

Ebony (Diospyros crassiflora) » horror, power

Echinacea (Echinacea purpurea) » higher self, strength, physical strength, immunity, healing, dignity, wholeness, integrity

Edelweiss (Leontopodium alpinum) » dedication, bravery, new direction, life purpose, positive change, education, I am only dedicated to you

Eggplant (Solanum melongena) » money, spirituality, achieving greatness, promotion, smile, happiness, good luck, fertility

Elder (Sambucus nigra) » inner strength, self-esteem, courage, fortitude, calm fears, nurturing, stabilise inner energy, vigour, resilience, joy, recovery, renewal of energy, protection from evil, good luck, release sins, prolong life, peaceful sleep

Elm (Ulmus) » dignity, love, faeries, stability, grounding

Emu Bush (Eremophila duttonii) » partnership, fairness, join me

Endive (Cichorium endivia) » frugality, love, lust

European Sycamore » see Great Maple

Evening Primrose (Oenothera) » you are safe, emotional warmth, female balance, calm, soothing, light in the darkness, insight, transformation, sweet memories, faithlessness, fickleness

Everlasting Daisy (Rhodanthe chlorocephala) » I wish this moment would last forever, endurance, fortitude, independence

Eyebright (Euphrasia officinalis) » I can see you, insight, gladdens the eye, inner vision, see reality, memory, perception, mental clarity, clear perspective

F

Fairies' Fire (Pieris japonica) » mysteriously lovely

Fairy Aprons (Utricularia dichotoma) » guidance, you are in my thoughts, trust me, self-healing

Fairy Fan Flower (Scaevola aemula) » responsibility, self-confidence, you can do this, support, I support you

Fairy Iris » see Iris, Fairy

Fennel (Foeniculum vulgare) » force, praiseworthy, strength, encourage trust, love, purification, repel evil, uncrossing

Fern (Tracheophyta) » invisibility, sincerity, secrecy, secret

Feverfew (Tanacetum parthenium) » good health, calm, healing, purification, flexibility, tenacity, strength

Field Poppy (Papaver rhoeas) » memory, continuance, sacrifice, revelations, you are always in my memory

Fig (Ficus carica) » argument, longevity, prolific, divination, fertility, love

Fir (Abies) » time, elevation, suffering, inspiration, mother and baby blessing, harmony, happiness, peace, wisdom

Firethorn (Pyracantha) » solace in adversity, suppressed emotions, release anger, sex, warning, the devil

Fireweed (Chamerion angustifolium) » earth healing, transformation, change, restoration of self, hope, rebuild

Five Corners (Styphelia laeta) » development, alignment, life purpose, I'm ready to progress

Flame Lily (Gloriosa rothschildiana) » glory, success, exhuberant delight

Flame of the Forest (Butea monosperma) » break through

Flame Tree (Brachychiton acerifolius) » confidence, commitment, inner strength

Flamingo Flower (Anthurium) » hardworking, hospitality, welcome, think of me

Flannel Flower (Actinotus helianthi) » calm, healing, I'm sorry, I want to be closer to you, I trust you

Flax (Linum usitatissimum) » Bbe patient, domestic life, fate, patience grounding

Flor de Maga » see Puerto Rican Hibiscus

Fly Orchid (Ophrys insectifera) » deceit, error, releasing negativity

Fool's Parsley (Aethusa cynapium) » silliness

Forget-Me-Not (Myosotis) » I will not forget you, don't forget me, speak up, true love, memories, remembrance

F

Forsythia (Forsythia) » anticipation, patience, energy, good use of energy, appreciation for life, habit breaker, life force

Four O'Clock » see Marvel of Peru

Foxglove (Digitalis purpurea) » I believe in you, beware, stateliness, communication, insincerity, magic, confidence, creativity, youth

Frankincense (Boswellia sacra) » faithful heart, blessing, consecration, courage, divination, energy, exorcism, psychic development, love, luck, meditation, power, protection, purification, spiritual growth, spirituality, strength, success, visions

Fraxinella (Dictamnus) » ardour, fire

Frangipani (Plumeria alba) » confidence, youth, freedom, you are beautiful

Freesia (Freesia) » I trust you, life is worthwhile, trust, inner guidance, friendship, innocence, optimism, hope, thoughtfulness

Fringed Violet (Thysanotus tuberosus) » restoration, healing

Frog Orchid (Coeloglossum) » disgust, prayers answered

Fuchsia (Fuchsia magellanica) » true feelings, freeing deep emotions, amiability, confiding love, good taste

Fumitory (Fumaria officinalis) » anger, ill at ease, exorcism, money

G

Galangal (Alpinia galangal) » hex breaking, legal matters, luck, lust, protection, psychic development, uncrossing

Gardenia (Gardenia jasminoides) » awareness, secret love, divine message

Garlic (Allium sativum) » good fortune, protection, strength, courage, aphrodisiac, wholeness, immunity, avert envy

Gayfeather (Liatris) » enthusiasum

Gazania (Gazania) » focus, vitality

Gentian (Gentiana) » I have faith, I have faith in you, depression, self-belief, emotional healing, trust, faith, belief in the future, ingratitude

Geranium (Geranium) » I want to meet you, peace of mind, elegance, comfort, I prefer you, I miss you, fertility, love, virility

Geranium, Ivy-Leafed (Pelargonium peltatum) » I choose you, yes, favour

Geranium, Native (Geranium solanderi) » protection, grounding, come home, welcome home, get well

Geranium, Oak Leaf (Pelargonium quercifolium) » true friendship, strong partnership

Geranium, Rose (Pelargonium graveolens) » I will comfort you, calm down, stress relief, comfort, calm

Geranium, Scarlet (Pelargonium) » folly, comforting, consolation, duplicity, I do not trust you, preference, stupidity

German Iris » see Iris, German

G

Germander (Teucrium canadense) » opportunities

Geraldton Wax (Chamelaucium uncinatum) » assertiveness, independence, keep going

Gerbera Daisy (Gerbera jamesonii) » I appreciate you, I wish you happiness, cheerfulness, sudden happiness, love, happy life, celebration

Gerbera Daisy, Orange (Gerbera jamesonii) » clears negative emotions

Gerbera Daisy, Pink (Gerbera jamesonii) » protected heart

Gerbera Daisy, Red (Gerbera jamesonii) » emotional strength

Gerbera Daisy, White (Gerbera jamesonii) » emotional development

Gerbera Daisy, Yellow (Gerbera jamesonii) » emotional clarity

Gilia-Scarlet (Ipomopsis aggregata) » harmony

Gillyflower » see Stock

Ginger (Zingiber officinale) » you are loved, clarity, determination, intelligence, courage, warm feelings, tension relief, sensitivity, perception, sensory awareness

Ginseng (Panax) » love, wishes, beauty, protection, lust, grounding, balance, disconnection, longevity, mental powers

Ginkgo (Ginkgo biloba) » beauty, business, calling spirits, dreams, fertility, longevity, love

Gladiola (Gladiolus) » never give up, strength of character, constancy, faith, boundary setting, creative growth, ego

Globe Artichoke » see Artichoke, Globe

Globe Flower (Trollius) » welcome

Gloxinia (Gloxinia) » I loved you at first sight, proud spirit, beautiful relationships, sense of self, relationship balance

Goat's Rue (Galega officinalis) » reason, healing, health

Godetia (Clarkia amoena) » you please me, pleasing, revealing, tempering, patience, completion, simplicity

Golden Chalice (Solandra nitida zucs) » enlightenment

Golden Shower Tree » see Ratchaphruek

Golden Trumpet Tree (Tabebuia alba) » happiness, opportunity, abundance, exhuberance, optimism

Golden Wattle (Acacia pycnantha) » joy, optimism, the answer is yes

Goldenrod (Solidago virgaurea) » be cautious, good luck, risky venture, encouragement, good fortune

Gooseberry (Ribes uva-crispa) » anticipation

Goosegrass (Galium aparine) » binding, commitment, ensure survival

Goldenseal (Hydrastis canadensis) » healing, money

Gorse (Ulex europaeus) » anger, enduring affection, finances, protection

Gotu Kola (Hydrocotyle asiatica) » self-awareness

Grape (Vitis) » I am devoted to you, independence, freedom, abundance, inner growth, attachment, love, devotion

Grapefruit (Citrus paradisi) » health, purification, clarity

Grass (Gramineae) » submission, utility, protection, psychic powers

Grass Tree (Xanthorrhoea resinosa) » enlightenment, I understand, clarity

Great Maple (Acer pseudoplatanus) » imagination, great energy, personality, creativity, creative thought

Great Rhododendron (Rhododendron maximum) » ultimate joy, beyond limits, prosperity

G

Greater Celandine (Chelidonium majus) » vision, clarity, sharpen sight, information, telepathic communication, understanding dreams

Greek Valerian (Polemonium caeruleum) » war

Grevillea (Grevillea banksii) » creativity, let's work it out

Grey Spider Flower (Grevillea buxifolia) » faith, I believe in you, do not fear, belief, anxiousness, courage

Guarana (Paullinia cupana) » wishes, energy

Guava (Psidium guajava) » cheer up, fantasy, purification, romance

Guelder-Rose (Viburnum opulus) » age, autumn love, good news, winter

Gymea Lily (Doryanthes excelsa) » awareness, consequences, I have noticed you

Gypsophila see Baby's Breath

G

H

Harebell (Campanula rotundifolia) » aspire, grief, resignation, submission, thankfulness

Harvest Brodiaea (Brodiaea elegans) » release bitter feelings

Heartsease (Viola tricolor) » I am thinking of you, peace of mind, merriment, comfort, compassion, self-forgiveness

Hawkweed (Hieracium) » clarity of mind, grounding, decisions, self-sufficiency, day-dreaming, unconditional love, rejuvenation

Hawthorn (Crataegus monogyna) » balance, duality, purification, sacred union, hope, heart protection

Hazel (Corylus) » peace, reconciliation, faerie realm access, wisdom, inspiration, creativity, beauty, fertility, knowledge, skill with words, poetry

Heal-All (Pedicularis canadensis) » good luck, healing, sleep, youth

Heath (Erica) » tranquility, meditation, protection from supernatural energies

Heath Bell (Erica cinerea) » quiet reflection, gentle question, beware, faerie realm entrance, summon the devil, shape-shifting

Heather, Lavender (Calluna vulgaris) » you are beautiful, I admire you, beauty, admiration, peaceful sleep, removal of negative energies, good luck, solitude

Heather, White (Calluna vulgaris) » be brave, confidence, courage, faith, trust, I hope our wish is granted, protection from danger

Heilala » see Red Blossomed Heilala

Heliconia (Heliconia) » I am proud of you, adoration, pride, sunshine, attention seeking, realisation of ideas

Heliotrope (Heliotropium) » I am devoted to you, I am intoxicated with pleasure, you please me, devotion, faithfulness, eternal love, self-forgiveness

Hellebore (Helleborus) » mental healing, insanity cure, protection, invisibility, plant alchemy, banishing, exorcism, increased intelligence

Hemlock (Conium maculatum) » you will be my death, this must end, no, stop, letting go, transition

Hemp (Cannabis sativa) » I want to share my intention with you, fate, clarity, intention, sense of purpose, life purpose

Henbane (Hyoscyamus niger) » let me go, I am leaving, release, rest

Henna (Lawsonia inermis) » healing, luck, joy, beauty

Hens and Chickens (Sempervivum tectorum) » love, luck, protection

Hepatica (Hepatica) » your love makes me happy, confidence, cleansing, channel opening

Herb Christophe » see Wood Betony

Herb Paris (Paris quadrifolia) » betrothal

Hibbertia (Hibbertia pedunculata) » confidence

Hibiscus (Hibiscus) » you are perfect, delicate beauty, youth, fame, joy, happiness, personal glory

Hibiscus, Native Yellow (Hibiscus brackenridgei) » cheerfulness, positive self-image, empowerment

H

Hibiscus, Purple (Hibiscus rosa-sinensis) » wealth, royalty

Hibiscus, Pink (Hibiscus rosa-sinensis) » rare beauty

Hibiscus, Red (Hibiscus rosa-sinensis) » love, desire, passion, youth, beautiful

Hibiscus, White (Hibiscus rosa-sinensis) » enlightenment

Hibiscus, White (Hibiscus arnottianus) » I respect you, you belong here, consideration, female healing, progression, respect, belonging

Hickory (Carya) » legal matters, balance, strength, flexibility, persistence

Hippeastrum (Hippeastrum) » communication, miracle, possibilities, stability, detox, vitality, clarity

Himalayan Blue Poppy (Meconopsis grandis) » potential, possibilities, you make my dreams come true, psychic skills

Holly (Ilex aquifolium) » I wish you peace, good luck, defense, protection, domestic happiness, cheerfulness, homemaking, balance of mind, peace, am I forgiven?, am I forgotten?, resurrection, recovery

Hollyhock (Alcea rosea) » I will succeed, ambition, fruitfulness, joy, optimism, self-assuredness

Hollyhock, White (Alcea rosea) » female ambition

Honesty (Lunaria annua) » you fascinate me, peace, sincerity, honesty, fascination, protection, abundance, prosperity, alchemy

Honey Grevillea (Grevillea eriostachya) » creation, reward, creativity, achievement, will you be my partner?, will you marry me?

Honeysuckle (Lonicera) » be happy, I am devoted to you, happiness, sweet disposition, sweet life, end arguments, homesickness, intimacy, unity

Hop (Humulus lupulus) » apathy, injustice, passion, pride, healing, sleep, mirth

Horehound (Marrubium vulgare) » mental powers, mind clearing, quick thought, fire, frozen kindness

Hornbeam (Carpinus) » ornamentation, immortality

Horse-Chestnut (Aesculus hippocastanum) » learn from your mistakes, habit breaking, aware of present, stop recurrent thoughts

Hound's Tongue (Cynoglossum officinale) » tenacity

H

Hoya (Hoya australis) » alignment, breakthroughs, I am with you, broken promise

Hyacinth (Hyacinthus) » let's play, playfulness, sport, games, rashness, tension relief

Hydrangea (Hydrangea) » you are unfeeling, please understand, perseverance, understanding, interconnectedness, wholeness

Himalayan Balsam (Impatiens glandulifera) » ardent love, I can't wait to see you, impatience

Hyssop (Hyssopus officinalis) » I forgive you, cleanliness, sacrifice, breath, forgiveness, purification, shame, guilt, pardon, repentance

I

Ice Plant (Carpobrotus edulis) » you freeze me, idleness, old flame, rejection, frigidity, eloquence, openness, lighten mood

Icicle Plant (Mesembryanthemum crystallinum) » idleness

Impatiens (Impatiens walleriana) » motherly love, tolerance

Indian Paintbrush (Castilleja miniata) » inspiration, self-expression, new ideas, I see your inner beauty

Indian Pink (Spigelia marilandica) » sexuality

Ipecac (Gillenia stipulata) » emotional balance, calm down

Iris, Black (Iris nigricans) » royalty, creative power, valour, inspirational thoughts, quiet appreciation

Iris, Blue Flag (Iris versicolor) » I believe in you, faith, wisdom, valour, purification, spirit messages, creativity, inspiration, ability to be happy, release blocks, eliminate negative feelings

Iris Croatica (Iris perunika) » change in goals, quick decision, higher wisdom, truth

Iris, Fairy (Dietes grandiflora) » I hope your wishes are heard, I'm sorry you are hurt, discovery, gentle healing, belief in own gifts, working with the fae, new creative opportunities, success with creative ideas, plagiarism, confidences betrayed

Iris, German (Iris germanica) » love, message of love, faith, wisdom, valour

Iris, Siberian (Iris sibirica) » you inspire me, speak up, plagiarism, inspiration, failure to change, discovery, creativity

Ithuriel's Spear (Triteleia laxa) » love of others, comfort, increased trust, self-sufficiency, trust

Ivy (Hedera) » I desire you above all else, nothing will separate us, ambition, bonds, elegance, fidelity, friendship, immortality, marriage, tenacity

Ixora (Ixora coccinea) » positive outlook

J

Jack-in-the-Pulpit (Arisaema triphyllum) » authentic spirituality, service, leadership, spiritual path, life purpose, release love addiction

Jacaranda (Jacaranda acutifolia) » wisdom, luck, love

Jacobinia (Jacobinia) » acceptance

Jade (Crassula ovata) » good luck, I offer you friendship, strong presence, friendship, prosperity, fatigue, new beginning, optimism, energy expansion, focused intention

Jade Vine (Strongylodon macrobotrys) » communication, regeneration, travel opportunities, I understand you

Japanese Cherry » see Sakura

Japanese Toad Lily (Tricyrtis tojen) » freedom

Jasmine (Jasminum officinale) » abundance, victory, congratulations, hope

Jerusalem Artichoke » see Artichoke, Jerusalem

Jerusalem Thorn (Parkinsonia aculeata) » mental expansion

Jessamine, Yellow » see Yellow Jessamine

Job's Tears (Coix lacryma-jobi) » healing, luck, wishes

Jojoba (Simmondsia chinensis) » physical beauty, soothing

Jonquil (Narcissus jonquilla) » returned desire, ease of worry, desire, power, sorrow, death

Juniper (Juniperus) » journey, protection, anti-theft, love, exorcism, health, healing, cleansing, puritying spaces

K

Kava-Kava (Piper methysticum) » visions, protection, psychic development

Kalanchoe (Kalanchoe) » I still love you, endurance, lasting affection, friendship

Kangaroo Paw (Anigozanthos manglesii) » forgiveness, healing, I am sorry, understanding, truce

Kantuta (Cantua buxifolia) » I am sorry, please forgive me, let's start again, unity, hope, forgiveness

Kapok (Bomliax ceilia) » survival

Karee (Rhus pendulina) » love of life, assuredness, decision making, perseverance

Khat (Catha edulis) » life purpose

King Protea (Protea cynaroides) » creativity, courage, illumination, I am here, criticism

King's Mantle (Thunbergia erecta) » energy control

Kinnick-Kinnick (Arctostaphylos ursi) » break connections

Kiwi (Actinidia chinensis) » courage, optimism, gratitude

Kennedia (Kennedia) » mental beauty

Knapweed » see Cornflower

Knotweed (Polygonum aviculare) » binding, health, prosperity

Kowhai (Sophora) » growth, light in the darkness, personal development, brightness

Kudzu (Pueraria montana) » cursing, withholding, overshadowing

Kumquat (Citrus japonica) » luck, prosperity, wealth, better times

K

L

Lady's Mantle (Alchemilla vulgaris) » love attraction, soften rigidity, female healing, feminine strength, protection, solace, release barriers

Lady's Slipper (Cypripedioideae) » calm, sleep, spiritual purpose, energy healing, sexual interest

Lady's Smock » see Cuckoo Flower

Lantana (Lantana camara) » rigour, sharpness

Lantern Bush (Abutilon halophilum) » challenge, delays, wait for me, strength, warning, competition

Larch (Larix decidua) » durability, self-confidence, dissolve negativity, hidden abilities, self-esteem, challenges, exam support, perseverance, immortality, incorruptibility, protection from evil, protection against witchcraft, protection from disease

Larkspur » see Delphinium

Laurel (Laurus nobilis) » I change but in death, I admire you but cannot love you, victory, protection from disease, protection from witchcraft, merit, glory

Laurustinus (Viburnum tinus) » a token, I die if neglected

Lavender (Lavandula stoechas) » cleansing, protection, grace, trust, I admire you

Lechenaultia (Lechenaultia formas) » success, self-belief, luck, yes, celebration, cleansing

Leek (Allium ampeloprasum) » victory, protection

Lemon (Citrus limon) » I promise to be true, discretion, prudence, fidelity in love, cleansing, space cleansing, banish negative thoughts, zest

Lemon Balm (Melissa officinalis) » lift spirits, renewed youth, calm, strengthen mind, restore health, vigour, balance emotions, relax, courage, inner strength

Lemon Mint (Monarda citriodora) » forgiveness

Lemon Myrtle (Backhousia citriodora) » space, travel, safe travel, cleansing, I release you

Lemon Verbena (Aloysia triphylla) » attractiveness, love, protection from nightmares, sweet dreams, marriage, purification

Lemongrass (Cymbopogon citratus) » friendship, lust, psychic awareness, purification, protection from snakes

Lettuce (Lactuca sativa) » chastity, diviniation, cleansing, love, purity, protection, sleep

Lewis Mock Orange (Philadelphus lewisii) » gentleness, nuture, mothering, feminine qualities, deceit

Lilac (Syringa vulgaris) » let go of the past, let's move on, humility, confidence, vitality, chakra alignment, brotherly love, first emotion of love, forsaken memory, space clearing, divination

Lilac, White (Syringa) » a tribute to your beauty and spirituality, innocence, majesty, modesty, purity, virginity, youth, youthful innocence, peace, reincarnation

Lily (Lilium) » I am proud of you, long-lasting relationship, partnership, majesty, truth, honour, pride, mother, maternal, partnership, fertility, union

Lily, Easter » see Easter Lily

Lily of the Valley (Convallaria majalis) » be happy, choose the right path, life purpose, happiness, innocence, purity of heart, physical heart health, humility, chastity, sweetness, luck in love, physical transition, calming

Lily, Prairie » see Prairie Lily

Lily, Sego » see Sego Lily

Lily, Stargazer Pink » see Stargazer Lily, Pink

Lily, Stargazer White » see Stargazer Lily, White

Lily, Tiger » see Tiger Lily

Lime (Tilia x europaea) » grace, restoration, beauty, happiness, conjugal love, sweetness, peace, expansion, learning, wisdom, release emotional blocks, warmth, openness

Lime, Key West (Citrus aurantifolia) » passionate love, healing discussion

Linnaea (Linnaea borealis) » improved relationships, inner conflicts, patience, common ground, sense of self

L

Lint » see Cotton

Liquid Amber (Liquidambar styraciflua) » protection, integrity

Liquorice (Glycyrrhiza glabra) » I declare against you, fidelity, love, lust, revenge

Lisianthus (Eustoma grandiflorum) » will you marry me?, I appreciate you, outgoing nature, appreciation, calming, romantic desire, wedding, gratitude, comfort

Litchi (Litchi chinensis) » problem solving

Live Forever (Dudleya farinosa) » guidance

Liverwort (Marchantiophyta) » confidence

Lobelia (Lobelia inflata) » malevolence, clairvoyance, storms, faeries, love

Lobelia, Blue (Lobelia) » dislike

L Lobelia, White (Lobelia inflata) » rebuff

Lobster Claws » see Heliconia

Locust (Gleditsia triacanthos) » elegance

Locust, Green (Gleditsia triacanthos) » enduring affection

London Pride (Saxifraga x urbium) » fliratation, frivolity

Loquat (Eriobotrya japonica) » do not worry, luck

Lords and Ladies (Arum maculatum) » ardour, my heart is full of passion, zeal

Lotus » see Sacred Lotus

Loosestrife, Purple (Lythrum salicaria) » forgiveness, peace offering, harmony, friendship

Loosestrife, Yellow (Lythrum salicaria) » I am sorry, regret, peace

Love-in-a-Mist (Nigella damascena) » kiss me, you puzzle me, love, perplexity, femininity, emotional clarity, openness to love

Love Lies Bleeding (Amaranthus caudatus) » love lost, broken heart, desertion, hopeless not heartless

Love Seed (Adenanthera pavonina) » friendship, love, togetherness

Loveage (Levisticum officinale) » alleviate, love, attract love, travel safe, new friendships

Luffa (Luffa aegyptiaca) » physical cleansing

Lucky Hand (Orchis) » employment, travel, wishes

Lupin (Lupinus perennis) » creative arts, imagination, awareness, new direction, dejection, over-assertiveness

M

Macadamia (Macadamia integrifolia) » strengthen friendship, release negative patterns, money

Mace (Myristica fragrans) » creativity, divination, intelligence, mental work

Madagascar Jasmine » see Stephanotis

Madder (Rubia tinctorum) » calumny, slander, unchecked ego

Madder, Wild (Galium mollugo) » perseverance, resilience

Madonna Lily (Lilium candidum) » healing, secrets revealed, encouragement, I promise, protection against negativity

Magnolia (Magnolia campbellii) » wisdom, acceptance, strength, female energies, changes, I will always love you

Maguey (Agave americana) » family, fertility, growth

Mahogany (Swietenia macrophylla) » emotional healing, spirituality

Madia (Madia elegans) » perspective

Maize » see Corn

Mallow (Malva sylvestris) » grace, true self

Maltese Centaury (Paleocyanus crassifoleus) » self-determination, trust, progress

Maltese Cross (Lychnis chalcedonica) » religious enthusiasm, spirituality

Mandevilla (Mandevilla splendens) » worthy

Mandrake (Mandragora officinarum) » rarity, horror, activation, catalyst, shape-shifting, magic

Mango (Mangifera indica) » enlightenment, fertility, sex

Mangrove, Freshwater (Barringtonia acutangula) » new opportunities

Manzanita (Arctostaphylos manzanita) » inner feelings

Maple (Acer) » promise, balance, practical magic, love, longevity, abundance, success, generosity, offering, practicality

Marguerite Daisy (Argyranthemum frutescens) » faith, simplicity, loyal love, beauty, gentleness, youth, heart-centred wisdom

Marigold (Tagetes evecta) » vitality, vigour, renewal, life force, magic, irrational expectations, you ask too much of me, honesty, passion, creativity, grief

Marjoram (Origanum majorana) » cleansing, happiness, protection, you make me blush, innocence, modesty

Marsh Marigold (Caltha palustris) » wealth, desire for riches, abundance, connection to earth, grounding, security

Marshmallow (Althea officinalis) » to cure, humanity, dispel evil spirits, attract good spirits, beneficence, mother, maternal energies, protection

Marvel of Peru (Mirabilis jalapa) » I am shy, my love burns for you, timidity, flame of love, wonderful

Masterwort (Peucedanum ostruthium) » courage, strength

Mastic (Pistacia lentiscus) » positive energy, manifestation

Mayflower (Epigaea repens) » transition, change, defense, protection, confidence in decisions

Mburucuya » see Passionflower

Meadow Rose » see Rose, Meadow

Meadow Rue (Thalictrum) » divination, future, ease

Meadow Saffron (Colchicum autumnale) » my best days are over, transcendence, higher consciousness

Meadowsweet (Filipendula ulmaria) » healing, love, divination, peace, happiness, protection from evil, balance, harmony

Melati (Jasminum sambac) » purity, strength, divine hope, simplicity, humility

Melilot (Melilotus officinalis) » I remember, release

Melissa (Melissa officinalis) » friendship, success

Mesquite (Prosopis) » healing, abundance, warmth, compassion

Mercury » see Dog's Mercury

Mexican Orange Blossom (Choisya ternata) » eternal love, fruitfulness, innocence, loveliness, marriage, purity

Mezereum (Daphne mezereum) » coquette, desire to please

Michaelmas Daisy (Aster amellus) » afterthought, happiness/cheerfulness in old age, daintiness, farewell, love, patience

Mignonette (Reseda odorata) » dull virtues, your qualities surpass your charms

Milkmaids (Dentaria californica) » self-esteem

Milkweed (Asclepias) » heartache cure

Milkvetch (Astragalus) » your presence softens my pain

Milkwort (Polygala vulgaris) » hermitage

Mimosa (Acacia dealbata) » you are too rough, sensitive love, politeness, courtesy, manners

Mint (Mentha) » warmth of feeling, protection from illness, virtue, strength for challenges

Mistletoe (Viscum album) » kiss me, will you marry me?, divine union, love bond, marriage, affection, overcoming difficulties, magic, all heal, romance, major change, transformation

Mock Orange (Philadelphus) » I remember, recollection, gentleness, new ideas, nurturing, feminine qualities, counterfeit, deceit

Money Plant (Lunaria annua) » ability

Moneywort (Bacopa monnieri) » release, fidelity

Monkey Flower (Mimulus guttatus) » confidence, personal power

Monk's Aster (Aster) » personal truth

Monkshood (Aconitum) » divine communication, dreams, chivalry, misanthropy, knight-errantry, protection, invisibility, judgement, fearlessness, clairvoyance

Moon Orchid (Phalaenopsis amabilis) » I desire you, attraction, sexuality, charisma

Moonflower » see Queen of the Night

Moonwort » see Honesty

M

Moschatel (Adoxa moschatellina) » insignificance, weakness

Moss Rose (Portulaca grandiflora) » ecstasy, shy love, voluptuous love

Morning Glory (Ipomoea purpurea) » habit breaking, consistency, mortality, love in vain, affection, enthusiasum, vitality, love

Moth Orchid (Phalaenopsis) » communication

Motherwort (Leonurus cardiaca) » concealed love, female healing, inner trust, spiritual healing, astral projection, immortality, longevity, relationship balance, mothering issues, sedation, calm anxiety

Mountain Ash » see Rowan

Mountain Devil (Lambertia formosa) » happiness, forgiveness

Mountain Laurel (Kalmia latifolia) » protection, guidance, support, clarity when challenged

Mountain Pride (Penstemon newberryi) » acceptance

Mournful Widow (Scabiosa atropurpurea) » I have lost all, lucklessness, unfortunate attachments

Moving Plant (Mimosa pudica) » agitation, I am shy, withdrawal

Mugwort (Artemisia vulgaris) » prophecy, protection, strength, psychic abilities, prophetic dreams, healing, astral projection, awkwardness, creative visualisation, visions, clairvoyance, divination

Mountain Avens (Dryas octopetala) » self-confidence, release of fear, belief in self

Mulberry, Black (Morus nigra) » I will not survive you, sadness, protection, strength, release of emotions

Mulberry, Red (Morus rubra) » wisdom, warming of feelings

Mulberry, White (Morus alba) » wisdom, study, earth-to-heaven connection, wealth, defeat

Mulla Mulla » (Ptilotus exaltatus) » recovery, move on, new beginning

Mullein (Verbascum thapsus) » stay strong, I wish you success, courage, protection, protection from curses, protection from negative spirits, comfort, take courage

Mullein, White (Verbascum thapsus) » friendship, good nature

Mums » see Chrysanthemum, Florist's

Musk Rose » see Rose, Musk

Musk Thistle (Carduus nutans) » over-adornment

Mustard (Sinapis arvensis) » depression recovery, protection from evil spirits, fertility, transform darkness, inner stability, joy, peace, indifference

Myrtle (Myrtus) » love, marriage, immortality, will you marry me?

N

Naked Lady (Lycoris squamigera) » self-forgiveness

Narcissus, Poet's » see Poet's Narcissus

Nasturtium (Tropaeolum majus) » I believe you can succeed, I support you, let's have fun, creative freedom, vitality, fun challenges, independence, over-thinking, jest

Native Geranium (Geranium solanderi) » protection, grounding, come home, welcome home, get well

Native Passionflower (Passiflora herbertiana) » love, adaptation, breaking negative patterns, balanced emotions

Native Violet (Viola papilionacea) » independence, inner voice, self-reliance

Native Wood Violet (Viola odorata) » independence, intuition development, shield from interference

Neoporteria Cactus (Neoporteria paucicostata) » motivation

Nettle (Urtica) » you are cruel, you are spiteful, cruelty, pain, slander, clear choices, decision making, protection against evil spirits, health recovery

Nigella » see Love-in-a-Mist

Nightshade (Solanaceae) » you lie, enchantment, witchcraft, sorcery, scepticism, no, falsehood, dark thoughts

Nightshade, Deadly » see Belladonna

Noble Star Cactus (Stapelia nobilis) » compassion, service

O

Oak (Quercus robur) » strength, pride, steadfastness, great achievement, durability, courage, protection, truth, masculine strength, steadfastness in faith, virtue, protection from lightning, ward off ill health, immortality, heritage, endurance, willpower, devotion to duty, high ideals, fulfillment of commitments

Oats (Avena sativa) » your voice is beautiful, fertility

Okra (Abelmoschus esculentus) » protection from negative energy, magical powers awakened, curse breaking, release fear

Old Maid (Catharanthus roseus) » connection

Old Man Banksia (Banksia serrata) » life, enthusiasm, I am interested

Oleander (Nerium oleander) » caution, respect, calculated risks, lust, notice me

Olive (Olea europaea) » congratulations, you have won, peace, purity, harmony, goodwill, life, hope, inner strength, joy, wisdom, victory

Onion (Allium cepa) » protection, purification, detox, hibernationg energy, potential

Opium Poppy (Papaver somniferum) » I would die for you, beauty, magic, pleasure, loyalty, vitality, rememberance, heartbreak healing, fertility

Opoponax (Commiphora erythraea) » acquiring knowledge, I know, intuition, secrets revealed, necromancy

Orange Banksia (Banksia ashbyi) » enthusiasm, education, learning, you excite me

Orange Blossom (Citrus x sinensis) » will you marry me?, I will love you forever, you bring me joy, innocence, eternal love, marriage, fruitfulness, fertility, excitement, enthusiasm

Oregano (Origanum vulgare) » joy, happiness, honour

Orchid (Orchidaceae) » you are sexy, love yourself, uniqueness, sensuality, rare beauty, refinement, enchantment, grace, sex, self-love, self-assured

Orchid, Bee » see Bee Orchid

Orchid, Butterfly » see Butterfly Orchid

Orchid, Christmas » see Christmas Orchid

Orchid, Fly » see Fly Orchid

Orchid, Frog » see Frog Orchid

Orchid, Moon » see Moon Orchid

Orchid, Moth » see Moth Orchid

Orchid, Purple » see Purple Orchid

Orchid, Spider » see Spider Orchid

Orchid, Tropicbird Orchid » Tropicbird Orchid

Orchid, White Nun » see White Nun Orchid

Oregon Grape (Mahonia aquifolium) » cleansing, self-love, acceptance, trust, goodwill

Osier (Salix viminalis) » frankness

Osmanthus (Osmanthus fragrans) » happiness, inspiration, life energy, preservation of beauty, rejuvenation, stress relief

Owl's Clover (Orthocarpus purpurascense) » artistic expression

Ox-Eye Daisy (Leucanthemum vulgare) » obstacle, patience, true self, visual clarity

P

Pagoda Flower (Clerodendrum speciosissimum) » relationship security

Pansy (Viola tricolor var. hortensis) » I am thinking of our love, love in idleness, remembrance, immunity, loving thoughts

Parsley (Petroselinum crispum) » entertainment, fest, protection of food, festivity, to win, useful knowledge

Pansy, Wild » see Wild Pansy

Papaya (Carica papaya) » love, protection, contentment

Paper Daisy » see Everlasting Daisy or Straw Flower

Parosela (Dalea) » to seek

Passion Flower (Passiflora incarnate) » I am pledged to another, belief, passion, religious superstition, religious work, stability, spiritual balance, higher consciousness

Passionflower, Native (Passiflora herbertiana) » love, adaptation, breaking negative patterns, balanced emotions

Passionfruit (Passiflora edulis) » friendship, love, peace, purity

Pasqueflower (Pulsatilla vulgaris) » you must let go, calm down, you have no claims, scattered thoughts, relaxation, balanced energy, calming

Patchouli (Pogostemon cablin) » defense, fertility, releasing, love, wealth, sexual power

Patience Dock (Rumex patientia) » patience, I will wait

Paw Paw (Asimina triloba) » new ideas, learning

Pea (Pisum sativum) » meeting, I long for a tryst, lasting pleasure, money

Peach Blossom (Prunus persica) » romantic partnership, altruism, release of tensions, immortality, longevity, prosperity, luck, romance

Peanut (Arachishypogaea)»aggressiveenergy,beauty,promises,maleenergy, birth, prosperity, grounding

Pear (Pyrus communis) » affection, comfort, faeries, love, lust

Pelargonium (Pelargonium cucullatum) » I am ready, eagerness, overwork, acquaintance

Pennyroyal (Mentha pulegium) » run away, leave me quickly, stand firm, fight or flight

Penstemon (Penstemon x mexicali) » spirituality

Pentas (Pentas lanceolata) » awareness

Peony (Paeonia officinalis) » I wish you a happy marriage, happy wedding anniversary, wealth, honour, good health, prosperity, romance, compassion, shame, female fertility, nobility

Pepper (Piper nigrum) » strengthen energy, satire, purification, healing, protection

Peppermint (Mentha piperita) » friendship, love, clarity, refreshment, concentration, clear thinking, inspiration, energy, alert mind, study support

Periwinkle (Vinca minor) » my heart was mine until we met, first love, new friendship, sweet memories, possession cure, immortality

Persicaria (Persicaria lapathifolia) » restoration

Persimmon (Diospyros virginiana) » surround me in natural beauty, changing sex, healing, transformation, enlightenment

Peruvian Lily (Alstroemeria) » I wish you success, I am devoted to you, I am your friend, strength, wealth, good fortune, abundance, prosperity, friendship, devotion

Peyote (Lophophora williamsii) » visions, life, sustenance, health, success, good luck, shamanic powers

Pasqueflower, American » see American Pasqueflower

Petra Vine (Petra valubilis) » wellbeing

Petunia (Petunia) » your presence soothes me, I want to be with you, do not give up hope, protection, anger, resentment, enthusiasm, clarity, priorities

Pheasant's Eye (Adonis vernalis) » painful memories, sorrowful remembrance

Phlox (Phlox) » agreement, I think we could be friends, united souls, unanimity

Phlox, Pink (Phlox) » friendship

Phlox, White (Phlox) » interest

Pine (Pinus sylvestris) » self-forgiveness, faithfulness, constancy in adversity, courage, pity, immortality, mourning, uprightness, strength of character, earth-to-heaven connection, longevity, vitality, happy old age

Pine Drops (Pterospora andromedea) » clear perspective

Pine, White » see White Pine

Pineapple (Ananas comosus) » you are perfect, welcome, chastity, luck

Pink (Dianthus plumarius) » always lovely, boldness, lasting beauty, perfection, woman's love

Pink, Clove-Scented (Dianthus caryophyllus) » dignity, how sweet you are

Pink, Variegated (Dianthus plumarius) » refusal

Pink Heath (Epacris impressa) » direction, goal setting, focus, travel, I need an answer

P

Pink Knotweed (Persicaria capitata) » stand tall, confidence, spatial awareness

Pink Poui (Tabebuia pentaphylla) » delight

Pistachio (Pistacia vera) » promiscuity

Pitcher Plant, California » see California Pitcher Plant

Pitcher Plant, Purple » see Purple Pitcher Plant

Plane Tree (Platanus) » genius, magnificence, shelter

Plantain (Plantago major) » well-trodden path, life path, strength

Plum (Prunus domestica) » keep your promise, I do not care, fidelity, independence, promise, indifference

Plum, Chinese » see Chinese Plum

Poinciana (Delonix regia) » I understand, sacrifice, empathy

Poinsettia (Euphorbia pulcherrima) » appreciation, thank you, true feelings

Poison Ivy (Rhus toxicodendron) » strength

Poet's Narcissus (Narcissus poeticus) » confidence, hope, self-love, conceit, I have confidence in you

Pohutukawa (Metrosideros excelsa) » strength, inner strength, transformation, I am staying with you

Poke Weed (Phytolacca americana) » end of sadness

Pomegranate Blossom (Punica granatum) » prosperity, ambition, grace, mature elegance, perfection

Poppy » see Field Poppy

Pot of Gold (Winteria aureispina) » coming together

Potato (Solanum tuberosum) » benevolence

Puerto Rican Hibiscus (Thespesia grandiflora) » I love your beauty, self-confidence, passion in love

Prairie Crocus (Pulsatilla patens) » balance emotions, endurance, will to live, releasing emotional drama

Prairie Lily (Lilium philadelphicum) » summer, happiness, strength, return of joy

Prairie Rose » see Rose, Prairie

Prayer Plant (Maranta leuconeura) » intuition

Prickly Pear (Opuntia ficus-indica) » satire, chastity, endurance, inspiration, warmth

Pride of Barbados (Poinciana pulcherrima) » female healing, sisterhood, womanhood, joyful encouragement, exuberance, pride, flamboyance

Pride of China (Koelreuteria bipinnata) » dissension

Primrose (Primula vulgaris) » patience, kindness, gentleness, belonging, nurturing, courage, peaceful sleep, bashfulness, youth, first love, stages of life, flow, opening, cleansing, lightening

Primrose, Evening » see Evening Primrose

Primula » see Primrose

Princess Flower Tree (Tibouchina semidecandra) » trust, ascension

Privet (Ligustrum vulgare) » defense, mildness, prohibition

Psyllium (Plantago ovata) » enhancement, strength

Pumpkin (Cucurbita pepo) » to increase, bulkiness, moon, the world, abundance

Purple Orchid (Cattleya skinneri) » I respect your uniqueness, strengthen desire, find new paths, royalty, respect, admiration

Purple Pitcher Plant (Sarracenia purpurea) » female healing, female protection, sexual vitality, sexual trust

Purple Saxifrage (Saxifraga oppositifolia) » birth, beginning, relief, hardiness, clear personal energies

Purslane (Portulaca oleracea) » dreams, happiness, psychic development, intimacy, expanded horizons

Pussytoes (Antennaria) » I will never forget you, soul purpose, commitment, deepen relationships, devotion, overlooked

Puti Tai Nobiu (Bougainvillea spectabilis) » it hurts not to have a sweetheart, hidden protection, grace, beauty, release of hurt

Pyramidal Orchid (Anacamptis pyramidalis) » unity, legacy, you need to choose

Pyrethrum (Anacyclus pyrethrum) » bravery

P

Q

Queen Anne's Lace (Daucus carota) » you are safe, protection, sanctuary, awareness, female energies

Queen of the Meadow (Filipendula ulmaria) » bride blessing, will you marry me?, properity, happiness

Queen of the Night (Selenicereus grandiflorus) » power, intuition, dreams, I dream of you

Queen's Rocket (Hesperis matronalis) » fashionable, you are the Queen of coquettes

Quince (Cydonia oblonga) » I cannot resist you, I only want you, temptation, enticement, strength in love, balance of male and female energies

Quinoa (Chenopodium quinoa) » balance, compassion

R

Rabbit Bush (Chrysothamnus nauseosus) » discipline

Radish (Raphanus sativus) » love, positive change, fringe benefits

Ragweed » see Ambrosia

Ragwort (Jacobaea vulgaris) » free thoughts, resilience

Ragged Robin (Lychnis flos-cuculi) » wit

Ranunculus (Ranunculus) » I hold you close to my heart, romantic rendezvous, charm, attractiveness, everlasting love, commitment, meaningful secret

Rabbit Orchid (Leptoceras menziesii) » abundance, improvement, career, fertility, congratulations on birth of baby, new job

Rafflesia (Rafflesia arnoldii) » consciousness, reconnection, answered questions, progression

Raspberry (Rubus idaeus) » compassion, generosity, envy, remorse

Ratchaphruek (Cassia fistula) » pray, protection from disease, royalty

Red Blossomed Heilala (Garcinia sessilis) » reverence, high-ranking, honour

Red Bud (Cercis siliquastrum) » lift spirits

Red Clover (Trifolium pratense) » good fortune, good luck, fertility, domestic virtue, protection from danger, psychic protection, cleansing, clear negativity, balance, calmness, clarity, enhance self-awareness

Red Dock (Rumex sanguineus) » fertility, money

Red Hot Poker (Kniphofia) » new habits, end self-sabotage, attitude, abuse, withdrawal, true self-awakening, death

Red Whortleberry (Vaccinium) » I happily await your return, patience, anticipation

Redbay (Persea borbonia) » love's memory

Redwood (Sequoiadendron giganteum) » inspiration, mystical powers, revelation, balance, wisdom, independence, communication

Rhododendron (Rhododendron) » heart healer, beware of excess, consolation, limits, danger, self-insight, shadow self, inner wisdom

Rhododendron, Coast » see Coast Rhododendron

Rhododendron, Great » see Great Rhododendron

Rhubarb (Rheum rhabarbarum) » fidelity, advice

Robina (Pseudoacacia) » vitality

Rock Rose (Helianthemum) » first aid, courage, extended potential, mental calmative

Rocky Mountain Columbine (Aquilegia caerulea) » pride, peace, folly, mental peace, understanding unknown, learning

Rocket (Eruca sativa) » deceit, rivalry

Rockmelon (Cucumis melo) » calm, joyful living

Rosa Mundi (Rosa) » variety

Rose, Austrian (Rosa) » very lovely

Rose, Beach (Rosa rugosa) » beauty, beauty is your only attraction

Rose, Briar (Rosa rubiginosa) » simplicity, poetry, sweet words, divine love

Rose, Bridal (Rosa) » happy love

R

Rose, Burgundy (Rosa) » simplicity, unconscious beauty, pensive beauty

Rose, Cabbage (Rosa x centifolia) » ambassador of love

Rose, Campion » see Campion Rose

Rose, Carolina (Rosa carolina) » love is dangerous

Rose, Cecil Brunner (Rosa Mlle. Cecile Brunner) » boundaries, security, goals, achievement, realistic goals

Rose, Cherokee (Rosa laevigata) » female strength, hope, pray, pain, suffering, female healing, adaptability, healing ability

Rose, China (Rosa chinensis) » beauty always new, departure, everlasting loveliness, transient brilliance

Rose, Dark Pink (Rosa) » thank you, I am grateful, gratitude, appreciation, I agree with you, I want to be with you

R

Rose, Damask (Rosa x damascena) » beauty ever new, beautiful complexion

Rose, Deep Red (Rosa) » bashful love

Rose, Dog » see Dog Rose

Rose, Green (Rosa chinensis viridiflora) » vitality

Rose, Lavender (Rosa) » our love is pure, purity of heart

Rose, Maiden's Blush (Rosa) » if you love me you will find it out

Rose, Mauve (Rosa) » you enchant me, I loved you at first sight, love at first sight, enchantment, magic

Rose, May (Rosa) » precocity

Rose, Meadow (Rosa blanda) » release energies, untie bonds, release

Rose, Miniature (Rosa) » childhood memories, begin again

Rose, Moss » see Moss Rose

Rose, Musk (Rosa moschata) » let's stop fighting, I am sorry, improved relationships, compassion, higher self, resolution

Rose of Jerico (Anastatica hierochuntica) » resurrection, protection, repels negativity

Rose of Sharon » see Althea

Rose, Orange (Rosa) » you fascinate me, enthusiasm, happiness, fascination

Rose, Pale Pink (Rosa) » I am sorry, get well, healing, grace

Rose, Peach (Rosa) » I appreciate you, I am sincere, I agree with you, I want to be with you, union, deal, appreciation, agreement, sincerity

Rose, Pink (Rosa) » chaste love, friendship

Rose, Prairie (Rosa arkansana) » transform emotions, development, growth, awareness, new journey, travel, new growth

Rose, Provence » see Rose, Cabbage

Rose, Pompon (Rosa) » pretty, genteel

Rose, Red (Rosa) » I love you, I respect you, you are beautiful, respect, love, courage, passion, lust, relationship, beauty

Rose, White (Rosa) » I am telling the truth, I will protect you, protection, purity, honesty, truth

Rose, Yellow (Rosa) » I am your friend, can we be friends?, I am falling in love with you, falling in love, welcome back, come back to me, I will return, friendship, new beginning

Rose, Wild (Rosa acicularis) » I trust you, will you marry me?, new path, trust, promises, contracts, betrayal

Rosebay Willowherb (Chamerion angustifolium) » celibacy, pretension

Rosemary (Rosmarinus officinalis) » I remember you, your presence revives me, psychic awareness, mental strength, accuracy, clarity, remembrance, memory

Rosella Flower (Hibiscus heterophyllus) » strength, opportunity, energy boost, I am ready

Rosewood (Pterocarpus indicus) » compassion, spirituality, feminine grace, nourishing, beauty, intuitive healing

Rowan (Sorbus aucuparia) » protection from evil, magical protection, protection from enchantment, visions, protection, vitality, spiritual strength, reawakening, psychic intuition, power, healing

Royal Bluebell (Wahlenbergia gloriosa) » generosity, trust, integrity, I trust you

Rue (Ruta graveolens) » vision, spiritual protection, energy protection, repentance, disdain, higher self

Rush (Juncaceae) » docility, meekness

R

S

Sacred Blue Lily (Nymphaea caerulea) » rebirth, sacredness, consciousness, victory, second chance, disconnection, I understand you

Sacred Lotus (Nelumbo nucifera) » detachment, spiritual growth, stand strong, think again

Safflower (Carthamus tinctorius) » do not abuse, care

Saffron (Crocus sativus) » strength, restoration of trust

Sainfoin (Onobrychis) » agitation

Saint Barnaby's Thistle (Centaurea solstitialis) » resistance, self-defense

Saint John's Wort (Hypericum perforatum) » protection, fertility, animosity, superstition, longevity, protection of home, protection from illness, calm, reduced fear, removal of evil spirits, removal of negativity

Sakura (Prunus serrulata) » peace, harmony, return to me

Sage (Salvia officinalis) » purification, longevity, good health, long life, wisdom, cleansing, protection, higher purpose, reflection, inner peace, esteem, domestic virtue

Sagebrush (Artemisia tridentate) » cleansing, purification, protection, psychic protection, protection from evil, personal evolution

Saguaro Cactus Blossom (Carnegiea gigantean) » will to live, inner wisdom, compassion, endurance, self-empowerment

Sallow (Salix cinerea) » flexibility, psychic vision, intuition

Sand Lily (Leucocrinum montanum) » persistence

Sandalwood (Santalum album) » clear negativity, mental focus, reincarnation, wishes

Sassafras (Sassafras variifolium) » personal success

Sarsaparilla (Smilax ornata) » virility

Sarsaparilla, Wild (Aralia nudicaulis) » perseverance, endurance, flexibility

Satin Flower (Olsynium douglasii) » sincerity

Savory (Satureja hortensis) » mental powers

Saxifrage, Purple » see Purple Saxifrage

Scabiosa (Scabiosa) » admiration, origins, mourning, new possibilities, gentle healing

Scammony (Convolvulus scammonia) » revenge

Scarlet Fritillary (Fritillaria recurva) » movement

Scarlet Pimpernel (Anagallis arvensis) » will you meet me?, faithfulness, rendezvous, change, laughter, mirth, childhood, protection from witchcraft

Scleranthus (Scleranthus annus) » decide

Scotch Thistle » see Thistle, Scotch

Scotch Thistle (Onopordum acanthium) » retaliation, inner strength, willpower, command, positive action

Scots Pine (Pinus syvestris) » immortality, divine light, fertility

Scottish Primrose (Primula scotica) » I love you completely, I'm sorry, compassion, acceptance, anxiety, forgiveness, unconditional love, patience

Sea Holly (Eryngium maritimum) » austerity, independence, sternness

Sego Lily (Calochortus nuttallii) » I am receptive, cosmic connection, feminine aspects, sensitivity, soul, nuture

Self-Heal (Prunella vulgaris) » get well, healing, will to live, immune system strength, understanding self, wellness, motivation, independence

Service Tree (Sorbus) » prudence, from bad to good

Sesame (Sesamum indicum) » lust, abundance

Shallot (Allium cepa var. aggregatum) » end misfortune

Shamrock (Trifolium dubium) » fairies, elves, luck, success

Shasta Daisy (Leucanthemum maximum) » be happy, can we be friends?, cheerfulness, integration, friendship, stability, innocence, sympathy, wholeness, happiness, modesty

Sheep Sorrel (Rumex acetosella) » banish ill will

Shepherd's Purse (Capsella bursa-pastoris) » I offer you my all, centered, grounding

Shooting Star (Dodecatheon meadia) » consciousness

S

Showy Lady Slipper (Cypripedium reginae) » spiritual purpose, soothe, emotional balance, release tension, service

Shrimp Plant (Justicia) » perfection of female loveliness

Siberian Iris » see Iris, Siberian

Silversword (Argyroxiphium sandwicense) » spiritual knowledge

Skullcap (Scutellaria) » relaxation, psychic healing, relaxation of nerves, self-esteem, ability to cope

Skunk Cabbage (Symplocarpus foetidus) » let me go, relrease, clear stagnant energy, attitude adjustment, light in the dark

Sky Vine (Thunbergia alata) » creativity, stability

Slippery Elm (Ulmus rubra) » stop gossip

Snakesfoot (Rauvolfia serpentina) » horror, warning

Snake's Tongue (Sansevieria) » slander

Snapdragon (Antirrhinum majus) » I'm sorry for what I did, grace under pressure, inner strength, expression of emotions, increased perception, spell breaker, deviousness, grace

Snowdrop (Galanthus nivalis) » I am here for you, hope, new beginnings, illumination, self-neglect, inner peace, renewal, solutions

Snowplant (Sarcodes sanquinea) » change

Solomon's Seal (Polygonatum) » banishing unwanted spirits, disdain, heal wounds, difficult decisions, accepting change, summon spirits, increase wisdom, protection

Soaproot (Chlorogalum pomeridianum) » understanding

Sorrel (Rumex acetosa) » paternal affection, affection

Sorrel, Wild (Rumex acetosella) » wit, ill-timed

Southern Cross (Xanthosia rotundifolia) » influence, responsibility

Southernwood (Artemisia abrotanum) » constancy, bantering, jest

Soy Bean (Glycine max) » good luck, banish evil spirits, protection

Spanish Moss (Tillandsia usneoides) » business, clearing, luck

Spearmint (Mentha spicata) » warmth of sentiment

S

Speedwell (Veronica officinalis) » do not forget me, I remain faithful, fidelity, thrive, honour, insight, slow down, intuition, calming

Spider Flower (Cleome) » elope with me, creativity

Spider Orchid (Caladenia) » adroitness, skill

Spiderwort (Tradescantia) » esteem but not love, transient happiness

Spikenard (Aralia racemosa) » lessons

Spinach (Spinacia oleracea) » fortitude, health, strength, prosperity

Spindle (Euonymus) » charming

Spirulina (Arthrospira) » fertility, detox, male strength

Spoonwood (Kalmia latifolia) » treachery

Spring Beauty (Claytonia virginica) » shifting energy

Spring Onion (Allium fistulosum) » loyal protection

Spruce (Picea) » boldness, fidelity, farewell, pity

S

Spurge Laurel (Daphne laureola) » victory through adversity, beginning, first

Stamonium (Datura stramonium) » disguise

Star Anise (Illicium verum) » consecration, psychic powers, calm

Star of Bethlehem (Ornithogalum) » I forgive you, self forgiveness, innocence, purity, honesty, hope, forgiveness, self-belief, blockages cleared

Stargazer Lily, Pink (Lilium orientalis) » expanded horizons, abundance, spontaneity, wealth, prosperity, ambition

Stargazer Lily, White (Lilium orientalis) » purity, innocence, simplicity

Starwort (Stellaria) » cheerfulness in old age, optimistic

Statice (Limonium) » I miss you, rememberance, sympathy, changing needs, centered, stillness, calm, adaptation

Stephanotis (Stephanotis floribunda) » let's travel, I wish you a happy marriage, good luck, marital bliss, desire to travel, cooperation, communication, respect for differences

Stevia (Stevia rebaudiana) » energy

Stock (Matthiola incana) » I have affection for you, slow down, lasting beauty, affection, happy life, contented existence, slowing of pace, focus, completion of projects

Stonecrop (Sedum) » tranquillity

Straw Flower (Xerochrysum bracteatum) » I am here for you, I will always treasure you, happy memories, unconditional love, eternal happiness

Strawberry (Fragaria x ananassa) » luck, love, purity, sensuality, fertility, abundance, humility, modesty

Sturt's Desert Pea (Swainsona formosa) » I am sorry, overcoming, grief, you have hurt me

Sturt's Desert Rose (Gossypium sturtianum) » courage, decision, I am sorry, forgive me, self-confidence

Sumac (Rhus) » splendour

Suncup (Lonicera ovata) » self-confidence, inner strength

Sundew (Drosera auriculata) » stay strong, focus, optimism, congratulations, be alert

Sunflower (Helianthus annuus) » get well, be strong, strength, happiness, male healing, confidence, self-esteem, assertiveness

Swallow-Wort (Cynanchum louiseae) » medicine, heal

Swamp Lily (Crinum pedunculatum) » energy, regret, get well, I will help you

Swamp Onion (Allium validum) » purifying

Swan Plant (Asclepias physocarpa) » ideas

Sweet Alyssum (Alyssum maritimum) » I love more than just your beauty, I understand, mental anguish released, clarity

Sweet Bugle (Lycopus virginicus) » wedding blessings

Sweet Chestnut (Castanea sativa) » virtue, chastity, victory over temptation, stress relief, inner transformation

Sweet Gale » see Bayberry

Sweet Marjoram (Origanum marjorana) » let go of fear, self-reliance, comforting, relieve physical tension, relieve mental tension, consolation, protection from lightning, comfort grief, comfort, fertility, love, joy, honour, good fortune, long life

Sweet Pea (Lathyrus odoratus) » you are beautiful, good luck, gratitude, greed, harmony, protection, responsibility, comfort, social responsibility

Sweet Pepper » see Capsicum

Sweet Potato (Ipomoea batatas) » comfort, nurture, sex, peace, resolution

Sweet Sultan (Amberboa moschata) » felicity, happiness

Sweet Violet (Viola odorata) » steadfastness, loyalty, humility, constancy, shyness, protection from deception, protection from inebriation, love otions

Sweet William (Dianthus barbatus) » gallantry, I was only teasing

Sydney Rock Rose (Boronia serrulata) » acceptance, you are loved, you are not alone

Sycamore (Acer pseudoplatanus) » curiosity, reserve, natural beauty

T

Tabacco (Nicotiana tabacum) » purification, visions, spirituality, bond with creator, bond between worlds

Tagua (Phytelephas macrocarpa) » longevity

Tall Yellow Top (Senecio magnificus) » acceptance

Tamarisk (Tamarix) » crime, risks, inspiration

Tamarind (Tamarindus indica) » faithfulness, durability, forbearance

Tangerine (Citrus tangerina) » dispel negativity, vitality, mental powers

Tansy (Tanacetum vulgare) » war, declaration of war

Tarragon (Artemisia dracunculus) » I want to share my life with you, sharing, partnership

Tea (Camellia sinensis) » peace, simplicity, enlightenment, courage, strength, prosperity

Tea Tree (Leptospermum myrsinoides) » attainment, congratulations, luck, good luck

Teasel (Dipsacus) » importunity, misanthropy, protection from evil

Teuila (Alpinia purpurata) » true love, fiery passion, strength, warmth, diversity, prosperity

Texas Bluebonnet (Lupinus texensis) » pride, destiny, service, survival, forgiveness, sensory awareness

Thistle, Common (Cirsium vulgare) » independence, austerity, protection from distraction, habit breaking, spiritual desires, courage, inner strength, coping

Thistle, Scotch (Onopordum acanthium) » retaliation, integrity, truth, pride, self-respect

Thorn Apple (Datura stamonium) » initiation, detachment, identity, ease confusion, courage to change

Thrift (Armeria maritima) » dauntlessness, interest, sympathy

Throatwort (Trachelium caeruleum) » neglected beauty

Thyme (Thymus vulgaris) » bravery, affection, courage, strength, let's do something, activity

Tiare (Gardenia taitensis) » welcome, I love you, love, hospitality, youthful beauty

Tiger Lily (Lilium tigrinum) » I am proud of you, resurrection, female healing, healthy competition, inner calm, security, relationship harmony, unity, protection from spirits, pride

Toadflax (Linaria vulgaris) » hex breaking, presumption, reluctance in love

Toothwort (Lathraea squamaria) » secret love

Tomato (Solanum lycopersicum) » endurance, courage, own power, faith, trust, breaking free, love

Tonka (Dipteryx odorata) » courage

Torch Ginger » see Teuila

Tormentil (Potentilla erecta) » protection of love, protection from evil spirits

Tradescantia (Tradescantia zebrina) » esteem but not love, momentary happiness

Traveller's Joy (Clematis vitalba) » mature-aged love, safety

Tree Houseleek (Aeonium) » grounding, calm, strength

Tree of Life (Guaiacum officinale) » reliability, substance, old age

Tree Peony (Paeonia suffruticosa) » good luck, I wish you good health, harmonious relationships, physical healing, physical temptation, happy anniversary, birth

Tree Spider Orchid (Dendrobium tetragonum) » you can do this, I believe in you, resolve, intuition, secrets

Treasure Flower (Gazania rigens) » personal gifts

Trillium (Trillium) » modest ambition, modest beauty, birth, awaken, oneness, celebration, compassion, support birth, passion

Trillium, White » see White Trillium

Trilobed Violet (Viola palmata) » trust new opportunities, courage to explore, happiness, openess

Tropicbird Orchid (Angraecum eburneum) » our passion will survive, freedom of expression, survival, self-reliance

Trout Lily (Erythronium americanum) » I understand you, positive transformation, clarity, understanding, co-operation, helpful relationships, happy attitude, gratitude

Trumpet Creeper (Campsis radicans) » purify, release attachments

Tuberose (Polianthes tuberosa) » I desire you, dangerous pleasures, sex, intimacy, protection, strength

Tulip, Purple (Tulipa) » undying love

Tulip, Red (Tulipa) » believe in me, declaration of love, passion, desire

Tulip, Variegated (Tulipa) » beautiful eyes, I see your beauty

Tulip, White (Tulipa) » forgiveness, forgive me

Tulip, Wild (Tulipa sprengeri) » I want you, desire, passion, reunion, self-improvement

Tulip, Yellow (Tulipa) » hopeless love

Tulip Tree (Liriodendron) » fame, rural happiness

Turkey Bush (Calytrix exstipulata) » inspiration, faith, creativity, imagination, you inspire me

Turk's Cap (Lilium superbum) » transition

T

Turmeric (Cucurma longa) » purification, warmth, lift emotions

Turnip (Brassica rapa subsp. rapa) » charity, grounding, ending relationships

Twin Flower » see Linnaea

V

Valerian (Polemonium caeruleum) » accommodating disposition, concealed merit, I want to marry you

Variegated Box (Buxus sempervirens) » good deeds, too good to be true, shadow and light, opportunities with equal challenges

Vanilla (Vanilla planifolia) » affinity, love, lust, you can do this, balance, peace, protection

Venus Flytrap (Dionaea muscipula) » I am ready for you, preparation, broad perpective, solutions, deceit

Venus' Looking Glass (Triodanis perfoliata) » flattery, gratitude, self-perception, self-worth

Verbena » see Vervain

Vervain (Verbena officinalis) » enchantment, divination, spellcasting, ritual cleansing, protection from evil, love, immunity from enemies, peaceful settlement, open attitude, harmonious life

Vetch (Vicia) » shyness

Violet, African » see African Violet

Violet, Blue » faithfulness, modesty, answers within, subconscious

Violet, Dog » see Dog Violet

Violet, Native » see Native Violet

Violet, Native Wood » see Native Wood Violet

Violet, Purple » I was thinking of you

Violet, Sweet » see Sweet Violet

Violet, Trilobed » see Trilobed Violet

Violet, Yellow (Viola pubescens) » rare worth, rural happiness

Violet Nightshade (Solanum brownii) » power, responsibility, challenges, mentorship

Virginia Creeper (Parthenocissus quinquefolia) » ever changing, variety, I will stay with you in good times and bad

W

Wake Robin (Trillium pendulum) » self-confidence, voice

Wallflower (Erysimum) » misfortune, fidelity, fidelity in adversity

Walnut (Juglans regia) » royalty, wisdom, fertility, longevity, strength in adversity, support during change, link breaking, protection from outside influences, new relationships, inner strength, stability, mental stability

Wand Flower (Sparaxis grandiflora) » happy work, life path

Wandering Jew » see Tradescantia

Waratah (Telopea speciosissima) » survival, courage, passion, I love you completely, be brave, bravery

Water Hyacinth (Eichbornia crassipes) » inner growth, transition

Water Lily (Nymphaea) » unity, creation, enlightenment, resurrection, purity, gracefulness, seperation

Water Lily, Blue (Nymphaea) » wisdom, sharing knowledge

Water Lily, Pink (Nymphaea) » teaching, knowledge, grace

Water Lily, Purple (Nymphaea) » psychic development, mystic power

Water Lily, Red (Nymphaea) » love, passion, estranged love, new love, lust

Water Lily, White (Nymphaea) » mental purity, new ideas, enlightenment

Water Ribbons (Triglochin procerum) » freedom, new path, trust, don't give up on us, go with the flow

Watermelon (Citrullus lanatus) » creative effort, creative energy, fullness, encouragement

Wax Plant » see Hoya

Wedding Bush (Ricinocarpos pinifolius) » commitment, dedication, life purpose, join me, will you marry me?

Weeping Willow (Salix babylonica) » melancholy, mourning

Wheat (Triticum) » fruitfulness, I offer you all I have, prosperity

Whiteweed » see Ageratum

White Flag (Spathiphyllum) » comfort in social situations

White Mulberry » see Mulberry, White

White Nun Orchid (Lycaste skinneri alba) » beauty, peace, art

White Pine (Pinus strobus) » peace, legacy, conflict resolution

White Trillium (Trillium grandiflorum) » beauty, purity, healing

Whortleberry » see Bilberry

Wild Banana Orchid (Schomburgkia thomsoniana) » sexual relationships, balancing sexuality, joy in new experiences, psychic awareness

Wild Pansy (Viola tricolor) » open your heart, resonance, strong heart, inner strength, heartbreak healing

Wild Yam » (Dioscorea villosa) » willpower, distant healing

Willow (Salix alba) » be mine again, forsaken love

Willowherb (Epilobium) » control, protection from storms, mindfulness, optimism during difficult times

Wisteria (Wisteria sinensis) » enduring love, clinging clove, endurance, love, honour, creative expansion, patience, longevity, fertility

Witchhazel (Hamamelis virginiana) » stop pleasing others, divination, physical strength, protection from infection, healthy ego

Wolf's Bane » see Monkshood

Wood Anemone (Anemone nemerosa) » forlornness, letting go, protection from disease

Wood Betony (Stachys betonica) » magic, detachment, emotional wellbeing, resolve conflicts, celibacy, inner calm, expel evil spirits, end despair, purification, protection

Wood of Life (Guaiacum sanctum) » magic, magical strength, endurance, heritage, physical strength

Woodbine (Lonicera periclymenum) » please keep this secret, fraternal love, peace of mind, secrets, material objects, wealth, strength, honesty, family strength

Woodruff (Galium odoratum) » modest worth

Wooly Sunflower (Eriophyllum lanatum) » gentle strength

Wormwood (Artemisia absinthium) » do not be discouraged, absence, authenticity, sorrowful parting

X

Xeranthemum (Xeranthemum bracteatum) » cheerfulness in adversity, never say die

Xu Duan (Dipsacus japonica) » ward off evil, care

Y

Yam, Wild » see Wild Yam

Yarrow (Achillea millefolium) » friendship, war, elegance, banishing, relaxation

Yellow Dock (Rumex crispus) » prosperity, understanding, change habits

Yellow Elder (Tecoma stans) » critique, change for the better, regeneration, possibilities

Yerba Buena (Satureja douglasii) » meditation

Yerba Santa (Eriodictyon glutinosum) » holy, emotional release, unresolved grief, life restoration, natural feelings

Yellow Jessamine (Gelsemium sempervirens) » purification, joy, friendship, misunderstandings cleared

Yew (Taxus baccata) » death, longevity, magic, wisdom, knowledge, transcendence, immortality, rebirth, protection

Yesterday, Today and Tomorrow (Brunfelsia) » breakthroughs, healing transformation

Ylang-Ylang (Cananga odorata) » gratitude, love, peace, sex, attraction

Yucca (Yucca filamentosa) » transformation, shape-shifting, protection from evil, purification, removal of curses

Z

Zedoary (Curcuma zedoaria) » confidence, passion

Zephyr Lily (Zephyranthes) » I am waiting, expectation, healing past hurts

Zinnia (Zinnia elegans) » absence, missing you

Z

SECTION THREE

RESOURCES

ANNIVERSARY FLOWERS

1st   Carnation (Dianthus caryophyllus)
2nd   Lily of the Valley (Convallaria majalis)
3rd   Sunflower (Helianthus annuus)
4th   Hydrangea (Hydrangea)
5th   Daisy (Leucanthemum maximum, Bellis perennis)
6th   Calla Lily (Zantedeschia aethiopica)
7th   Freesia (Freesia)
8th   Lilac (Syringa vulgaris)
9th   Bird of Paradise (Strelitzia reginae)
10th   Daffodil (Narcissus pseudonarcissus)
11th   Tulip (Tulipa)
12th   Peony (Paeonia officinalis)
13th   Chrysanthemum (Chrysanthemum)
14th   Orchid (Orchidaceae)
15th   Rose (Rosa)
20th   Aster (Aster)
25th   Iris (Iris)
30th   Lily (Lilium)
40th   Gladiolus (Gladiolus)
50th   Violet (Viola), Yellow Rose (Rosa)

FLOWERS FOR DAYS OF THE WEEK

SUNDAY California Poppy (Eschscholzia californica)
Chrysanthemum (Chrysanthemum)
Day Lily (Hemerocallis)
Sunflower (Helianthus annuus)
Marigold (Tagetes evecta)

MONDAY Honesty (Lunaria annua)
Lily of the Valley (Convallaria majalis)
White Rose (Rosa)
Snowdrop (Galanthus nivalis)
Phlox (Phlox)

TUESDAY Nasturtium (Tropaeolum majus)
Geranium (Geranium)
Dahlia (Dahlia)
Red Hot Poker (Kniphofia)

WEDNESDAY Lupin (Lupinus perennis)
Columbine (Aquilegia)
Vervain (Verbena officinalis)

THURSDAY Lilac (Syringa vulgaris)
Lavender (Calluna vulgaris)
Violet (Viola)
Stock (Matthiola incana)
Cyclamen (Cyclamen)

FRIDAY Forget-Me-Not (Myosotis)
Carnation (Dianthus caryophyllus)
Love-in-a-Mist (Nigella damascena)
Pink Rose (Rosa)

SATURDAY Wallflower (Erysimum)
Chrysanthemum (Chrysanthemum)
Fuchsia (Fuchsia magellanica)
Dahlia (Dahlia)

FLOWERS OF THE MONTH

You may like to select flowers to match the birth month of a person or that align with the month of an event you are planning.

TRADITIONAL WESTERN CULTURE FLOWERS OF THE MONTH

JANUARY	Carnation (Dianthus caryophyllus), Snowdrop (Galanthus nivalis)
FEBRUARY	Primrose (Primula scotica), Iris (Iris)
MARCH	Daffodil (Narcissus pseudonarcissus)
APRIL	Shasta Daisy (Leucanthemum maximum), Daisy (Bellis perennis)
MAY	Lily (Lilium), Lily of the Valley (Convallaria majalis)
JUNE	Rose (Rosa)
JULY	Waterlily (Nymphaea), Sweet Pea (Lathyrus odoratus), Delphinium (Delphinium)
AUGUST	Gladiolus (Gladiolus)
SEPTEMBER	Aster (Aster)
OCTOBER	Dahlia (Dahlia), Marigold (Tagetes evecta)
NOVEMBER	Chrysanthemum (Chrysanthemum)
DECEMBER	Holly (Ilex aquifolium), Poinsettia (Euphorbia pulcherrima)

CHINESE FLOWERS OF THE MONTH

JANUARY	Plum Blossom (Prunus mume)
FEBRUARY	Peach Blossom (Prunus persica)
MARCH	Tree Peony (Paeonia suffruticosa)
APRIL	Cherry Blossom (Prunus serrulata)
MAY	Magnolia (Magnolia campbellii)
JUNE	Pomegranate (Punica granatum)
JULY	Lotus (Nelumbo nucifera)
AUGUST	Pear Blossom (Pyrus)
SEPTEMBER	Mallow Blossom (Malva sylvestris)
OCTOBER	Chrysanthemum (Chrysanthemum)
NOVEMBER	Gardenia (Gardenia jasminoides)
DECEMBER	Poppy (Papaver rhoeas)

JAPANESE FLOWERS OF THE MONTH

JANUARY	Pine (Pinus)
FEBRUARY	Plum Blossom (Prunus mei)
MARCH	Cherry Blossom (Prunus serrulata), Peach Blossom (Prunus persica), Pear Blossom (Pyrus)
APRIL	Cherry Blossom (Prunus serrulata), Wisteria (Wisteria sinensis)
MAY	Azalea (Rhododendron Tsutsusi), Peony (Paeonia officinalis)
JUNE	Iris (Iris)
JULY	Morning Glory (Ipomoea purpurea), Mountain Clover (Trifolium montanum)
AUGUST	Lotus (Nelumbo nucifera)
SEPTEMBER	*Seven Grasses of Autumn:*
	Hagi Bush » Japanese Clover (Lespedeza)
	Susuki » Pampas Grass (Cortaderia selloana)
	Kuzu » Arrowroot (Maranta arundinacea)
	Nadeshiko » Wild Carnation (Dianthus)
	Ominaeschi » Maiden Flower (Patrinia Scabiosifolia)
	Fujibakama » Chinese Agrimony (Agrimonia pilosa)
	Hirogao » Wild Morning Glory (Ipomoea)
OCTOBER	Maple (Acer), Chrysanthemum (Chrysanthemum)
NOVEMBER	Maple (Acer), Willow (Salix alba)
DECEMBER	Camellia (Camellia japonica), Empress Tree (Paulownia tomentosa)

AUSTRALIAN FLOWERS OF THE MONTH

JANUARY	Billy Buttons (Pycnsorus globosus)
FEBRUARY	Blue Gum Flower (Eucalyptus globulus)
MARCH	Orange Banksia (Banksia ashbyi)
APRIL	Tea Tree (Leptospermum myrsinoides)
MAY	Crowea (Crowea exalata)
JUNE	Geraldton Wax (Chamelaucium uncinatum)
JULY	Gymea Lily (Doryanthes excelsa)
AUGUST	Waratah (Telopea speciosissima)
SEPTEMBER	Golden Wattle (Acacia pycnantha)
OCTOBER	Flannel Flower (Actinotus helianthi)
NOVEMBER	Kangaroo Paw (Anigozanthos manglesii)
DECEMBER	Rosella Flower (Hibiscus heterophyllus)

FLOWERS OF THE ZODIAC

AQUARIUS 20 January ~ 18 February
Snowdrop (Galanthus nivalis), Foxglove (Digitalis purpurea),
Mullein (Verbascum thapsus), Orchid (Orchidaceae),
Gentian (Gentiana)

PISCES 19 February ~ 20 March
Violet (Viola), Carnation (Dianthus caryophyllus),
Heliotrope(Heliotropium)OpiumPoppy(Papaversomniferum),
Peruvian Lily (Alstroemeria)

ARIES 21 March ~ 19 April
Gorse (Ulex europaeus), Holly (Ilex aquifolium),
Nasturtium (Tropaeolum majus), Scotch Thistle (Onopordum
acanthium), Common Thistle (Cirsium vulgare),
Tulip (Tulipa), Wild Rose (Rosa acicularis),
Woodbine (Lonicera periclymenum)

TAURUS 20 April ~ 20 May
Apple (Malus domestica), Cherry (Prunus serrulata),
Coltsfoot (Tussilago farfara), Lily (Lilium), Lily of the Valley
(Convallaria majalis), Lovage (Levisticum officinale),
Violet (Viola), Wild Rose (Rosa acicularis),
Almond (Prunus amygdalus), Ash (Fraxinus)

GEMINI 21 May ~ 20 June
Dill (Anethum graveolens), Iris (Iris), Rose (Rosa),
Parsley (Petroselinum crispum), Snapdragon (Antirrhinum
majus), Hazel (Corylus)

CANCER 21 June ~ 22 July
Delphinium (Delphinium), Honesty (Lunaria annua),
Moonwort (Botrychium lunaria), Poppy (Papaver rhoeas),
Waterlily (Nymphaea), Rose, White (Rosa),
Willow (Salix alba), Agrimony (Agrimonia eupatoria)

LEO 23 July ~ 22 August
Angelica (Angelica archangelica), Borage (Borago officinalis), Cowslip (Primula veris), Forsythia (Forsythia), Heliotrope (Heliotropium), Hops (Humulus), Laurel (Laurus nobilis), Marigold (Tagetes evecta), Peony (Paeonia officinalis), Sunflower (Helianthus annuus)

VIRGO 23 August ~ 22 September
Cornflower (Centaurea cyanus), Daisy (Leucanthemum maximum), (Bellis perennis), Madonna lily (Lilium candidum), Rosemary (Rosmarinus officinalis), Valerian (Polemonium caeruleum)

LIBRA 23 September ~ 22 October
Almond (Prunus amygdalus), Apple (Malus domestica), Hydrangea (Hydrangea), Love-in-a-Mist (Nigella damascena), Plum (Prunus domestica), Violet (Viola), Rose, White (Rosa)

SCORPIO 23 October ~ 21 November
Basil (Ocimum basilicum), Chrysanthemum (Chrysanthemum), Heather (Calluna vulgaris), Holly (Ilex aquifolium), Celandine (Ficaria verna), Peony (Paeonia officinalis)

SAGITTARIUS 22 November ~ 21 December
Carnation (Dianthus caryophyllus), Mulberry (Morus), Sage (Salvia officinalis), Wallflower (Erysimum)

CAPRICORN 22 December ~ 19 January
Holly (Ilex aquifolium), Nightshade (Solanaceae), Rue (Ruta graveolens), Snowdrop (Galanthus nivalis), Solomon's Seal (Polygonatum), Violet (Viola), Yew (Taxus baccata)

NATIONAL FLOWERS

Antigua & Barbuda » Dagger's Log (Agave karatto miller)
Argentina » Ceibo (Erythrina crista-galli)
Australia » Golden Wattle (Acacia pycnantha)
Austria » Edelweiss (Leontopodium alpinum)
Bahamas » Yellow Elder (Tecoma stans)
Bangladesh » Water Lily (Nymphaea nouchali)
Barbados » Pride of Barbados (Poinciana pulcherrima)
Belaus » Flax (Linum usitatissimum)
Belgium » Red Poppy (Papaver rhoeas)
Belize » Black Orchid (Trichoglottis brachiata)
Bermuda » Blue-Eyed Grass (Sisyrinchium montanum)
Bhutan » Blue Poppy (Meconopsis betonicifolia)
Bolivia » Kantuta (Cantua buxifolia)
Brazil » Golden Trumpet Tree (Tabebuia alba)
Bulgaria » Rose (Rosa)
Canada » Maple (Acer)
Cayman Islands » Wild Banana Orchid (Schomburgkia thomsoniana)
Chile » Copihue (Lapageria rosea)
China » Chinese Plum Blossom (Prunus mume)
Colombia » Christmas Orchid (Cattleya trianae)
Costa Rica » Purple Orchid (Cattleya skinneri)
Croatia » Iris Croatica (Iris perunika)
Cuba » Butterfly Jasmine (Mariposa)
Cyprus » Rose (Rosa)
Czech Republic » Rose (Rosa)
Denmark » Marguerite Daisy (Argyranthemum frutescens)
Ecuador » Rose (Rosa)
Egypt » Lotus (Nymphaea lotus)
Estonia » Cornflower (Centaurea)
Ethiopia » Calla Lily (Zantedeschia aethiopica)
France » Iris (Iris)
French Polynesia » Tiare (Gardenia taitensis)
Finland » Lily of the Valley (Convallaria majalis)
Germany » Knapweed (Centaurea cyanus)

Greece » Bear's Breech (Acanthus mollis)

Greenland » Willowherb (Epilobium)

Guam » Puti Tai Nobiu (Bougainvillea spectabilis)

Guatemala » White Nun Orchid (Lycaste skinneri alba)

Guyana » Waterlily (Victoria regia)

Honduras » Orchid (Brassavola digbiana)

Hong Kong » Orchid (Bauhinia blakeana)

Hungary » Tulip (Tulipa)

Iceland » Mountain Avens (Dryas octopetala)

India » Lotus (Nelumbo nucifera)

Indonesia » Melati (Jasminum sambac), Moon Orchid (Phalaenopsis amabilis), Rafflesia (Rafflesia arnoldii)

Iran » Red Rose (Rosa)

Iraq » Rose (Rosa)

Ireland » Shamrock (Trifolium)

Italy » Daisy (Bellis perennis)

Jamaica » Wood of Life (Guaiacum sanctum)

Japan » Chrysanthemum (Chrysanthemum), Sakura (Prunus serrulata)

Jordan » Black Iris (Iris nigricans)

Laos » Champa (Calophyllum)

Kazakhstan » Lily (Lilium)

Kuwait » Arfaj (Rhanterium epapposum)

Kyrgyzstan » Tulip (Tulipa germanica)

Latvia » Ox-Eye Daisy (Leucanthemum vulgare)

Lebanon » Cedar of Lebanon (Cedrus libani)

Liberia » Pepper (Piper nigrum)

Libya » Pomegranate Blossom (Punica granatum)

Lithuania » Rue (Ruta graveolens)

Luxembourg » Rose (Rosa)

Madagascar » Poinciana (Delonix regia)

Maldives » Pink Rose (Rosa)

Malta » Maltese Centaury (Paleocyanus crassifoleus)

Netherlands » Tulip (Tulipa)

New Zealand » Kowhai (Sophora microphylla)

Paraguay » Mburucuya (Passiflora caerulea)

Peru » Kantuta (Cantua buxifolia)

Philippines » Sampaguita (Jasminum sambac)
Poland » Corn Poppy (Papaver rhoeas)
Portugal » Lavender (Lavandula angustifolia)
Puerto Rico » Puerto Rican Hibiscus (Thespesia grandiflora)
Romania » Dog Rose (Rosa canina)
Russia » Chamomile (Matricaria recutita)
Samoa » Teuila (Alpinia purpurata)
San Marino » Cyclamen (Cyclamen)
Scotland » Scotch Thistle (Cirsium altissimum)
Seychelles » Tropicbird Orchid (Angraecum eburneum)
Sicily » Carnation (Dianthus caryophyllus)
Singapore » Vanda Miss Joaquim Orchid (Vanda x 'Miss Joaquim')
Slovakia » Rose (Rosa)
Slovenia » Carnation (Dianthus caryophyllus)
Spain » Red Carnation (Dianthus caryophyllus)
Sri Lanka » Nil Mahanel Waterlily (Nymphaea stellata)
South Africa » Protea (Protea cynaroides)
South Korea » Rose of Sharon (Hibiscus syriacus)
Sweden » Linnaea (Linnaea borealis)
Switzerland » Edelweiss (Leontopodium alpinum)
Syria » Jasmine (Jasminium)
Taiwan » Plum Blossom (Prunus mume)
Thailand » Ratchaphruek (Cassia fistula)
Trinidad & Tobago » Chaconia (Warszewiczia coccinea)
Tonga » Red Blossomed Heilala (Garcinia sessilis)
Turkey » Tulip (Tulipa)
Ukraine » Sunflower (Helianthus annuus)
United States Of America » Rose (Rosa)
United Kingdom, England » Tudor Rose (Rosa)
United Kingdom, Wales » Daffodil (Amaryllidaceae)
Uruguay » Ceibo (Erthrina crista-galli)
Venezuela » Orchid (Cattleya mossiae)
Virgin Island » Yellow Elder (Tecoma stans)
Yemen » Arabian Coffee (Coffea arabica)
Yugoslavia » Lily of the Valley (Convallaria majalis)
Zimbabwe » Flame Lily (Gloriosa rothschildiana)

SCOTTISH CLANS
FLOWERS AND PLANTS ASSOCIATED
WITH THE MOST COMMON CLANS

Buchanan » Birch (Betula)
Cameron » Oak (Quercus)
Campbell » Myrtle (Myrtus)
Chisholm » Alder (Alnus)
Colquhoun » Hazel (Corylus)
Cumming » Sallow (Salix cinerea)
Drummond » Holly (Ilex aquifolium)
Farquharson » Purple Foxglove (Digitalis purpurea)
Ferguson » Poplar (Populus)
Forbes » Broom (Genisteae)
Fraser » Yew (Taxus)
Gordon » Ivy (Hedra)
Graham » Spurge Laurel (Daphne laureola)
Grant » Cranberry Heath (Astroloma humifusum)
Gunn » Rosewood (Pterocarpus indicus)
Lamont » Crab Apple Tree (Malus sylvestris)
McDonald » Heath Bell (Erica cinerea)
McDougall » Cloudberry (Rubus chamaemorus)
MrGregor » Scots Pine (Pinus syvestris)
McIntosh » Boxwood (Buxus)
McKay » Bulrush (Scirpoides holoschoenus)
McKenzie » Deer Grass (Trichophorum cespitosum)
McKinnon » St John's Wort (Hypericum perforatum)
McLachlan » Mountain Ash (Sorbus aucuparia)
McLeod » Red Whortleberry (Vaccinium)
McNeil » Bladder Fucus (Fucus vesiculosus)
McPherson » Variegated Box (Buxus sempervirens)
McQuarrie » Blackthorn (Prunus spinosa)
McRae » Clubmoss (Lycopodium)
Menzies » Ash (Fraxinus)
Murrey » Juniper (Juniperus)
Ogilvie » Hawthorn (Crataegus)

Oliphant » Great Maple (Acer pseudoplatanus)
Robertson » Fern (Tracheophyta)
Rose » Briar Rose (Rosa rubiginosa)
Ross » Bearberry (Arctostaphylos uva-ursi)
Sinclair » Clover (Trifolium)
Stewart » Thistle (Onopordum acanthium)
Sutherland » Cat's Tail Grass (Phleum pratense)

STATES AND TERRITORIES OF AUSTRALIA
OFFICIAL FLORAL EMBLEMS

Australian Capital Territory » Royal Bluebell (Wahlenbergia gloriosa)
New South Wales » Waratah (Telopea speciosissima)
Northern Territory » Sturt's Desert Rose (Gossypium sturtianum)
Queensland » Cooktown Orchid (Vappodes phalaenopsis)
South Australia » Sturt's Desert Pea (Swainsona formosa)
Tasmania » Tasmanian Blue Gum (Eucalyptus globulus)
Victoria » Common Heath (Epacris impressa)
Western Australia » Kangaroo Paw (Anigozanthos manglesii)

AMERICAN STATES
OFFICIAL FLORAL SYMBOLS

Alabama » Camellia (Camellia japonica)
Alaska » Forget-Me-Not (Myosotis alpestris)
Arizona » Saguaro Cactus Blossom (Carnegiea gigantean)
Arkansas » Apple Blossom (Malus domestica)
California » California Poppy (Eschscholzia californica)
Carolina (North) » Dogwood (Cornus florida)
Carolina (South) » Yellow Jessamine (Gelsemium sempervirens)
Colorado » Rocky Mountain Columbine (Aquilegia caerulea)
Connecticut » Mountain Laurel (Kalmia latifolia)
Dakota (North) » Prairie Rose (Rosa blanda, Rosa arkansana)
Dakota (South) » American Pasqueflower (Pulsatilla hirsutissima)
Delaware » Peach Blossom (Prunus persica)
Florida » Orange Blossom (Citrus x sinensis)
Georgia » Cherokee Rose (Rosa laevigata)
Hawaii » Aloalo (Hibiscus brackenridgei)
Idaho » Lewis Mock Orange (Philadelphus lewisii)
Illinos » Native Wood Violet (Viola)
Indiana » Paeony (Paeonia)
Iowa » Wild Prairie Rose (Rosa arkansana)
Kansas » Sunflower (Helianthus annuus)
Kentucky » Goldenrod (Solidago gigantea)
Louisiana » Southern Magnolia (Magnolia grandiflora)
Maine » Pine Cone, White Pine (Pinus strobus)
Maryland » Black-Eyed Susan (Rudbeckia hirta)
Massachusetts » Mayflower (Epigaea repens)
Michigan » Apple Blossom (Malus domestica)
Minnesota » Showy Lady Slipper (Cypripedium reginae)
Mississippi » Southern Magnolia (Magnolia grandiflora)
Missouri » Downy Hawthorn (Crataegus mollis)
Montana » Bitter Root (Lewisia rediviva)
Nebraska » Goldenrod (Solidago gigantean)
Nevada » Sagebrush (Artemisia tridentate)
New Hampshire » Purple Lilac (Syringa vulgaris)

New Jersey » Violet (Viola sororia)
New Mexico » Yucca (Yucca glauca)
New York » Rose (Rosa)
Ohio » Scarlet Carnation (Dianthus caryophyllus)
Oklahoma » Mistletoe (Phoradendron serotinum)
Oregon » Oregon Grape (Berberis aquifolium)
Pennsylvania » Mountain Laurel (Kalmia latifolia)
Rhode Island » Trilobed Violet (Viola palmata)
Tennessee » Iris (Iris germanica)
Texas » Texas Bluebonnet (Lupinus texensis)
Utah » Sego Lily (Calochortus nuttallii)
Vermont » Red Clover (Trifolium pratense)
Virginia » Flowering Dogwood (Cornus florida)
Washington » Coast Rhododendron (Rhododendron macrophyllum)
West Virginia » Great Rhododendron (Rhododendron maximum)
Wisconsin » Native Violet (Viola papilionacea)
Wyoming » Indian Painbrush (Castilleja linariifolia)

CANADIAN PROVINCES AND TERRITORIES
OFFICIAL FLOWER SYMBOLS

Alberta » Wild Rose (Rosa acicularis)
British Columbia » Pacific Dogwood (Cornus nuttallii)
Manitoba » Prairie Crocus (Pulsatilla patens)
New Brunswick » Purple Violet (Viola)
Newfoundland » Purple Pitcher Plant (Sarracenia purpurea)
Northwest Territories » Mountain Avens (Dryas octopetala)
Nova Scotia » Mayflower (Epigaea repens)
Nunavut » Purple Saxifrage (Saxifraga oppositifolia)
Ontario » White Trillium (Trillium grandiflorum)
Prince Edward Island » Lady's Slipper (Cypripedium acaule)
Quebec » Blue Flag Iris (Iris versicolor)
Saskatchewan » Prairie Lily (Lilium philadelphicum)
Yukon Territory » Fireweed (Chamerion angustifolium)

GODS, GODDESSES & OTHER BEINGS

A selection of flowers and plants with close associations to deities, revered people and entities from religions, beliefs and folklore throughout the world

Acacia (Acacia) » Allat, Al Uzzah, Astarte, Diana, Ishtar, Osiris, Ra

Acanthus (Acanthus mollis) » Acantha

Adonis (Adonis) » Adonis

Agaric (Amanita) » Bacchus, Dionysus, Wontan

Agave (Agave) » Agave

Agrimony (Agrimonia) » The Goddess

Alder (Alus) » Bran, Cronus, Ellerkonig, The Goddess, Gwern, Helice, Phoroneus, Proteus, Saturnus

Almond (Prunus dulcis) » Artemis Caryatis, Attis, Carmenta, Hermes, Mercury, Metis, Thorth

Amaranth (Amaranthus) » Artemis

Anemone (Anemone) » Adonis, Aphrodite, Flora, Venus

Angelica (Angelica archangelica) » Sophia, Venus

Apple (Malus domestica) » Aphrodite, Apollo, Athene, Diana, Dionysus, Eve, The Goddess, Hera, Iduna, Olwen, Venus, Vertumnus, Zeus

Apricot (Prunus armeniaca) » The Goddess

Arbutus (Arbutus) » Cardea

Ash (Fraxinus) » Achilles, Andrasteia, Cerridwen, The Goddess, Gwydion, Mars, Nemesis, Neptune, Odin, Poseidon, Thor, Uranus, Wotan

Asparagus (Asparagus officinalis) » Zeus

Aspen (Populus tremula) » Hercules, Leuce, Diarmuid Ua Duibhne, Ilak

Asphodel (Asphodelus) » Persephone

Bael (Aegle marmelos) » Aegle, Shiva

Bamboo (Bambusoideae) » Hina, Thoth

Banana (Musa) » Kanaloa

Banyan (Ficus benghalensis) » Maui, Shiva

Barley (Hordeum vulgare) » Adonis, Alphito, Ariadne, Ceres, Cerridwen, Cronus, Damuzi, Dionysus, Isis, Osiris

Basil (Ocimum basilicum) » Erzulie, Krishna, Vishnu

Bean (Phaseolus) » Cardea, Ceres, Demeter

Beech (Fagus) » Athena, Ammon, Apollo, Diana, Zeus

Belladonna (Atropa belladonna) » Atropos, Bellona, Circe, Hecate

Birch (Betula) » Berkana, Thor

Bitterwort (Gentiana lutea) » The Goddess

Black Hellebore (Helleborus niger) » The Goddess

Blackberry (Rubus fruticosus) » Blodeuwedd, Brigid, The Goddess

Blackthorn (Prunus spinosa) » Eris

Bodhi Tree (Ficus religiosa) » Buddha, Krishna, Vishnu

Box (Buxus) » Pluto

Buttercup (Ranunculus) » Hymen

Cannabis (Cannabis sativa) » Bast, Shiva

Cardamom (Elettaria cardamomum) » Erzulie

Carnation (Dianthus caryophyllus) » Jupiter

Cauliflower (Brassica oleracea) » Luna, Selene

Cedar (Cedrus) » Arinna, Baalat, Osiris, Aegir, Amun Ra, Baalat, Cernunnos, Forseti, Helios, Indra, Isis, Jupiter, Njord, Odin, Osiris, Pan, Poseidon, Sol, Sunnu, Wotan

Celery (Apium graveolens) » Cadmilus, Helios, Hermes, Jupiter, Kadmilos, Mercury, Sol, Zeus

Centaury (Centaurea cyanus) » Chiron, Helios, Sol

Chamomile (Chamaemelum nobile) » Baldur, Cernunnos, Cerridwen, Gullveig, Helios, Hermes, Karnayna, Mercury, Mimir, Oshun, Ra, Sif, Sol

Champa (Calophllum) » Laxmi

Chaste Tree (Vitex agnus-castus) » Asclepius

Cherry (Prunus serrulata) » The Goddess, Vertumnus

Chilli (Capsicum) » Ares, Mars

Cinnamon (Cinnamomum verum) » Aphrodite, Ch'ang-o, Venus

Clover (Trifolium) » Artemis, Diana, Olwen, Rowen

Cocoa (Theobroma cacao) » Ek Chuah

Columbine (Aquilegia vulgaris) » Freya

Corn (Zea mays) » Abuk, Acca Laurentia, Adonis, Anath, Ashnan, Attis, Bhim Deo, Bhimsen, Ceres, Cerridwen, Chitariah Tubueriki, Cronus, Dagon, Damuzi, Danae, Demeter, Dionysus, Enlil, Ezinu, Fornax, Gauri, Heqet, Ino, Isis, Jehovah, Jesus, Kore, Lugh, Maneros, Metsik, Nebri, Neper Ninlil, Ninhursag, Nisaba, Osiris, Persephone, Robigus, Sita, Sud, Tailtiu, Chitariah Tubueriki, Tammuz, Uma, Viribius, Volos

Coconut (Cocos nucifera) » Te Tuna

Costmary (Tanacetum balsamita) » Mary

Cow parsley (Anthriscus sylvestris) » Mary

Crocus (Crocus sativus) » Britomartis, Jove, Juno

Cucumber (Cucumis sativus) » Luna, Selene, Uttu

Cupid's Dart (Catananche caerulea) » Cupid

Cyclamen (Cyclamen persicum) » Hecate, Aphrodite, Venus

Cypress (Cupressus sempervirens) » Aphrodite, Apollo, Artemis, Ashtoreth, Astarte, Cranae, Cupid, Diana, Hebe, Heqet, Hercules, Jupiter, Mithras, Osiris, Pluto, Zoroaster

Daisy (Bellis perennis) » Artemis, Freya, Thor

Dandelion (Taraxacum) » Hecate

Date Palm (Phoenix dactylifera) » Apollo, Artemis, Damuzi, Diana, Hecate, Isis, Latona, Tammuz

Dog Rose (Rosa canina) » The Goddess

Dogwood (Cornus) » Cire, Cronus, Proteus, Saturn

Elder (Sambucus nigra) » Hulda, The Goddess, Venus

Elm (Ulmus) » Dionysus, Hoenin, Lodr, Odin

Fennel (Foeniculum vulgare) » Dioysus, Prometheus

Fenugreek (Trigonella foenum-graecum) » Apollo

Fig (Ficus carica) » The Apsaras, Dionysus, The Goddess, Isis, Juno

Fir (Abies) » Adonis, Artemis, Attis, Bacchus, Cybele, Diana, Dionysus, Druantia, Erigone, Hathor, Io, Isis, Neptune, Osiris, Pan

Flax (Linum usitatissimum) » Apollo, The Goddess, Hulda, Isis, Linda

Frankincense (Boswellia sacra) » Baal, Bel, Ra

Galangal (Alpinia galangal) » Vulcan

Garlic (Allium sativum) » Hecate

Geranium (Pelargonium) » The Goddess

Gorse (Ulex) » Jupiter, Thor

Hawthorn (Crataegus) » Blodeuwedd, Cardea, Flora, Hymen, Maia, Olwen

Hazel (Corylus) » Aengus, Artemis, Diana, Hermes, MacColl, Mercury, Thor

Heather (Calluna vulgaris) » Aphrodite, Erycina, Cybele, Eryx, Isis

Heliotrope (Heliotropium) » Apollo

Hemlock (Tsuga) » Hecate

Holly (Ilex aquifolium) » Tannus, Taranis, Thor

Hollyhock (Alcea) » Althea

Horehound (Marrubium vulgare) » Horus

Houseleek (Sempervivum) » Jupiter, Thor

Hyacinth (Hyacinthus) » Hyacinthus, Zeus

Iris (Iris) » Hera, Iris, Isis, Juno

Iris Croatica (Iris perunika) » Perun

Ivy (Hedera) » Artemis Tridaria, Attis, Bacchus, Cissia, Dionysus, The Goddess, Hymen, Osiris, Rhea

Jasmine (Jasminum) » Vishnu

Kava Kava (Piper methysticum) » Kaneloa

Lady's Bedstraw (Galium verum) » Mary

Lady's Mantle (Alchemilla) » Mary

Lady's Smock (Cardamine pratensis) » Mary

Larkspur (Delphinium) » Apollo

Laurel (Laurus nobilis) » Asclepius, Apollo, Ceres, Daphne, Eros, Faunus

Lavender (Lavandula) » Aradia

Lettuce (Lactuca sativa) » Min, Venus

Lily (Lilium) » Astarte, Britomartis, Hera, Juno, Kwan Yin, Nephthys, Venus

Lily of the Valley (Convallaria majalis) » Apollo, Asclepius, Maia, Mercury

Linden (Tilia) » Lada, Venus

Lotus (Nelumbo nucifera) » Buddah, Hapy, Isis, Nissa, Sarasvati

Madonna lily (Lilium candidum) » Mary

Maize (Zea mays) » Chicomecohuatl, Cinteotl, Xipe Totec, Yum Caz

Mallow (Malva) » The Goddess

Mandrake (Mandragora officinarum) » Aphrodite, Cire, Harthor, Hecate, Selene, Venus

Manila Palm (Adonidia) » Adonis

Marigold (Tagetes erecta) » Artemis, Sarasvati, Tages

Marjoram (Origanum majorana) » Aphrodite, Venus

Marshmallow (Althaea officinalis) » Althea

Meadowsweet (Filipendula ulmaria) » Blodeuwedd, The Goddess

Milk Thistle (Silybum marianum) » Mary

Mint (Mentha) » Hecate, Minthe, Pluto

Mistletoe (Viscum album) » Apollo, Asclepius, Baldur, Freya, Frigg, Ischys, Ixion, Jove, Manannan, MacLir, Odin, Venus

Monkshood (Aconitum) » Hecate, Hercules, Monerva, Saturn

Mugwort (Artemisia vulgaris) » Artemis, Diana

Mulberry (Morus) » Brahma, Diana, Minerva, San Ku Fu Jen

Mullein (Verbascum) » Jupiter

Mustard (Sinapis) » Asclepius

Myrrh (Commiphora myrrha) » Adonis, Astarte, Isis, Mariamne, Marian, Mary, Myrrha, Ra

Myrtle (Myrtus) » Aphrodite, Artemis, Ashtoreth, Astarte, Hathor, Mariamne, Marian, Marina, Miriam, Myrrha, Myrto, Venus

Narcissus (Narcissus poeticus) » Atropos, Clotho, The Fates, Hades, Lachesis, Narcissus, Persephone, Pluto

Nettle (Urtica) » Thor

Nutmeg (Myristica fragrans) » Myrrha

Oak (Quercus) » Ariadne, Artemis, Athena, Baldur, Belenos, Blodeuwedd, Cardea, Cernunnos, Circe, Cybele, the Dagda, Demeter, Dia, Diana, Dianus, Dione, Donar, Egeria, El, Erato, Esus, Hecate, Hercules, Herne, Hou, Janicot, Janus, Jehovah, Jove, Jupiter, Mars, Mary, the Morrigan, Pan, Peirun, Perkunas, Picus, Tara, Taranis, Teutates, Thor, Thunor, Viribus, Zeus

Oats (Avena sativa) » Brigid

Olive (Olea europaea) » Apollo, Athene, Hercules, Irene, Minerva, Ra, Zeus

Onion (Allium cepa) » Hecate, Isis

Opium Poppy (Papaver somniferum) » Dionysus

Orange (Citrus x sinensis) » Juno, Jupiter

Ox-Eye Daisy (Leucanthemum vulgare) » Artemis, Thor

Pansy (Viola tricolor var. hortensis) » The Goddess

Peony (Paeonia) » Apollo, Paeon

Papyrus (Cyperus papyrus) » Baalat, Hapy, Hathor

Parsley (Petroselinum crispum) » Persephone

Pasqueflower (Pulsatilla) » Adonis, Venus

Peach (Prunus persica) » The Goddess, Harpocrates, Horus, Vertumnus

Pear (Pyrus) » Athene, Hera, Priapus

Pennyroyal (Mentha pulegium) » Demeter

Peppermint (Mentha x piperita) » Pluto

Pine (Pinus) » Artemis, Astarte, Attis, Bacchus, Cybele, Diana, Dionysus

Plane Tree (Platanus) » Apollo, Xerxes

Pomegranate (Punica granatum) » Adonis, Attis, Cere, Damuzi, Hera, Judah, Ninib, Persephone, Rimmon, Tammuz

Poplar, Black (Populus nigra) » Egeria, Hecate

Poplar, White (Populus alba) » Apollo, Juno, Leuce, Persephone

Poppy (Papaver) » Aphrodite, Ceres, Demeter, Hypnos, Somnus

Pumpkin (Cucurbita) » Chicomecohuatl

Quince (Cydonia oblonga) » Aphrodite

Reed (Phragmites) » Coventia

Rhubarb (Rheum rhabarbarum) » Gayomart

Rice (Oryza sativa) » Antaboda, Ch'ang-o

Rose (Rosa) » Adonis, Aphrodite, Aurora, Cupid, Demeter, Eros, Harpocrates, Hathor, Horus, Hulda, Isis, Mary, Venus

Rosemary (Rosmarinus officinalis) » Mary, Venus

Rowan (Sorbus) » Akka/Mader, Akka/Rauni, Aphrodite, Brigantia, Brigid, Elis, Oeagrus, Ran, Thor

Rue (Ruta graveolens) » Aradia, Diana

Saffron (Crocus sativus) » Ashtoreth, Eos, Thoth

Saint John's Wort (Hypericum perforatum) » Baldur, The Goddess

Sesame (Sesamum indicum) » Ganesha

Snowdrop (Galanthus) » Brigid

Southernwood (Artemisia abrotanum) » Artemis, Diana

Spurge (Euphorbia) » Munsa

Strawberry (Fragaria x ananassa) » Freya, Frigg

Sycamore (Ficus sycomorus) » Isis, Osiris

Tamarisk (Tamarix) » Anu, Isis, Osiris

Tansy (Tanacetum vulgare) » Ganymede

Tarragon (Artemisia dracunculus) » Artemis, Diana

Thistle (Cirsium vulgare) » Minerva, Thor

Ti (Cordyline fruticosa) » Kaneloa, Lono, Pele

Tiare (Gardenia taitensis) » tea

Tormentil (Potentilla erecta) » Thor

Vervain (Verbena officinalis) » Aradia, Cerridwen, The Goddess, Isis, Juno, Jupiter, Mars, Mercury, Persephone, Thor, Venus

Violet (Viola) » Aphrodite, Attis, Diana, Io, Priapus, Venus, Zeus

Walnut (Juglans regia) » Artemis, Car, Carmenta, Carya, Jupiter, Metis

Waterlily (Nymphaea) » Coventia

Wheat (Triticum) » Adonis, Ceres, Demeter, Ishtar, Isis, Min, Osiris

Willow (Salix) » Anatha, Arawn, Artemis, Athena, Bel, Belenos, Belili, Cerridwen, Circe, Diana, Europa, Geshtinanna, Gwydion, Hecate, Helice, Hera, Ishtar, Jehovah, Lunsa, Mercury, Minerva, Orpheus, Psiris, Persephone, Zeus

Wormwood (Artemisia absinthium) » Artemis, Diana, Iris
Yarrow (Achillea millefolium) » Achilles
Yew (Taxus) » Banba, Hecate, Saturn

SAINTS
FLOWERS AND PLANTS DEDICATED TO SAINTS

St Alban » Rose (Rosa)
St Augustine » Rhododendron (Rhododendron)
St Augustine of England » Canterbury Bells (Campanula medium)
St Barnabas » St Barnaby's Thistle (Centaurea solstitialis)
St Boniface » Three-Leafed Rose (Rosa)
St Brigid » Rush (Juncaceae)
St Cedd » Oak (Quercus robur)
St Christopher » Herb Christophe (Stachys betonica)
St Congar » Yew (Taxus baccata)
St David » Daffodil (Narcissus pseudonarcissus)
St Fintan » Sycamore (Acer pseudoplatanus)
St George » Valerian (Polemonium caeruleum)
St James » Tulip (Tulipa)
St John » St John's Wort (Hypericum perforatum)
St John the Baptist » Lychnis (Lychnis)
St Margaret » Daisy (Bellis perennis)
St Mary Magdalene » Blush Rose (Rosa)
St Mary the Virgin » Lady's Smock (Cardamine pratensis)
St Nicomede » Yellow Rose (Rosa)
St Paul » Carnation (Dianthus caryophyllus)
St Peter » Carnation (Dianthus caryophyllus)
St Philip » Tulip (Tulipa)
St Valentine » Crocus (Crocus)

CHINESE ROSE NUMBERS

**In China, the number of roses you receive, give or display
will have different meanings.**

1	You are my only love; love at first sight
2	To be deeply attached to each other
3	I love you
4	Promise; a solemn pledge of love
5	I love you with no regret
6	Everything else goes smoothly
7	Happy encounter; endless wishes
8	Let us make up
9	Steadfast love
10	You are perfect; sincerity
11	You have my best love and heart and soul
12	All my love; good luck this year; minds agreeing
13	Secret crush
14	Easy come, easy go
15	Young and beautiful
16	The color of love
17	Love will never change
18	Best love
19	Love forever
20	I will love you forever and my love will never change
22	Pairs and couples
24	I miss you twenty-four hours a day
27	Little darling wife
29	Love forever
30	Please accept my love; you do not need to say anything
33	I affectionately love you; I love you for three generations and three lifetimes
36	I have romance because of you
44	I love you till my last breath
48	I affectionately love you
50	I have no regrets about my love
51	You are the only one in my heart

66	True love never changes
77	Will you marry me?
88	I will try hard to recompense everything I've done wrong
99	Enduring love as expansive as the sky and earth
100	A harmonious union lasting 100 years; hold my hand and together we will grow old
101	You're my only love and I will love you forever
108	Marry me!
110	Endless love
111	I will love you all my life
144	Love you for the rest of my life
365	Miss you every day; love you every day
999	Endless love
1000	I will love you for a thousand years
1001	Forever

BOTANICAL NAME INDEX

A Rockpool book
PO Box 252
Summer Hill
NSW 2130
Australia
rockpoolpublishing.com
Follow us! f ⦾ rockpoolpublishing
Tag your images with #rockpoolpublishing

ISBN 9781925429466

First published in 2017
Copyright text © Cheralyn Darcey 2017
This edition published in 2017

National Library of Australia Cataloguing-in-
Publication entry
    Darcey, Cheralyn, author.

    Flowerpaedia : 1,000 flowers and their
    meanings / Cheralyn Darcey.

    9781925429466 (paperback)

    Includes index.

    Flowers–Dictionaries.
    Flowers–Australia–Dictionaries.
    Flowers–Handbooks, manuals, etc.

Cover design by Jessica Le, Rockpool Publishing
Cover image by Shutterstock
Internal design and layout by Seymour Designs
Illustrations page 235 by Cheralyn Darcey;
    page iv, vi, 11, 214, 233 by Jessica Le
Printed and bound in China

10 9 8 7 6

BIBLIOGRAPHY
BOOKS

Clarke, Ian and Lee, Helen, Name That Flower: The Identification of Flowering Plants (Melbourne University Press 1987)

Coombes, Allen J, Dictionary of Plant Names (Timber Press 2002)

Crane, Walter, Flowers From Shakespeare's Garden (Cassell & Co. Ltd. 1906)

Cunningham, Scott, Encyclopedia of Magical Herbs (Llewellyn Publications 2010)

Graves, Julia, The Language of Plants (Lindisfarne Books 2012)

Hanson, J. Wesley, Flora's Dial (Jonathan Allen 1846)

Harrison, Lorraine, RHS Latin for Gardeners (Mitchell Beazley 2012)

Hemphill, John & Rosemary, Myths and Legends of the Garden (Hodder & Stoughton 1997)

Jay, Roni, Sacred Flowers (Thorsons 1997)

Kear, Katherine, Flower Wisdom (Thorsons 2000)

Kelly, Frances, The Illustrated Language of Flowers (Viking O'Neil 1992)

MacOboy, Stirling, What Flower Is That? (Lansdowne Press 2000)

Mac Coitir, Niall, Irish Wild Plants (The Collins Press 2008)

Olds, Margaret, Flora's Plant Names (Gordon Cheers 2003)

Pavord, Anna The Naming of Names, The Search for Order in the World of Plants (Bloomsbury 2005)

Phillips, Stuart, An Encyclopaedia of Plants in Myth, Legend, Magic and Lore (Robert Hale Limited 2012)

Potter, Jennifer, Seven Flowers and How They Shaped the World (Atlantic Books 2013)

Sanders, Jack, The Secrets of Wildflowers (Lyons Press 2014)

Sulman, Florence, Wild Flowers of New South Wales (Angus & Robertson Ltd 1926)

Telesco, Patricia, A Floral Grimoire (Citadel Press 2001)

Vickery, Roy, A Dictionary of Plant-Lore (Oxford University Press 1995)

Ward, Bobby J, A Contemplation Upon Flowers (Timber Press 1999)

White, Ian, Australian Bush Flower Healing (Bantam Books 1999)